Learning Joomla! Extension Development

A practical tutorial on creating Joomla! 1.5 extensions with PHP, written and tested against the final release of Joomla! 1.5

Joseph L. LeBlanc

BIRMINGHAM - MUMBAI

Learning Joomla! 1.5 Extension Development

First published: December 2008

Production Reference: 1051208

Published by Packt Publishing Ltd.
32 Lincoln Road
Olton
Birmingham, B27 6PA, UK.

ISBN 978-1-847196-20-0

www.packtpub.com

Cover Image by Vinayak Chittar (vinayak.chittar@gmail.com)

Credits

Author

Joseph L. LeBlanc

Reviewer

Daniel Chapman

Senior Acquisition Editor

Douglas Paterson

Development Editor

Swapna V. Verlekar

Technical Editor

Rakesh Shejwal

Editorial Team Leader

Akshara Aware

Project Manager

Abhijeet Deobhakta

Project Coordinator

Lata Basantani

Indexer

Monica Ajmera

Proofreader

Dirk Manuel

Copy Editor

Sumathi Sridhar

Production Coordinator

Rajni R. Thorat

Cover Work

Rajni R. Thorat

About the Author

Joseph L. LeBlanc started with computers at a very young age. His independent education gave him the flexibility to experiment with and learn computer science. Joseph holds a bachelor's degree in Management Information Systems from Oral Roberts University.

Joseph is a freelance Joomla! extension developer. He released a component tutorial in May 2004, which was later translated into French, Polish, and Russian. Work samples and open-source extensions are available at www.jlleblanc.com. In addition to freelancing, he is an active member of the Washington, DC tech community and Joomla! Bug Squad.

I would like to thank the following people for making this book possible:

- Packt Publishing, for giving me the opportunity to author this work.

- Everyone who bought the first edition of this book, for offering both praise and critiques. By speaking up, you helped make this edition a reality.

- The Joomla! team, for developing some of the best software in the world.

- The DC PHP community, for showing me different ways people are solving similar problems.

- Steve and Sue Meeks, for their flexibility with my schedule during the writing process and for giving Joomla! a shot.

- Everyone who has downloaded and used my open-source components.

- My professors, for taking me on the Journey of a Byte and showing me how to write effectively.

- Mom and Dad, for teaching me how to learn.

About the Reviewer

Daniel Chapman started his career as an Oracle database consultant and trainer, working for various Australian Universities and Telecommunication Companies, and also for Oracle Australia, developing a keen sense of the value of development standards and analysis processes. After ten years in this arena he wanted a change and moved into web development in 2004, quickly picking up PHP, JavaScript, HTML, and CSS, while experimenting with various CMSes.

Finally deciding on Joomla! as his CMS of choice, Daniel initially began working as a consultant developing sites and producing a few small extensions, before starting one of the first Open Source Extension Clubs—Ninjoomla.com, which eventually changed it's name to NinjaForge.com, and has become quite well known in the Joomla! sphere.

I would like to thank my wife Kyoko, for her seemingly endless support of my work, even when it takes away time from us being together. I can't thank her enough for being there for me.

Table of Content

Preface

Although Joomla! has all of the basic content management tools you need to build a website, it is also designed to also run custom-built extensions written in PHP. This book steps through working examples of PHP code written to work seamlessly in Joomla!. Topics covered in this book include libraries for generating user interface elements, database table classes, Model-View-Controller design, configuration panels, the use of JavaScript libraries, and URL routing. After all of the code has been written, it is bundled in `.zip` files, ready to be installed by Joomla! site webmasters.

What this book covers

Chapter 1 gives you an overview of how Joomla! works. The example project used throughout the book is also introduced. The three types of extensions (components, modules, and plug-ins) are covered, along with a description of how they work together.

Chapter 2 begins with the development of the component used in the project. Initial entries are made in the database and toolbars are built for the backend. The general file structure of Joomla! is also introduced.

Chapter 3 walks through the creation of the backend interface for creating, editing, and deleting records in the project through the Model-View-Controller design pattern. Database table classes are also introduced.

Chapter 4 builds a frontend interface for listing and viewing records. Additionally, code to generate and interpret search engine friendly links is covered. The project is also expanded slightly, as a commenting feature is added.

Chapter 5 takes a closer look at the methods provided by the JTable, JHTML, and JUser classes. The JTable class allows you to manage a list of ordered records, while JHTML helps generate common HTML elements. Also, the concept of checking out records when JTable and JUser are used together is introduced.

Chapter 6 introduces a module used to list records on every page of the site. The module takes advantage of layouts, where the same data can be formatted differently depending on how the code is called. Some of the code is also separated out into a helper class so that the main code generating the module stays simple.

Chapter 7 continues development of the component, adding elements from the JTHML class that make the component blend in with the rest of the Joomla! interface. Controls over the publishing of records are introduced, as well as an interface for removing offensive comments. More toolbars are added, and multiple controllers are introduced.

Chapter 8 shows how to add many common JavaScript effects to your extensions. This chapter also explains how to create a Google Map and interact with it using MooTools. Finally, a way of using jQuery alongside MooTools is covered.

Chapter 9 develops three plug-ins. The first plug-in finds the names of records in the database and turns them in to links to those records. A second plug-in displays a short summary of the record when certain code is added to content articles. Finally, another plug-in is designed so that records are pulled up alongside Joomla! content searches.

Chapter 10 adds configuration parameters to the components, modules, and plug-ins. These are handled through XML and generate a predictable interface in the backend for setting options. Retrieving the value of these parameters is standardized through built-in functions.

Chapter 11 adds links and functionality to the component where users can email pages to their friends. It also prepares the user interface for internationalization and does a partial translation into French. Additionally, the chapter provides a solution for handling uploaded files.

Chapter 12 expands the XML files used for parameters and adds a listing of all the files and folders in each extension. Once this file is compressed along with the rest of the code into a ZIP archive, it is ready to be installed on another copy of Joomla! without any programmer intervention. Custom installation scripts and SQL code are also added to the component.

Who is this book for

This book is suitable for PHP programmers who want to take their first steps in customizing and extending the features of Joomla! through custom PHP development. It is not a reference guide for advanced Joomla! developers.

You only need to understand the basics of PHP programming; no experience of developing Joomla! extensions is assumed. You are expected to be familiar with the general operation of Joomla!.

Conventions

In this book, you will find a number of styles of text that distinguish between different kinds of information. Here are some examples of these styles, and an explanation of their meaning.

Code words in text are shown as follows: "We do not need to specify the directory where the framework is located; jimport() takes care of this."

A block of code will be set as follows:

```
function edit()
    {
        JRequest::setVar('view', 'single');
        $this->display();
    }
```

When we wish to draw your attention to a particular part of a code block, the relevant lines or items will be shown in bold:

```
switch($task)
{
    case 'add':
    addSingle();
    break;
    case 'save':
    saveSingle();
    break;
}
```

Any command-line input or output is written as follows:

```
UPDATE jos_critic SET ordering = id;
```

New terms and important words are shown in bold. Words that you see on the screen, in menus or dialog boxes for example, appear in our text like this: "clicking the **Next** button moves you to the next screen".

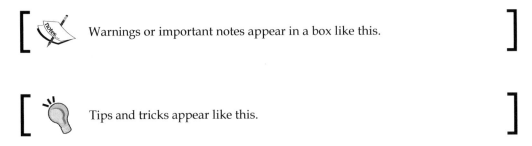

Warnings or important notes appear in a box like this.

Tips and tricks appear like this.

Reader feedback

Feedback from our readers is always welcome. Let us know what you think about this book—what you liked or may have disliked. Reader feedback is important for us to develop titles that you really get the most out of.

To send us general feedback, simply drop an email to feedback@packtpub.com, and mention the book title in the subject of your message.

If there is a book that you need and would like to see us publish, please send us a note in the **SUGGEST A TITLE** form on www.packtpub.com or email suggest@packtpub.com.

If there is a topic that you have expertise in and you are interested in either writing or contributing to a book, see our author guide on www.packtpub.com/authors.

Customer support

Now that you are the proud owner of a Packt book, we have a number of things to help you to get the most from your purchase.

Downloading the example code for the book

Visit http://www.packtpub.com/files/code/6200_Code.zip to directly download the example code.

The downloadable files contain instructions on how to use them.

Errata

Although we have taken every care to ensure the accuracy of our contents, mistakes do happen. If you find a mistake in one of our books—maybe a mistake in text or code—we would be grateful if you would report this to us. By doing so you can save other readers from frustration, and help us to improve subsequent versions of this book. If you find any errata, please report them by visiting http://www.packtpub.com/support, selecting your book, clicking on the **let us know** link, and entering the details of your errata. Once your errata are verified, your submission will be accepted and the errata added to any list of existing errata. Any existing errata can be viewed by selecting your title from http://www.packtpub.com/support.

Piracy

Piracy of copyright material on the Internet is an ongoing problem across all media. At Packt, we take the protection of our copyright and licenses very seriously. If you come across any illegal copies of our works in any form on the Internet, please provide us with the location address or website name immediately so that we can pursue a remedy.

Please contact us at copyright@packtpub.com with a link to the suspected pirated material.

We appreciate your help in protecting our authors, and our ability to bring you valuable content.

Questions

You can contact us at questions@packtpub.com if you are having a problem with any aspect of the book, and we will do our best to address it.

1
Joomla! Extension Development: An Overview

You have developed dynamic websites in the past, but a friend of yours told you about Joomla!, so you decide to give it a try. You want to start a simple website about restaurants after being inspired by the attractive celebrity chefs on the Food Network. The installation goes smoothly and more quickly than attempting to build a content management system from scratch. After finding a delicious template, adding some menus, and banging out a couple of reviews, you begin to think of some of the features that will draw in more visitors and even some cash. Within minutes, you install a shopping cart for selling books, a forum for gathering suggestions of places to review, and some advertising affiliate programs for the sidebars.

However, as you glance through the home page, you feel that something is missing. Then suddenly a brilliant idea hits you for something entirely new. Once it is executed, you know others will want to use it for their sites as well. You look around Joomla!'s source files and start looking for a way of building code that will slide right into place.

Why extend Joomla!?

Joomla! is not only designed to handle content articles, but also to allow a number of complex applications to be cleanly integrated. Shopping carts, forums, social networking profiles, job boards, and real estate listings are examples of the Joomla! extensions written by developers. All of these can run on a Joomla! site, and only a single database, template, and core need to be maintained. When you build an extension to Joomla!, it will inherit the look and feel of the overall site. Any type of program that can be coded in PHP is a potential extension waiting to be written.

Your extensions can also be portable. When coded correctly, you will easily be able to install your code on another copy of Joomla! without having to enter the database logins and other basic configuration information again. You will also be able to distribute your extensions to others as packages so they can install and enjoy them easily. End users will not need any programming or database knowledge to use your extensions.

Customization versus extension

Joomla!'s code is designed to be extended rather than hacked or directly modified. Rather than changing the core code, it is better to write an extension. When updates and patches are released for Joomla!, the core code will be updated, but your extensions will not be overwritten. These extensions are crafted in a self-contained manner, allowing you to develop your own code freely, without disturbing other items present in the Joomla! installation.

Although they are self-contained, extensions do not operate in a completely sealed environment; you can mix different extensions to get the functionalities you desire. Joomla!'s code allows extensions to share resources and sometimes perform actions on each other. Because we can write extensions, we will do this instead of customizing the core.

How to extend Joomla!

There are five types of extensions that Joomla! supports—templates, languages, components, modules, and plug-ins. Templates are used to control the overall look and feel of your site, using HTML and CSS. Languages are used to translate the text labels of the Joomla! user interface through the use of a simple text file. Components, modules, and plug-ins are primarily PHP-based, and will be the focus of this book.

Components

Of the extensions available, components are the most crucial. Components are essentially what you see in the "main" portion of the page. Joomla! is designed to load and run exactly one component for each page generated. Consequently, Joomla!'s core content management functionality itself is a component.

Components frequently have sophisticated backend controls. The backend is commonly used to create and update records in database tables; it can also run PHP code not specific to Joomla!. For instance, you may have an existing program that sends emails to a large list of subscribers. Instead of making your users log into this program separately, you can provide a link in the backend through which non-programmers can tell the program to send a message. You can also create component backends, which allow site administrators to upload pictures or videos.

Modules

In contrast to components, any number of modules can appear on a page. They are frequently used to create sidebars, banners, and menus. Modules complement the contents of a component; they are not intended to be the main substance of a page. Joomla! also allows administrators to add their own text into custom modules called content modules; these involve no programming and can be displayed alongside coded components. The backend controls for modules are limited, typically consisting of basic formatting.

Plug-ins

When a piece of code is needed throughout the site, it is best implemented as a plug-in (formerly called a Mambot). Plugins are commonly used to format the output of an article, component, or module when a page is built. Some examples of plug-ins include keyword highlighting, article comment boxes, and JavaScript-based HTML editors. Plugins can also be used to add different types of data to the results found in the core search component. The backend controls for plug-ins are similar to those of modules.

Topic overview

This book will cover the following topics regarding the development of extensions for Joomla!:

- Creating toolbars and list screens
- Maintaining a consistent look, and reducing repetitive code by using HTML functions
- Accessing the database and managing records
- Security, and the preferred way of getting request variables
- Menu item control
- Controlling the logic flow within a component

- Configuration through XML parameters
- Packaging and distributing

Let's take an overview of these topics.

Creating toolbars and list screens

Joomla! has a standard set of toolbar buttons that are used throughout the backend. These provide a consistent appearance across components so that users quickly become familiar with the corresponding functions. When necessary, the labeling and functions of these buttons can be changed, and new buttons can also be added.

As with the standard toolbars, Joomla! has a certain look for screens that list a set of records from the database. These lists usually have links to the edit screens for the individual records and have toggles that change the publishing status of the record. Automatic pagination is also available for lists.

Maintaining a consistent look, and reducing repetitive code by using HTML functions

Several standard CSS class names are used to format content and HTML elements within your extensions. This makes it easy for your extensions to seamlessly blend in with the rest of the website. Additionally, Joomla! includes many functions to automate the generation of checkboxes, dropdowns, select lists, and other common elements.

Accessing the database and managing records

A common database object is used in Joomla!, so that only one connection is made during every page request. This object also provides a set of functions to make queries and retrieve results. These functions are database-independent and are designed in such a way that you can install multiple copies of Joomla! into the same database when desired.

In addition to having a common database object, Joomla! has a standard database table class. Records can be created, read, updated, and deleted using the core functions. Logic can also be added so that child records in other tables are deleted when the parent is removed.

Security, and the preferred way of getting request variables

Because Joomla! is a web application deployed within public reach, it is necessary to protect it against security vulnerabilities. Joomla! employs a common method to make sure that scripts are called only within the framework, and not randomly executed.

Besides unintended script behavior, maliciously-submitted data can be used by hackers to gain access to your database. Joomla! provides functionality that prevents attacks of this kind.

Menu item control

A noteworthy feature of Joomla! is that navigation is separated from content. However, if a component is not built to take this into account, it is possible that website administrators will lose their templates and module selections. To take advantage of the system, it is necessary to refer to the intended menu item in generated links.

Also, it is possible to give administrators multiple options for linking to your component. This will allow the selection of different display options for the frontend without the need to construct long, confusing URLs manually. These options can additionally offer administrators some simple configuration controls.

Controlling the logic flow within a component

The same file is always called when a certain component is loaded, but different functions are called within it. Joomla! uses standard variables to determine which function to execute on each request. There are also classes available to automate the logic flow based on these variables.

At a minimum, components are designed to separate the output from the database and other processing functions. Larger components will separate the logic flow using a controller, the data access methods using a model, and the output using views. These conventions make it easier to maintain the code and help the component perform in a reliable and predictable way.

The elements of larger components come together to form what is called the **Model View Controller** (**MVC**) design pattern. Rather than being a specific piece of code that you include, MVC is a method to organize your project. The use of MVC helps you keep HTML markup, database queries, and user requests separate from one another so that code changes cause minimal disruption. Other software projects such as Ruby on Rails, CodeIgniter, Django, CakePHP, Zend Framework, and Qcodo also use MVC as a way of designing web applications.

When writing MVC code the first time, it may seem like unnecessary work up front. However, as your components grow, MVC makes your code easier to read and maintain. For instance, when an extra `<div>` tag must be added around your output, another programmer maintaining the component will automatically know to look amongst the views instead of deciphering the controller function that accepts uploaded files. Code that mixes processing and HTML output quickly becomes difficult to maintain; `if()` statements pile up and you never know if you are adding tags to the right place. Although the use of MVC in Joomla! components is optional, it is strongly recommended for nontrivial code.

Configuration through XML parameters

Rather than create a separate table to hold all of the configuration for an extension, Joomla! sets aside a place where short values can be held. These variables are defined through an XML file, which is installed with the extension. The XML file also provides default values and constraints for these parameters. The saving and retrieval of these values is automated-that is, handwritten queries are not needed.

Packaging and distributing

Once the coding is complete, it can be easily packaged for others to use. A listing of all the files involved is added to the XML file. Any queries needed for table creation are also included. All of the files are then compressed in an archive. The extension is then ready to be installed on any Joomla! based website.

Our example project

We will build extensions to create, find, promote, and cross-link restaurant reviews. A component will handle common data points seen across all reviews, such as price range, reservations, cuisine type, and location. Your visitors will be able to search and sort the reviews, and add their own criteria, to zero in on their dining options for the evening.

Some modules will highlight new reviews, and draw the attention of frequent visitors. Finally, one plug-in will pull pieces of the reviews into feature articles, and another will integrate them into searches.

To prepare for this project, you need to install a fresh copy of Joomla! 1.5 on a web server with PHP and MySQL. If you prefer to use one computer exclusively to complete this project (and do not have a local web server), the best thing to do would probably be to download and install a bundled and pre-configured package such as WAMP for Windows (`http://www.wampserver.com`) or MAMP for Mac (`http://mamp.info`). This way, you will be able to work with all of the files on your local file system.

Summary

In this introductory chapter, we first understood the need for extending Joomla! 1.5 and compared customization with extension. We learnt that Joomla! can be extended through components, modules, and plug-ins. This allows you to add functionality to a Joomla! site without hacking the core code. Joomla! can then be maintained and updated without disturbing the custom code. We also saw an overview of the topics that we will be covering in the chapters that follow.

2
Getting Started with Component Development

Before you begin with coding, there are a few files and folders that have to be created, as well as a query that has to be run. This will not only allow you to build the components, but will also help you try different features without extensive configuration. You will also get a quick overview of the way Joomla! organizes components and how they can be accessed. Finally, you will add some toolbars that work just like those in other components.

Joomla!'s component structure

Joomla! employs a specific naming convention, which is used by all components. Each component in the system has a unique name with no spaces. The code is split into two folders, each bearing the component name prefixed by `com_`. The component in this book will be called `restaurants`. Therefore, you will have to create two folders named `com_restaurants`:

- Create one in the folder named `components`, for the frontend
- Create one in the folder named `components` within the `administrator` folder for the backend

When the component is loaded from the frontend, Joomla! will look for a file with the component's unique name ending in a `.php` extension. Within the `components/com_restaurants` folder, create a `restaurants.php` file. Similarly, running it in the backend also assumes the presence of a file with the component name followed by `.php`. Add the `restaurants.php` file in `administrator/components/com_restaurants` folder. Leave both of the files empty for the moment.

Previous versions of Joomla! required you to use `admin.` as a prefix for your filename; in this case, you would have typed `admin. restaurants.php`. Although Joomla! 1.5 will execute a file named this way, it is no longer the preferred convention.

Executing the component

In the simplest style of PHP coding, webmasters link to individual `.php` files. A PHP website coded this way might have `index.php`, `aboutus.php`, `portfolio.php`, and `contact.php` as four pages linked directly via `<a>` tags. Although this makes it easy to locate the code generating a specific page, you need to be a programmer to be able to add more pages.

In contrast, every frontend page in Joomla! is dynamically-generated through a single `index.php` file. This makes it possible for user-created pages to be dynamically-generated without the need for new `.php` files, Apart from user content, different components can be loaded by setting the `option` variable in the URL. If you install Joomla! on a local web server in a directory named `joomla`, the URL for accessing the site will be `http://localhost/joomla/index.php` or something similar. Assuming that this is the case, you can load the component's frontend by opening `http://localhost/joomla/index.php?option=com_restaurants` in your browser.

At this point, the screen should be essentially blank, apart from the common template elements and modules. To make this component slightly more useful, open `restaurants.php` and add the following code, then save it and refresh the browser.

```php
<?php
defined( '_JEXEC' ) or die( 'Restricted access' );
echo '<div class="componentheading">Restaurant Reviews</div>';
?>
```

Your screen will look like the following:

You may be wondering why we called `defined()` at the beginning of the file. This is a check to ensure that the code is called through Joomla! instead of being accessed directly at `/components/com_reviews/restaurants.php`. Joomla! automatically configures the environment with some security safeguards that can be defeated if someone is able to directly execute the code for your component.

 Always add `defined( '_JEXEC' ) or die( 'Restricted access' );` at the beginning of every PHP file you write for Joomla! extensions. This prevents anonymous visitors from accessing the files directly and running code arbitrarily.

After the security check, there is a single line of PHP code outputting a `<div>` element with the class, `componentheading`. This is a standard CSS class used in Joomla! templates for the heading that appears above components. When you use this class for the markup, your HTML is automatically styled the way the template designer intended.

Creating code for the backend involves a similar process. Drop the following code into `/administrator/components/com_reviews/restaurants.php`:

```php
<?php
defined( '_JEXEC' ) or die( 'Restricted access' );
echo 'Restaurant Reviews';
?>
```

Save `restaurants.php`, then go to `http://localhost/joomla/administrator/index.php?option=com_restaurants` and compare your result with the following:

As in the frontend, the code first uses `defined( '_JEXEC' ) or die ( 'Restricted access' );` to make sure that `restaurants.php` is not being called directly. After this, the string **Restaurant Reviews** is the output with no extra formatting. Our text automatically appears within a rounded rectangle due to the design of the standard Joomla! administrator template. Because the administrator template is specifically designed for component backends, you do not need to add as many CSS classes to your markup.

Joomla!'s division of frontend and backend

For all of the Joomla! components, code empowering the backend portion is kept away from the frontend code. In some instances, the backend may use certain files from the frontend (and vice versa), but in general the two are separate. Security is enhanced as you are less likely to slip the administrative functions into the frontend code. This is an important distinction as the frontend and backend are similar in structure.

The following folder diagram shows the Joomla! root with the `administrator` folder expanded:

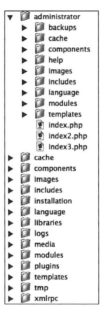

Note that the `administrator` folder has a structure similar to that of the root folder. It is important to differentiate between the two. If you accidently place your code in the wrong folder, it will fail to execute until you move it.

Registering your component in the database

You now know how to access both the frontend and the backend of the component. Although you could keep typing in the URLs each time you wanted to execute a piece of code, this will not be acceptable to your users. Navigation can be provided if you register the component in the database by adding a row to the components table.

We will perform this registration using the following query. It is assumed that your database prefix is `jos_`. If not, replace `jos_` with the prefix you chose. If you prefer to work directly with SQL statements via the command-line interface, enter the following query in your console:

```
INSERT INTO jos_components (name, link, admin_menu_link,
          admin_menu_alt, `option`, admin_menu_img, params)
VALUES (`Restaurant Reviews`, `option=com_restaurants`,
        `option=com_restaurants', `Manage Reviews`,
        `com_restaurants`, `js/ThemeOffice/component.png`, ``);
```

If you prefer to use a GUI or web-based database manager such as phpMyAdmin, enter **Restaurant Reviews** for **name**, **option=com_restaurants** for **link** and **admin_menu_link**, **Manage Reviews** for **admin_menu_alt**, **com_restaurants** for **option**, and **js/ThemeOffice/component.png** for **admin_menu_img**. Leave all of the other fields blank. The fields **menuid**, **parent**, **ordering**, and **iscore** will default to **0**, while **enabled** will default to **1**.

Field	Type	Function	Null	Value
id	int(11)			
name	varchar(50)			Restaurant Reviews
link	varchar(255)			option=com_restaurants
menuid	int(11) unsigned			0
parent	int(11) unsigned			0
admin_menu_link	varchar(255)			option=com_restaurants
admin_menu_alt	varchar(255)			Manage Reviews
option	varchar(50)			com_restaurants
ordering	int(11)			0
admin_menu_img	varchar(255)			js/ThemeOffice/component.png
iscore	tinyint(4)			0
params	text			
enabled	tinyint(4)			1

Adding this record gives the system some basic information about your component. It states the name you want to use for the component; this can contain spaces and punctuation. You can provide specific links to go to both the frontend and the backend. The image to be used on the **Components** menu can be specified. Also, the description in the browser status bar can defined. It is not necessary to add this query when developing the component—once you create the basic directories and files, your component is ready to be executed. However, this query does add a menu item in the backend and makes it possible to add an appropriate link in the frontend without hard-coding a URL.

After you have successfully entered the record, go to any page in the backend and refresh it. When you move the cursor over the **Components** menu you should see the new option.

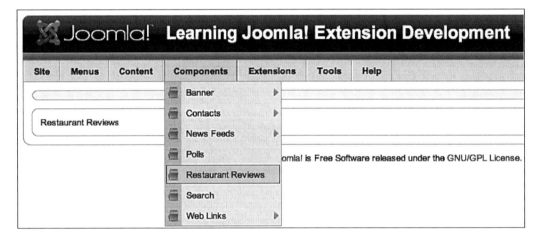

Now that the component is registered, you can also create a link for the frontend. Go to **Menus | Main Menu** and click **New**. From this screen, select **Restaurant Reviews**. Enter **Reviews** as the **Title**. Your screen will look similar to the following one:

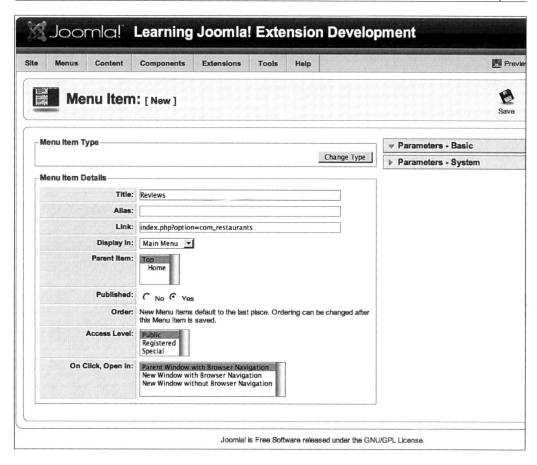

Now click **Save** and go to the frontend. You should now see **Reviews** listed as an option.

You could just break out your PHP skills and start coding the component, ensuring all frontend requests go through `http://localhost/joomla/index.php?option=com_restaurants` and all backend requests go through `http://localhost/joomla/administrator/index.php?option=com_restaurants`. Joomla! is flexible enough to let you do as you please. In some cases, you will have existing code that you want to use and you will need to split it into appropriate files. But for the restaurant reviews, you are building a new Joomla! component from scratch. You have the opportunity to design everything with Joomla's toolbars, users, database classes, and libraries in mind. These elements will save you a lot of time once you understand how they work.

Creating toolbars

Adding toolbar buttons to the backend of your component is quick and easy. Joomla! has a class named `JToolBarHelper` that allows you build the toolbar one button at a time, without having to touch HTML. The buttons consist of an image, HTML, and Javascript that interacts with `<form>` elements in your component.

To put `JToolBarHelper` to use, we will create a set of buttons that you would normally find on a screen for managing a list of records. Open `/administrator/components/com_restaurants/restaurants.php` and add the following code just before the line `echo 'Restaurant Reviews'`:

```
JToolBarHelper::title( JText::_( 'Restaurant Reviews' ), 'generic.png' );
JToolBarHelper::publishList();
JToolBarHelper::unpublishList();
JToolBarHelper::editList();
JToolBarHelper::deleteList();
JToolBarHelper::addNew();
```

Go to **Restaurant Reviews** on the **Components** menu or hit refresh if you're already there. You should see the title **Restaurant Reviews** on the left, with some icons on the right.

Because we added the toolbar code before the call to `echo`, you might assume that this positions the toolbar above our output. This is not actually the case; all Joomla! output is buffered before being sent to the browser. The calls to member functions of `JToolBarHelper` build the toolbar in memory as the code executes. When Joomla! assembles the backend template, the toolbar is called out of memory and the HTML output is then generated. Although the order of your calls to `JToolBarHelper` determines the ordering of the buttons on the toolbar, you can call `title()` at any time to set the heading on the left.

Creating a second toolbar

In addition to screens where you manage a set of records, you will also have screens for editing a single record or creating a new one. The toolbar for managing records will be of no use here, so we will create a second one. Wrap the toolbar code you wrote in the example above with the following `switch()` statement:

```
switch ($task)
{
    case 'edit':
    case 'add':
        JToolBarHelper::save();
        JToolBarHelper::apply();
        JToolBarHelper::cancel();
        break;
    default:
        JToolBarHelper::title( JText::_( 'Restaurant Reviews' ),
        'generic.png' );
        JToolBarHelper::publishList();
        JToolBarHelper::unpublishList();
        JToolBarHelper::editList();
        JToolBarHelper::deleteList();
        JToolBarHelper::addNew();
        break;
}
```

The `$task` variable is automatically registered as having global scope by Joomla!; this is a convention used for routing users through components. Joomla! will set `$task` to the value of the task in the **POST** or **GET** portion of your request. With this in mind, add `&task=add` on to the end of the URL, and then load the page so that you can see the other toolbar.

Your users will certainly not want to add the task variable to the end of the URL as they navigate through your component. How will they be able to use the second toolbar then? Each button on the toolbar represents a different task. When a button is clicked, the associated task is added to your form and it is automatically submitted. Once the appropriate form is in place, a click on the **New** button from the first screen will set **task** to **add** and pull up the toolbar seen in the second. Because we do not yet have any forms in the backend, these toolbar buttons will not function. These will start working in the next chapter when we build out the rest of the backend.

Available toolbar buttons

Joomla! allows you to override any button with your own task and label, passing them as the first and second parameters respectively. The following predefined buttons are among the ones available for use in your components:

[If you would like to create a custom button that looks and behaves like the core buttons, use the `custom()` member function of `JToolBarHelper`, passing in the task, icon, mouse-over image, and text description as the parameters.]

Summary

The basic files necessary to build the component are now in place. The rest of the Joomla! installation now knows that this component is available for frontend and backend use. By using standard HTML and CSS classes, the component has a look and feel similar to that of the other components in the system, making it easy to use with different templates. Basic toolbars are available for use with the component and can be assigned to different screens by using the `$task` variable.

3
Backend Development

Creating and managing restaurant reviews is our component's largest task. We will add forms and database functions to take care of this so that we can start adding reviews. The backend forms will be built according to the **Model-View-Controller (MVC)** design pattern, to keep our source code clean and organized. Developing the backend now will give us the chance to gather feedback from our restaurant reviewers. Designing this interface will carry us through the following topics:

- Creating a database table to hold the reviews
- Coding with MVC
- Setting up a basic form for data entry
- Processing the data and adding it to the database
- Listing the existing reviews
- Editing records

Creating the database table

Before we set up an interface for entering reviews, we need to create a place in the database where they will go. We will start with a table where one row will represent one review. Assuming that your database prefix is jos_ (check **Site | Global Configuration | Server** if you are unsure), enter the following query into your SQL console:

```
CREATE TABLE `jos_reviews`
(
    `id` int(11) NOT NULL auto_increment,
    `name` varchar(255) NOT NULL,
    `address` varchar(255) NOT NULL,
    `reservations` varchar(31) NOT NULL,
    `quicktake` text NOT NULL,
```

```
    `review` text NOT NULL,
    `notes` text NOT NULL,
    `smoking` tinyint(1) unsigned NOT NULL default `0`,
    `credit_cards` varchar(255) NOT NULL,
    `cuisine` varchar(31) NOT NULL,
    `avg_dinner_price` tinyint(3) unsigned NOT NULL default `0`,
    `review_date` datetime NOT NULL,
    `published` tinyint(1) unsigned NOT NULL default `0`,
    PRIMARY KEY (`id`)
);
```

If you're using phpMyAdmin, pull up the following screen and enter **jos_reviews** as the table name and specify that you want it to generate **13** fields.

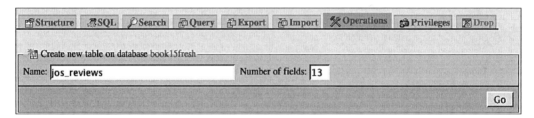

After clicking **Go**, you will see a grid; fill in the details of this grid so that it looks like the following screen:

Field	Type ⑦	Length/Values¹	Collation	Attributes	Null	Default²
id	INT	11			not null	
name	VARCHAR	255			not null	
address	VARCHAR	255			not null	
reservations	VARCHAR	31			not null	
quicktake	TEXT				not null	
review	TEXT				not null	
notes	TEXT				not null	
smoking	TINYINT	1			not null	0
credit_cards	VARCHAR	255			not null	
cuisine	VARCHAR	31			not null	
avg_dinner_p	TINYINT	3			not null	0
review_date	DATETIME				not null	
published	TINYINT	1			not null	0

Make sure that you make the field **id** into an automatically-incremented primary key:

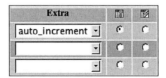

Creating a table class

We could write individual functions to take care of the queries necessary to add, update, and delete the reviews. However, these are rudimentary functions that you would prefer not to write. Fortunately, the Joomla! team has written code that you can use to automate these tasks. The JTable class provides functions for creating, reading, updating, and deleting records from a single table in the database.

To take advantage of JTable, we need to write an extension specific to the jos_reviews table. In the /administrator/components/com_restaurants folder, create a folder named tables. Within this new folder, create a review.php file and enter the following code:

```php
<?php
defined('_JEXEC') or die('Restricted access');
class TableReview extends JTable
{
    var $id = null;
    var $name = null;
    var $address = null;
    var $reservations = null;
    var $quicktake = null;
    var $review = null;
    var $notes = null;
    var $smoking = null;
    var $credit_cards = null;
    var $cuisine = null;
    var $avg_dinner_price = null;
    var $review_date = null;
    var $published = null;
    function __construct(&$db)
    {
        parent::__construct( '#__reviews', 'id', $db );
    }
}
```

When we extend the JTable class, we add all of the columns of the database table as member variables and set them to **null**. Also, we override the class constructor—the __construct() method. As a minimum, our __construct() method will take a database object as a parameter and will call the parent constructor using the name of the database table (where #__ is the table prefix), the primary key, and the database object.

Why use #___ as the Table prefix?

When writing queries and defining JTable extensions in Joomla!, use #___ instead of jos_. When Joomla! executes the query, it automatically translates #___ into the database prefix chosen by the administrator. This way, someone can safely run multiple installations of Joomla! from the same database. This also makes it possible for you to change the prefix to anything you like without changing the code. You can hard-code the names of legacy tables that cannot be renamed to follow this convention, but you will not be able to offer multiple installation compatibility.

Let's give TableReview a test. Because all of the table column names are member variables of the class, we can set them manually and then use the store() member function to add that data into our table. The restaurants.php file was added to /administrator/components/com_restaurants in Chapter 2, so you can use that to test your TableReview class. First, go to the bottom of the file and add a line that tells Joomla! where to look for your TableReview class:

```
JTable::addIncludePath(JPATH_COMPONENT.DS.'tables');
```

The addIncludePath() function of JTable tells Joomla! to look for table class files in the path that you provide. This makes it possible for you to add classes for multiple tables in the same folder, and make them available for use with one line of code.

A couple of preset constants are used in our function call above. The constant JPATH_COMPONENT is automatically set to the full path of our component's directory; in this case, this is your base Joomla! directory followed by /administrator/components/com_restaurants. For cross-platform compatibility, DS is used in place of slashes for directory separators.

Now that Joomla! knows where to look for our database table class, it's time to get a table object, based on that class. Add this line next:

```
$row =& JTable::getInstance('Review', 'Table');
```

The getInstance() function of JTable needs two parameters—the name of the specific table and the class prefix to be used. Note that Joomla! takes **Review** and **Table,** and assembles the class name TableReview from them. Separating them helps Joomla! know which file to load when creating the class instance.

The fields of the **jos_reviews** table can now be populated by using `$row`. Because the column names are matched up to member variables in `$row`, you can set these variables to whatever value you like. The following sample code sets some of the fields in the table, and then uses the `store()` function to generate an **INSERT** query.

```
$row->name = 'Salad Surprises';
$row->address = '283 Chestnut Street';
$row->quicktake = 'Salad lovers finally have a home.';
$row->review = 'This restaurant caters to salad lovers of all types,
                but sometimes the service is spotty.';
$row->notes = 'Diet friendly';
$row->credit_cards = 'Visa';
$row->cuisine = 'Salad';
$row->avg_dinner_price = '8';
$row->store();
```

To run the code, open **Components | Restaurant Reviews** in the backend. If you used the code above, part of a screen from phpMyAdmin, listing the records in **jos_reviews**, would look like this:

id	name	address	reservations	quicktake	review	notes	smoking	credit
1	Salad Surprises	283 Chestnut Street		Salad lovers finally have a home.	This restaurant caters to salad lovers of all type...	Diet friendly	0	Visa

Along with `store()`, the `TableReview` class inherits the `bind()`, `load()`, and `delete()` functions, among others. These four functions allow you to manage records in the database without writing a single line of SQL.

Coding with MVC

Our first few encounters with the component have involved simple code where each line executes sequentially. Many standalone PHP scripts are also initially coded this way. Although this is good for learning how the code executes, it will soon become cluttered if we attempt to add multiple screens and data processing.

This is where the MVC design pattern helps keep things organized. Views will primarily be used to handle HTML output. Each view in our component will represent a different screen. In Joomla!, each view has its own folder containing individual files with HTML output. The folders also contain files that perform final data formatting.

Although it would be possible to add database queries directly into the view code, this would get messy before long. To avoid this, we will use models that pair with our views. The model will contain a function that queries the database, and then sorts the results into a suitable data structure. By default, each view will look for a model with the same name, and use this if it exists. However, models are interchangeable—you can use the same model with more than one view, which avoids code duplication.

Finally, just as you cannot load the **Restaurant Reviews** component by going to `http://localhost/administrator/components/com_restaurants/restaurants.php`, views cannot be loaded directly by the browser. A controller will be placed in `restaurants.php` to handle this instead. The controller will determine what the incoming request is attempting to do (such as display a list or update a record), and will then act accordingly. By default, controllers in Joomla! assume that you want to load a view, and will attempt to display one based on the HTTP request variables passed to it.

In restaurant terms, you can think of MVC as the chef, your dinnerware, and a waitperson. The bulk of a waitperson's job involves taking your order and delivering your food. However, the waitperson also acts as a *controller* for your overall dining experience, handling tasks that do not involve the kitchen (such as fetching more silverware and presenting the bill).

Once you've ordered your meal, the waitperson takes the order to the kitchen. The chef cooks and *models* your food in such a way that it is ready to be presented and eaten. Your chef is solely focused on cooking food and does not think about the table arrangement or the temperature of the dining room.

When the food is delivered to you, it is *viewed* on a plate instead of in the pan where it is cooked. The same plates are washed between each meal and used for different foods. If asked nicely, the waitperson can bring the same food in a bowl or in to-go boxes instead of on a plate.

Contrast this restaurant to a street vendor making burritos from a cart. The street vendor rolls out a sheet of aluminum foil and places down a tortilla. The tortilla is then filled with rice and beans, then rolled up and wrapped in the foil. After you pay the vendor, the foil, tortilla, and toppings are handed to you in one pack. Although the burritos are delicious, the cart is a single-meal option where one customer is served at a time. The street vendor will never be able to turn the cart into a full restaurant without renting a storefront and hiring wait staff.

PHP programmers often start by writing code in a "street vendor" style, where one file takes care of all the logic, data, and presentation. Although this works well for simple single-use tasks, it becomes unmanageable as multiple screens and functions are added. Using the MVC pattern will help us to keep the code clean, and will make it easier to expand the component later.

Creating the review form

With a database table now in place, we need a friendly interface for adding reviews
into the database. To start, let's create a form for entering the review data. Because the
form will involve a large amount of HTML output, we will create a view for it. Inside
your /administrator/components/com_restaurants folder, create a new folder
called views. Because we are adding a form for entering single reviews, create a folder
inside views called single. Finally, create an additional folder in single called tmpl.
When you are done, the directory structure of com_restaurants should look like this:

Before displaying the HTML output there are some drop-downs, data, and other
elements that need to be pulled up. The logic to do this for the single view will
be contained in the view.html.php file in the /administrator/components/
com_restaurants/views/single folder. Create this file and add the following
code to it:

```php
<?php
defined( '_JEXEC' ) or die( 'Restricted access' );
jimport( 'joomla.application.component.view');
```

After making sure the code is being called within Joomla!, we use the jimport()
function to bring in code from the Joomla! framework. This function allows us to
bring up specific elements of the framework when we need them, instead of loading
all of the code into memory at once. We do not need to specify the directory where
the framework is located—jimport() takes care of this. Continue writing
view.html.php, adding the following code:

```php
class RestaurantsViewSingle extends JView
{
    function display($tpl = null)
    {
    $row =& JTable::getInstance('Review', 'Table');
    $this->assignRef('row', $row);
    $editor =& JFactory::getEditor();
    $this->assignRef('editor', $editor);
    $reservations = array(
```

```
        array('value' => 'None Taken', 'text' => 'None Taken'),
        array('value' => 'Accepted', 'text' => 'Accepted'),
        array('value' => 'Suggested', 'text' => 'Suggested'),
        array('value' => 'Required', 'text' => 'Required')
        );
    $this->assignRef('reservations', JHTML::_('select.genericList',
    $reservations, 'reservations', 'class="inputbox" '. '', 'value',
    'text', $row->reservations ));
    $this->assignRef('smoking', JHTML::_('select.booleanlist',
    'smoking', 'class="inputbox"', $row->smoking));
    $this->assignRef('published', JHTML::_('select.booleanlist',
    'published', 'class="inputbox"', $row->published));
    $this->assignRef('review_date', JHTML::_('calendar',
    $row->review_date, 'review_date', 'review_date'));
        parent::display($tpl);
    }
}
```

> **Where is the closing ?> tag?**
>
> You may have noticed that the PHP files in this chapter have not been closed with ?> tags. This is a newer convention that many PHP projects (including Joomla!) have adopted. The closing tag is not required by PHP and is not helpful unless you intend to add more HTML markup below your code. Leaving the closing ?> off prevents extraneous whitespace (frequently added by text editors) from being inadvertently added to the output.

This code creates a class based on JView called RestaurantsViewSingle. Note that the convention is to begin the class name with the name of the component, followed by View, and then ending with the name of the view. This class contains a single function called display(), which can be used to add data and elements to the view.

As with the sample JTable code shown earlier, we get an instance of the TableReview object. This instance is returned as $row, which is then assigned to the view using the assignRef() member function. The handling of $row is followed by bringing in and assigning the WYSIWYG editor. Next, several HTML elements are generated. The array $reservations defines a set of value and label pairs that are to be used in generating a <select> HTML drop-down. The JHTML class is then used to generate this drop-down along with a couple of radio buttons and a calendar. These are all assigned to the view, with the names **reservations, smoking, published**, and **review_date**, respectively.

What does JHTML::_() do?

Joomla! includes many HTML generation functions that can be used to automate the creation of elements, such as drop-down lists and checkboxes. In an effort to speed up performance, these functions are loaded into memory only when needed. This is accomplished through the _() function, which takes the function name as the first parameter and passes the remaining parameters (if any) to the desired function. Functions are organized by type, which is indicated by the first part of the name passed into the first parameter of _() before the period.

Once all of the elements are assigned to the view, we are ready to display the HTML output. The display() function from JView loads an output file based on the value of $tpl. In this case, $tpl defaults to null, which means that JView will look for a file called default.php in the tmpl folder. Because this file does not exist already, you need to create it, and add the following code:

```php
<?php
defined( '_JEXEC' ) or die( 'Restricted access' );
JHTML::_('behavior.calendar');
?>
<form action="index.php" method="post" name="adminForm"
id="adminForm">
  <fieldset class="adminform">
    <legend>Details</legend>
    <table class="admintable">
    <tr>
      <td width="100" align="right" class="key">
        Name:
      </td>
      <td>
        <input class="text_area" type="text" name="name" id="name"
        size="50" maxlength="250" value="<?php echo $this->
        row->name;?>" />
      </td>
    </tr>
    <tr>
      <td width="100" align="right" class="key">
        Address:
      </td>
      <td>
        <input class="text_area" type="text" name="address"
        id="address" size="50" maxlength="250" value="<?php echo
        $this->row->address;?>" />
      </td>
    </tr>
```

```
<tr>
  <td width="100" align="right" class="key">
    Reservations:
  </td>
  <td>
    <?php echo $this->reservations; ?>
  </td>
</tr>
<tr>
  <td width="100" align="right" class="key">
    Quicktake:
  </td>
  <td>
    <?php
    echo $this->editor->display( 'quicktake',
    $this->row->quicktake, '100%', '150', '40', '5' ) ;
    ?>
  </td>
</tr>
<tr>
  <td width="100" align="right" class="key">
    Review:
  </td>
  <td>
    <?php
    echo $this->editor->display( 'review',
    $this->row->review, '100%', '250', '40', '10' ) ;
    ?>
  </td>
</tr>
<tr>
  <td width="100" align="right" class="key">
    Notes:
  </td>
  <td>
    <textarea class="text_area" cols="20" rows="4" name="notes"
     id="notes" style="width:500px"><?php echo $this->row->notes;
     ?></textarea>
  </td>
</tr>
<tr>
  <td width="100" align="right" class="key">
    Smoking:
  </td>
  <td>
```

```
      <?php echo $this->smoking; ?>
    </td>
  </tr>
  <tr>
    <td width="100" align="right" class="key">
      Credit Cards:
    </td>
    <td>
      <input class="text_area" type="text" name="credit_cards"
          id="credit_cards" size="50" maxlength="250"
          value="<?php echo $this->row->credit_cards;?>" />
    </td>
  </tr>
  <tr>
    <td width="100" align="right" class="key">
      Cuisine:
    </td>
    <td>
      <input class="text_area" type="text" name="cuisine"
          id="cuisine" size="31" maxlength="31"
          value="<?php echo $this->row->cuisine;?>" />
    </td>
  </tr>
  <tr>
    <td width="100" align="right" class="key">
      Average Dinner Price:
    </td>
    <td>
      $<input class="text_area" type="text"
          name="avg_dinner_price"
          id="avg_dinner_price" size="5" maxlength="3"
          value="<?php echo $this->row->avg_dinner_price;?>" />
    </td>
  </tr>
  <tr>
    <td width="100" align="right" class="key">
      Review Date:
    </td>
    <td>
      <?php echo $this->review_date; ?>
    </td>
  </tr>
  <tr>
    <td width="100" align="right" class="key">
```

```
        Published:
      </td>
      <td>
        <?php echo $this->published; ?>
      </td>
    </tr>
    </table>
  </fieldset>
  <input type="hidden" name="id" value=
  "<?php echo $this->row->id; ?>" />
  <input type="hidden" name="option" value="<?php echo $option;?>" />
  <input type="hidden" name="task" value="" />
  <?php echo JHTML::_( 'form.token' ); ?>
</form>
```

The bulk of this file consists of HTML markup, with very little PHP code. Most of the PHP code in this file consists merely of using echo to output the member variables we assigned using the assignRef() member function in view.html.php. However, there are a few exceptions. First, as with all PHP files in Joomla!, we check to make sure that the file is being called within Joomla! rather than being called directly. Next, JHTML::_('behavior.calendar'); loads in the JavaScript necessary to run the pop-up calendar that will be displayed. Even though we are making the call here in the HTML output for our component, the JavaScript will automatically be loaded in the <head> portion of the HTML document. This is because Joomla! buffers all of the output while running the code, and then sends the output back to your web browser as the last step.

You might also notice that we are outputting the value of $option even though we never assigned this to the view. The JView parent class automatically pulls in this variable just before loading our HTML output. Finally, we output the results of JHTML::_('form.token');. This adds a randomly-generated token to the form that will be used later to verify the user's session.

Before we can view our work in the browser, we need to make some modifications to restaurants.php so that the view code will execute. Delete all of the code after JTable::addIncludePath(JPATH_COMPONENT.DS.'tables') and add the following:

```
switch($task)
{
    case 'add':
    addSingle();
    break;
}
function addSingle()
```

```
{
    include JPATH_COMPONENT.DS.
    'views'.DS.'single'.DS.'view.html.php';
    $view = new RestaurantsViewSingle();
    $view->display();
}
```

If the value of $task is edit or add, the addSingle() function is called. This function includes the view.html.php file, creates an instance of the RestaurantsViewSingle class, and then calls the display() member function. When you go to http://localhost/joomla/administrator/index. php?option=com_restaurants&task=add, your screen will appear similar to this:

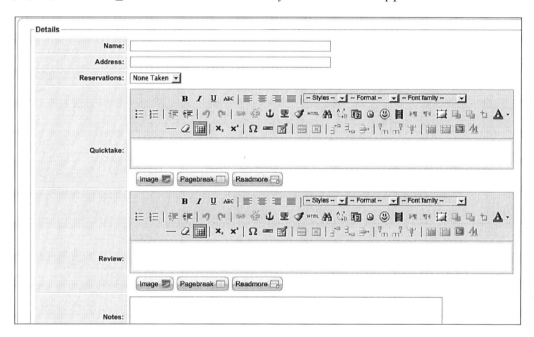

Processing the data

Once the data in the form has been filled out and the admin clicks the **Save** button, we need to save the information into the database. To start, create a new function of saveSingle() in restaurants.php:

```
function saveSingle()
{
    JRequest::checkToken() or jexit( 'Invalid Token' );
    global $mainframe, $option;
    $row =& JTable::getInstance('review', 'Table');
    if (!$row->bind(JRequest::get('post')))
```

```
{
    JError::raiseError(500, $row->getError() );
}
$row->quicktake = JRequest::getVar( 'quicktake', '', 'post',
                'string', JREQUEST_ALLOWRAW );
$row->review = JRequest::getVar( 'review', '', 'post', 'string',
                JREQUEST_ALLOWRAW );
if(!$row->review_date)
{
    $row->review_date = date( 'Y-m-d H:i:s' );
}
if (!$row->store())
{
    JError::raiseError(500, $row->getError() );
}
$mainframe->redirect('index.php?option=' . $option,
                'Review Saved');
}
```

Let's look at what this code is doing. First, `JRequest::checkToken()` determines whether a token has been passed in for the request. Because this function modifies the database, `checkToken()` is used to ensure that the request is legitimate. If the request is not legitimate, `jexit()` halts Joomla! immediately.

How does `checkToken()` ensure that a call is a legitimate request, and why is this a concern?

Cross-Site Request Forgeries (CSRF) have become a popular method of attacking web applications. These forgeries rely on the fact that authenticated users stay logged into websites as they use their browsers throughout the day. If a forger knows you are logged into a particular site, he or she can hijack your session using malicious HTML or JavaScript. To combat this, you can add a randomly-generated token for each session that is only displayed on forms and not stored in browser's cookies. `JHTML::_( 'form.token' )` generates this token for you and `JRequest::checkToken()` will attempt to match the submitted token with the one set for the session. If they do not match, you should halt Joomla! immediately. Use this code wherever you are performing database functions or any other sensitive operation where you are assuming the role of an authenticated user. You can read more about CSRF attacks and how to prevent them at `http://shiflett.org/articles/cross-site-request-forgeries`.

Next, we pull in the globals $mainframe and $option. The $mainframe object has many member functions that you can use to control session variables and headers. We also set $row as an instance of our TableReview class. The bind() member function of $row is called to load in all of the variables from the form.

The bind() function takes an associative array as the parameter and attempts to match all of the elements to member variables of the object. To reduce the risk of SQL injection attacks, we call JRequest::get() to sanitize the values from $_POST. This process escapes characters that could be used to control the SQL query. If bind() fails, the error is retrieved from the $row object and is raised using the raiseError() function of JError. Typically, this stops Joomla! and displays the error message.

After binding, we can manipulate the member variables of $row directly. Because the quicktake and review fields accept HTML content, they need special handling, as the bind() function automatically strips out HTML. To get around this, we use the getVar() member function of JRequest, passing into the form the variable name, the default value, the request array we wish to pull from, the expected data type, and the JREQUEST_ALLOWRAW flag.

In addition to recapturing the HTML data, we are also able to add default data or some other automatically-generated data after binding. In our code, we've set it to fill in the current date for the review, in case a specific date was not chosen.

Finally, we call the store() function, which takes all of the member variables and turns them into an UPDATE or INSERT statement, depending on the value of **id**. Because we are creating this record for the first time, it will not have a value for **id** and so an INSERT query will be constructed.

If there is an SQL error, an error is raised. Frequently, SQL errors at this level can be caused by the extraneous member variables of $row in the database table. If you run into a query error, first check to make sure that the spelling of your member variables matches the spelling of the table columns. Otherwise, if the SQL is successful, we use the redirect() function from $mainframe to send the user back to the main component screen with a confirmation message.

Currently, the switch() statement in restaurants.php only processes the add and edit tasks. Now that we have a form and a function in place, we can add a case to save our data. Add the highlighted code shown to the switch() statement:

```
switch($task)
{
    case 'add':
    addSingle();
    break;
```

```
        case 'save':
        saveSingle();
        break;
}
```

Save all of your files and go to `http://localhost/joomla/administrator/index.php?option=com_restaurants&task=add` in your browser. You should now be able to fill out the form and click **Save**. After you click **Save** you should see a screen similar to the following:

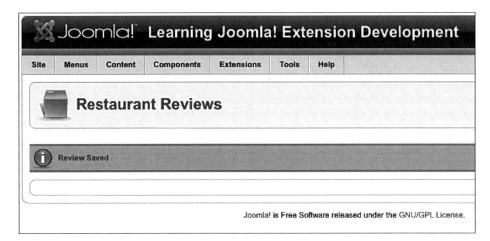

Why can't I click the 'New' button?

The buttons on the toolbar are designed to work with a form named `adminForm`. Because this screen does not yet have a form, clicking on any of the buttons will result in a JavaScript error. Once `adminForm` has been added with the hidden variable task, the buttons will function as expected.

You can check the results in the `jos_reviews` database table. If everything works correctly, a table listing in phpMyAdmin shows the following result after you click on **Browse**.

☐	✎	✕	2	The Daily Dish	180 Main Street	Accepted	This tried and true classic is always a sure bet.	Chicken fried steak, meatloaf, potatoes, string be...	Get there early on Friday nights, it's impossible ...	0	Visa, MasterCard, Discover

Creating a list screen

Because our administrators will not have access to phpMyAdmin, we need to build a screen that lists all of the reviews in the database. Accomplishing this will involve creating another folder inside the `views` folder and calling up the code from `restaurants.php`. Until now, we've been using `switch` statements to test the value of `$task` and to call an appropriate function. You could keep doing this, but it would be more convenient for you to combine these tasks. Remove the code below the call to `JTable::addIncludePath()` and insert the following code in its place:

```
jimport('joomla.application.component.controller');
class RestaurantsController extends JController
{
    function add()
    {
        JRequest::setVar('view', 'single');
        $this->display();
    }
    function save()
    {
        JRequest::checkToken() or jexit( 'Invalid Token' );
        global $option;
        $row =& JTable::getInstance('review', 'Table');
        if (!$row->bind(JRequest::get('post')))
        {
            JError::raiseError(500, $row->getError() );
        }
        $row->quicktake = JRequest::getVar( 'quicktake', '', 'post',
        'string', JREQUEST_ALLOWRAW );
        $row->review = JRequest::getVar( 'review', '', 'post',
        'string', JREQUEST_ALLOWRAW );
        if(!$row->review_date)
        {
            $row->review_date = date( 'Y-m-d H:i:s' );
        }
        if (!$row->store())
        {
            JError::raiseError(500, $row->getError() );
        }
        $this->setRedirect('index.php?option=' . $option,
                        'Review Saved');
    }
    function display()
    {
        parent::display();
    }
}
$controller = new RestaurantsController();
$controller->execute( $task );
$controller->redirect();
```

As with the `view.html.php` file in `views/single`, `jimport()` is used to load in a specific piece of the Joomla! framework. Doing this allows us to declare `RestaurantsController` as an extension of `JController`. Three functions are added to this class—`add()`, `save()`, and `display()`. Instead of writing an `include` statement that pulls in our view, the `setVar()` member function of `JRequest` is used to set the `view` environment variable to `single`. Setting `view` allows the parent `display()` function to automatically load in the correct files based on the variable name.

The `save()` function is identical to the `saveSingle()` function except that `$this->setRedirect()` is called instead of using the `$mainframe` global object. Finally, for the moment `display()` simply calls the parent `JController::display()` function for the moment. The `display()` function is called by default when the task called does not match any of the available functions.

Finally, an instance of the `RestaurantsController()` class is declared, and the `execute()` member function is called. The `execute()` function will attempt to match the variable passed in with a member function. Once `execute()` finishes, `redirect()` is called to re-load the browser if a landing URL was set with `setRedirect()`.

Go to `http://localhost/joomla/administrator/index.php?option=com_restaurants&task=add` in your browser, and make sure that the form for adding reviews comes up. If not, make sure that all of the code above is in place and try again.

Now that we have `RestaurantsController` handling the flow of our backend, we can concentrate on adding the list screen. This screen will need to get all of the records in the **jos_reviews** table and display them in a grid. Although our `TableReviews` class can load in single rows from the database, it will not help us to load the reviews all at once. To do this, we will need to create another class. In the `/administrator/components/com_reviews` folder, create another folder named `models`. Within this folder, create a file named `all.php` and enter the following code in it:

```php
<?php
defined( '_JEXEC' ) or die( 'Restricted access' );
jimport('joomla.application.component.model');
class RestaurantsModelAll extends JModel
{
    var $data = null;
    function getData()
    {
        if (empty($this->data)) {
            $query = "SELECT * FROM #__reviews";
```

```
            $this->data = $this->_getList($query);
        }
        return $this->data;
    }
}
```

After checking to make sure that we are calling this code within Joomla! and loading some code from the framework, `RestaurantModelAll` is declared as an extension of `JModel`. The member variable `$data` is declared and will be used to cache the list.

Finally, the `getData()` function checks to see if the `$data` member variable is empty. If it is, then a query is run through the `_getList()` member function inherited from `JModel` and `$data` is set. Otherwise, the query is skipped and the list is returned, so that extraneous database calls are not made.

With `RestaurantModelAll` written, we can now create another folder within `view` to hold our display code. Add the folder named `all` in `administrator/components/com_restaurants/views` folder, and use the following code in a new file called `view.html.php`, within this folder:

```php
<?php
defined( '_JEXEC' ) or die( 'Restricted access' );
jimport( 'joomla.application.component.view');
class RestaurantsViewAll extends JView
{
    function display($tpl = null)
    {
        $rows =& $this->get('data');
        $this->assignRef('rows', $rows);
        parent::display($tpl);
    }
}
```

This code is similar to `view.html.php` in the single view, but this time we call the `get()` member function to retrieve the data. The `get()` function first looks for a PHP file in the `models` directory that shares the name of our view. When it finds this file it loads it in `RestaurantsModelAll`, and calls the `getData()` function and returns the result. The `$rows` are assigned to the view and we call the parent `display()` function. To add the output that `display()` will use, add a `tmpl` directory to the `views/all` directory, and then create a `default.php` file which contains the following code:

```php
<?php
defined( '_JEXEC' ) or die( 'Restricted access' );
?>
<form action="index.php" method="post" name="adminForm">
```

```
<table class="adminlist">
  <thead>
    <tr>
      <th width="20">
        <input type="checkbox" name="toggle"
            value="" onclick="checkAll(<?php echo
            count( $this->rows ); ?>);" />
      </th>
      <th class="title">Name</th>
      <th width="15%">Address</th>
      <th width="10%">Reservations</th>
      <th width="10%">Cuisine</th>
      <th width="10%">Credit Cards</th>
      <th width="5%" nowrap="nowrap">Published</th>
    </tr>
  </thead>
  <?php
  $k = 0;
  for ($i=0, $n=count( $this->rows ); $i < $n; $i++)
  {
    $row = &$this->rows[$i];
    $checked = JHTML::_('grid.id', $i, $row->id );
    $published = JHTML::_('grid.published', $row, $i );
    ?>
    <tr class="<?php echo "row$k"; ?>">
      <td>
        <?php echo $checked; ?>
      </td>
      <td>
        <?php echo $row->name; ?>
      </td>
      <td>
        <?php echo $row->address; ?>
      </td>
      <td>
        <?php echo $row->reservations; ?>
      </td>
      <td>
        <?php echo $row->cuisine; ?>
      </td>
      <td>
        <?php echo $row->credit_cards; ?>
      </td>
      <td align="center">
        <?php echo $published;?>
      </td>
    </tr>
```

```
    <?php
    $k = 1 - $k;
  }
  ?>
</table>
<input type="hidden" name="option" value="<?php echo $option;?>" />
<input type="hidden" name="task" value="" />
<input type="hidden" name="boxchecked" value="0" />
</form>
```

This function starts by defining a form, with a name of **adminForm** (for JavaScript references) that points to index.php. A table with the adminlist class is then started and headers are added. All of the headers are typical, except for the first one that acts as a "select all" checkbox that automatically selects all of the records on the screen.

Once out of the header, we begin a loop through the rows. The variables $i and $n are initially set to 0 and the number of rows respectively; the loop runs for as long as there are rows available to be displayed. Once inside the loop, we get a reference to the current row so that we can display the contents. We switch the value of $k back and forth between 0 and 1; this is used to alternate between two different CSS classes with slightly different background properties.

Several of the member variables are output directly, but a couple of the columns warrant special treatment. Using the function JHTML::_('grid.id'), we can get the HTML code for a checkbox that will be recognized by the backend JavaScript. The JHTML::_('grid.published') function generates an image button based on the value of the published member variable in the row. When it is set to 1, we get a "check" image, whereas a value of 0 yields an "x" image.

Below the table, there are four hidden variables. The first one holds the value for option so that we are routed to the correct component. The task is made available so that the JavaScript in the toolbars can set it before submitting the form. When any of the checkboxes for the records are toggled, boxchecked is set to 1. It is set back to 0 when all of checkboxes are cleared. This aids the JavaScript in processing the list. Once the HTML output code is in place, update the RestaurantsController::display() function in the restaurants.php file with the code highlighted below.

```
function display()
{
$view = JRequest::getVar('view');
if (!$view) {
    JRequest::setVar('view', 'all');
}
    parent::display();
}
```

The `display()` function is called by default when `$task` does not match any of the functions, but it is also called by `add()`. If `add()` is called, `view` gets set to `single`, but if no task is specified, `view` isn't set. If `view` is not set, the call to `setVar` specifies `all` as the `view`. Let's try calling the component without setting a value for task. Load `http://localhost/joomla/administrator/index.php?option=com_restaurants`, and a screen similar to the following should appear:

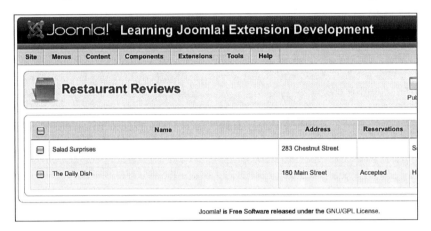

Editing records

Instead of writing a whole new set of functions for editing records, we can extend the existing code for the `single` view. In the `views/single/view.html.php` file, add the code highlighted below under `$row =& JTable::getInstance('Review', 'Table')`:

```
function display($tpl = null)
    {
        $row =& JTable::getInstance('Review', 'Table');
        $cid = JRequest::getVar( 'cid', array(0), '', 'array' );
        $id = $cid[0];
        $row->load($id);
        $this->assignRef('row', $row);
        $editor =& JFactory::getEditor();
        $this->assignRef('editor', $editor);
    }
```

As we did with the `save()` function in `RestaurantsController`, we get a `TableReview` object to handle the data for the record. We also pull in the form variable `cid`, which is an array of record IDs. Because we only want to edit one record at a time, we select the first ID in the array and load the corresponding row. This is all we have to do in order to populate the `single` view with data from the **jos_reviews** table.

To make the edit task active, we need to add the following function to
`RestaurantsController` class in the `restaurants.php` file:

```
function edit()
    {
        JRequest::setVar('view', 'single');
        $this->display();
    }
```

If you go to the list screen, select one of the checkboxes on the left and click **Edit.** The
selected record will be pulled up for editing. However, it is more convenient to have
links to the individual records in the **Name** field. To do this, go to the `default.php`
file in `/administrator/components/com_restaurants/views/all/tmpl`,
replace the code to display the name, and add the first two bits of highlighted code
as shown here:

```
jimport('joomla.filter.output');
    $k = 0;
    for ($i=0, $n=count( $this->rows ); $i < $n; $i++)
    {
      $row = &$this->rows[$i];
      $checked = JHTML::_('grid.id', $i, $row->id );
      $published = JHTML::_('grid.published', $row, $i );
      $link = JFilterOutput::ampReplace( 'index.php?option=
      ' . $option . '&task=edit&cid[]='. $row->id );
    ?>
    <tr class="<?php echo "row$k"; ?>">
      <td>
        <?php echo $checked; ?>
      </td>
      <td>
        <a href="<?php echo $link; ?>"><?php echo $row->name; ?></a>
      </td>
      <td>
        <?php echo $row->address; ?>
      </td>
      <td>
        <?php echo $row->reservations; ?>
      </td>
      <td>
        <?php echo $row->cuisine; ?>
      </td>
```

```
<td>
  <?php echo $row->credit_cards; ?>
</td>
<td align="center">
  <?php echo $published;?>
</td>
</tr>
```

To adhere to XHTML compliance, we need to make sure that ampersands are represented by the code &. We do this by using the ampReplace() function. This function is a member of the JFilterOutput class, which is loaded with the call to jimport('joomla.filter.output'). Joomla! has many different libraries for things such as XML processing and RSS output. Instead of loading the full set of libraries each time Joomla! loads, we use jimport() to load the code only when it is needed.

Save all of your files and then refresh the page http://localhost/joomla/administrator/index.php?option=com_restaurants. The record should now appear with a link. Click this link and you should get a screen that appears similar to this:

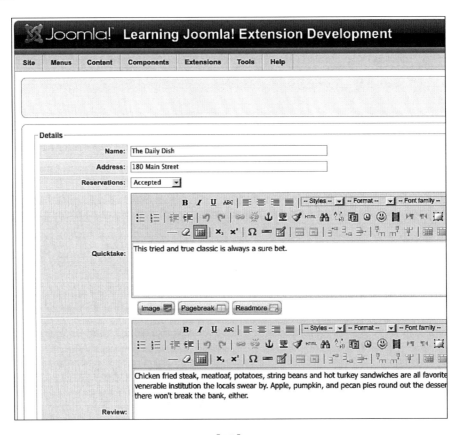

Summary

We used several specialized classes in this chapter to build the backend of the component in the MVC design pattern. Although we could have opted for something simpler, using MVC gives us the flexibility to add more functionality to our component later on, in a predictable and standardized way. Output, database queries, and decision logic are managed separately, making our component easier to maintain.

The backend is now fully functional for entering our restaurant reviews. We've saved ourselves from writing routine SQL statements by extending the JTable class. The HTML output is handled through views that generate add, edit, and list screens for the backend. These screens take advantage of back-end JavaScript to interact with the toolbar. Database queries populating these views are written separately in models.

Finally, functions have been added to the controller for saving and editing records. We call these functions by switching on the task variable. This variable is set on the form and submitted when an administrator clicks on one of the toolbar buttons in the backend. With these interface features in place, we can now get someone to start doing data entry while we build the rest of the component.

4
Frontend Development

Now that the reviewers have added some data in the backend, they're anxious to see how their reviews will appear to the visitors. Although we're still working on the backend, we will take a break from it for now to focus on the frontend visible to the outside world. We will learn how to incorporate the following features:

- Listing the reviews
- Displaying a review
- Generating search-engine friendly links
- Adding comments
- Displaying comments

Listing the reviews

In the *Executing the Component* section of Chapter 2, we follow the link `http://localhost/joomla/index.php?option=com_restaurants` (or follow the **Reviews** link we created) and get the following screen:

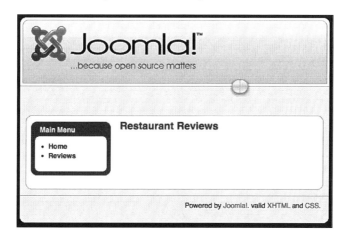

We will fill this screen with a list containing links that point to the individual reviews that we have added to the database, so that when visitors load the site, they can navigate through the reviews. As we did with the backend, we want to create a controller that we can use to organize our actions. Replace the code in the /components/com_restaurants/restaurants.php file with the following:

```php
<?php
defined( '_JEXEC' ) or die( 'Restricted access' );
jimport('joomla.application.component.controller');
class RestaurantsController extends JController
{
function display()
    {
        $view = JRequest::getVar('view');
        if (!$view) {
            JRequest::setVar('view', 'list');
        }
        parent::display();
    }
}
$controller = new RestaurantsController();
$controller->execute( $task );
$controller->redirect();
```

The jimport() function is first called to pull in the core controller code. Next, RestaurantsController is declared as an extension of JController. Inside the class, display() is the only function. If the view isn't set, it gets set to **list** and then the parent JContoller::display() function is called. After the class definition, we create a new instance of the controller and then use the current value of $task to execute it.

Before creating the **list** view for the frontend, let's write the query that we will use to pull the reviews out of the database. Create a folder called models in the /components/com_restaurants folder, then add the list.php file with the following code:

```php
<?php
defined( '_JEXEC' ) or die( 'Restricted access' );
jimport('joomla.application.component.model');
class RestaurantsModelList extends JModel
{
    var $_data = null;
    function &getData()
    {
        if (empty($this->_data)) {
            $query = "SELECT * FROM #__reviews WHERE published =
            '1' ORDER BY review_date DESC";
```

```
            $this->_data = $this->_getList($query);
        }
        return $this->_data;
    }
}
```

This model is very similar to the `RestaurantsModelAll` one that we used for the backend in Chapter 3. The difference here is that we only want to select the published reviews for display in the frontend, so we add a `WHERE` clause to make sure that **published** is set to **1**. We also want to show the most recent reviews first, so we `ORDER BY` the `review_date` field, in descending order.

Now that a controller and model are in place, all that is left to do is to add a view to display the reviews. The process for this is similar to what we did in the backend. Create a `views` folder in the `/components/com_restaurants` folder, and then create a `list` folder within that. The `list` folder will contain a file named `view.html.php` and a folder named `tmpl`, which will itself contain the `default.php` file. Your `views` folder structure will look like this:

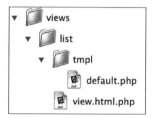

Add the following code into the `view.html.php` file. This code is almost identical to the code for the `all` view from the backend in Chapter 3, except that the name of the class is `RestaurantsViewList`:

```php
<?php
defined( '_JEXEC' ) or die( 'Restricted access' );
jimport( 'joomla.application.component.view');
class RestaurantsViewList extends JView
{
    function display($tpl = null)
    {
        $rows =& $this->get('data');
        $this->assignRef('rows', $rows);
        parent::display($tpl);
    }
}
```

Finally, we need to generate the HTML output that will be sent to the browser. Because $tpl is set to null, default.php is automatically loaded from the tmpl directory. Open /components/com_restaurants/views/list/tmpl/default.php and add this code:

```php
<?php defined( '_JEXEC' ) or die( 'Restricted access' ); ?>
<div class="componentheading">Restaurants we have reviewed</div>
<ul>
    <?php
    foreach ($this->rows as $row)
    {
        $link = 'index.php?option=com_restaurants&id=
        ' . $row->id . '&view=single';
        echo '<li><a href="' . $link . '">' .
        $row->name . '</a></li>';
    }
    ?>
</ul>
```

First, as with every PHP file we create in Joomla!, a check is added to make sure that the file is not being called directly. Next, the heading for the screen is added inside a **div** with the componentheading class. This class is a standard one used by template designers for CSS. The reviews are then listed one by one in an unordered list. The $rows that were assigned in view.html.php are cycled over, a link is built for each review and then it is output. Once all of this code is in place, save your files and then click the **Reviews** link (if you made one in Chapter 2) or go to http://localhost/joomla/index.php?option=com_restaurants. Your screen will look similar to this:

If you do not see any reviews listed, make sure that at least one of them is published in the backend. To publish a review, go to the list that was created in Chapter 3 and click on the title of one of the reviews. Then, set **Published** to **Yes** and click **Save**.

Displaying a review

If you were to click on any of the links at the moment, you would get a "**500**" error similar to the one below:

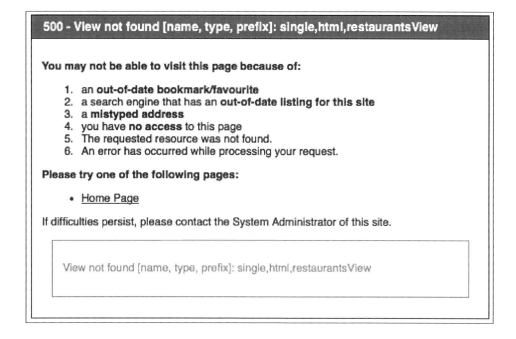

This is because we have not yet added the `single` view. By now, you are probably comfortable with creating the directory and file structure for a new view — you simply add the name of the view as a folder under `views`, and then create `view.html.php` and `tmpl/default.php` within this folder. Add this code for the view in the `view.html.php` file:

```php
<?php
defined( '_JEXEC' ) or die( 'Restricted access' );
jimport( 'joomla.application.component.view');
JTable::addIncludePath(JPATH_ADMINISTRATOR.
        DS.'components'.DS.'com_restaurants'.DS.'tables');
class RestaurantsViewSingle extends JView
{
    function display($tpl = null)
    {
        $id = (int) JRequest::getVar('id', 0);
        $review =& JTable::getInstance('review', 'Table');
        $review->load($id);
        if ($review->published == 0) {
            JError::raiseError(404,
            'The review you requested is not available.' );
        }
        if ($review->smoking == 1) {
            $smoking = 'Yes';
        } else {
            $smoking = 'No';
        }
        $date = JHTML::Date($review->review_date);
        $backlink = 'index.php?option=com_restaurants';
        $this->assignRef('review', $review);
        $this->assignRef('smoking', $smoking);
        $this->assignRef('date', $date);
        $this->assignRef('backlink', $backlink);
        parent::display($tpl);
    }
}
```

Before declaring the `view` class, we first pull in the framework code through `jimport()` and also add the include path for our `JTable` classes. In this case, we want to use the table classes that are in the backend folder of the component. To get the path of this folder, start with `JPATH_ADMINISTRATOR` and work your way to the `tables` folder.

Inside the `display()` function, **id** is extracted from the HTTP request using
`JRequest::getVar()`, then `$review` is set as an instance of `TableReview` using
`JTable::getInstance()`. The variable cast `(int)` is placed before the call to
`JRequest::getVar()` to make sure that the **id** variable is indeed an integer. This is
very important as requests are coming from unauthenticated users who could exploit
this if caution is not applied. If the **id** from the request is indeed an integer, it is used
to load the review. If the review is not published (or the load failed), an HTTP 404
error is returned and a screen similar to the following one is displayed:

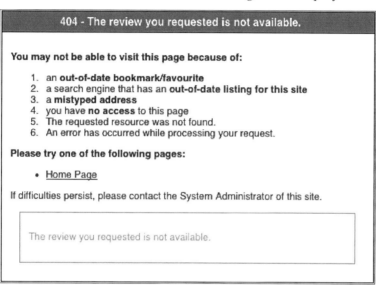

Instead of just assigning `$review` as a member variable of our view and outputting
everything directly in `tmpl/default.php`, some of the data is prepared so that it is
more presentable. First, the value of `smoking` is determined and the `$smoking` string
is set to **yes** or **no** accordingly. Next, `review_date` is passed into `JHTML::Date()`,
which returns the date in a human-readable and locale-specific format. Finally, a
link back to the main list of reviews is generated. All of these variables, along with
the `$review` object, are assigned to the view, and then `parent::display()` is called.
Because `$tpl` is set to **null**, Joomla! will look for a file named `default.php` in the
`tmpl` directory. Add the following code to this file:

```php
<?php defined( '_JEXEC' ) or die( 'Restricted access' ); ?>
<p class="contentheading"><?php echo htmlspecialchars($this->
review->name); ?></p>

<p class="createdate"><?php echo $this->date; ?></p>

<p><?php echo htmlspecialchars($this->review->quicktake); ?></p>

<p><strong>Address:</strong> <?php echo htmlspecialchars($this-
>review->address); ?></p>
```

```
<p><strong>Cuisine:</strong> <?php echo htmlspecialchars($this-
>review->cuisine); ?></p>

<p><strong>Average dinner price:</strong> $<?php echo
htmlspecialchars($this->review->avg_dinner_price); ?></p>

<p><strong>Credit cards:</strong> <?php echo htmlspecialchars($this-
>review->credit_cards); ?></p>

<p><strong>Reservations:</strong> <?php echo htmlspecialchars($this-
>review->reservations); ?></p>

<p><strong>Smoking:</strong> <?php echo $this->smoking ?></p>
<p><?php echo htmlspecialchars($this->review->review); ?></p>
<p><em>Notes:</em> <?php echo htmlspecialchars($this->review->notes);
?></p>

<a href="<?php echo htmlspecialchars($this->backlink); ?>">&lt; return
to the reviews</a>
```

After making sure that the call to `default.php` is within Joomla!, all of the member variables that were assigned back in `view.html.php` are output. Note that `htmlspecialchars()` is wrapped around every piece of output that was not generated by the Joomla! framework. This is used to help make sure that the HTML code sent to the browser is valid and that special characters (such as <, >, and &) are properly escaped and displayed on screen.

Once all of the files have been saved, click one of the review links again and you should see a nicely-formatted page.

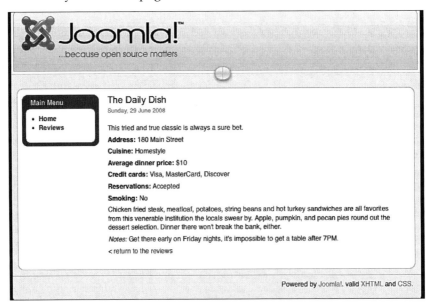

Generating search-engine-friendly links

Currently, the links to our reviews are generated as long GET strings, such as `http://localhost/joomla/index.php?option=com_resaurants&id=1&view=single&Itemid=2`. Our critics mentioned that they hate seeing links like these. Also, these links are not very helpful for search engines attempting to index our site. It would be preferable to have a link like—`http://www.ourdomain.com/reviews/view/1` instead. To accomplish this, we will define a route to both generate and decode **Search-Engine-Friendly (SEF)** links. Before we write any code, we will have to go to the administrator backend and enable SEF links. Go to **Site | Global Configuration** and make sure that **Search Engine Friendly URLs** is set to **Yes**. If you are using Apache as your web server and have `mod_rewrite` enabled, you can also set **Use Apache mod_rewrite** to **Yes**. This will remove `index.php` entirely from your URLs. With `mod_rewrite` enabled, the **SEO Settings** section of your **Global Configuration** screen should be as shown in the following image:

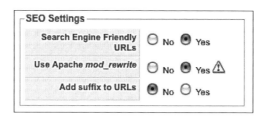

If you cannot use `mod_rewrite` with your configuration, the SEF links will still be built, but will have `index.php` in the middle, for example: `http://www.yoursite.com/index.php/search/engine/friendly/link`.

Click **Save** to change the configuration. If you're using `mod_rewrite`, make sure that you rename `htaccess.txt` to `.htaccess`. If you get a message saying that your configuration file is unwritable, open the `configuration.php` file in the Joomla! root and set the `$sef` member variable of `JConfig` to `1` instead of `0`.

Building URL segments

When creating internal links while building a page in Joomla!, components and modules will call the JRoute::_() function. This function takes a relative link as the parameter and returns an SEF version of the link. To build this version, JRoute::_() first parses the relative link into an array, then removes the option element and adds its value as the first segment of the new URL. The function will then look for router.php in the component directory that has the same name as option. If router.php is found, it will be included and the function beginning with the component name and ending with BuildRoute() will be called, in our case, RestaurantsBuildRoute(). To create this function, go back to the /components/com_restaurants folder and create a file named router.php. Fill this file with the following code:

```php
<?php
defined( '_JEXEC' ) or die( 'Restricted access' );
function RestaurantsBuildRoute(&$query)
{
    $segments = array();
    if (isset($query['view']))
        {
        $segments[] = $query['view'];
        unset($query['view']);
        }
    if (isset($query['id']))
        {
        $segments[] = $query['id'];
        unset($query['id']);
        }
    return $segments;
}
```

When JRoute::_() determines it is processing a link to a restaurant review, RestaurantsBuildRoute() will be called and an array of the URL variables (without the option element) will be passed in. To finish building the SEF link, we need to return an ordered array of the rest of the URL segments. First, we set $segments as an empty array. Next, we test the $query array to see if the view element is present. If it is so, we add the value of view as the first element of $segments and then remove view from $query. Next, we perform the same process with id. Finally, we return $segments so that JRoute::_() can finish building the URL.

There are two methods involved in the way this function is written that are crucial to getting SEF URLs built correctly. First, the $query array must be passed in by reference (preceded by & in the function definition). As we build the segments, we remove the processed elements from the $query array. Any element left in $query after our function will be processed back into the URL and will appear similar to GET elements. If we do not pass in $query by reference, the calls to unset() will only affect our local copy, and all of the URL elements will appear after the SEF segments.

In addition to handling $query correctly, the ordering of the elements in $segments matters. Because SEF URLs do not have any way of identifying the elements that the values are intended to set, the only way we can reliably map our values is to expect them in a predefined order. When we return $segments, JRoute::_() will add each element from this array to the URL, separating them by slashes. If there are any variables left in $query, these will be added to the end of the URL in GET string style.

Although we now have router.php in place with a function that will generate SEF URLs, our component's output functions are not set to use it. Open /components/com_restaurants/views/list/tmpl/default.php and replace the line where the value of $link is set, with the highlighted code:

```php
<?php
foreach ($this->rows as $row)
{
$link = JRoute::_('index.php?option=com_restaurants&id=
' . $row->id . '&view=single');
 echo '<li><a href="' . $link . '">' . $row->name . '</a></li>';
}

?>
```

Also, change the link back to the main list in /components/com_restaurants/views/single/view.html.php:

```php
$date = JHTML::Date($review->review_date);
$backlink = JRoute::_('index.php?option=com_restaurants');
$this->assignRef('review', $review);
```

The component will now generate SEF URLs according to the pattern we set in RestaurantsBuildRoute().

Parsing URL segments

If you attempt to click on one of the reviews right now, you will get a message similar to this one:

Fatal error: Call to undefined function restaurantsParseRoute() in **/Users/josephleblanc/Sites/book2ndChapter4 /includes/router.php** on line **247**

In addition to a function generating SEF URLs for reviews, we need a function capable of decoding these URLs. Go back to the `/components/com_restaurants/ router.php` file, and add the following function:

```
function RestaurantsParseRoute($segments)
{
    $vars = array();
    if (isset($segments[0])) {
        $vars['view'] = $segments[0];
    }
    if (isset($segments[1])) {
        $vars['id'] = $segments[1];
    }
    return $vars;
}
```

Once Joomla! determines that the page request is intended for the `restaurants` component, it will call `RestaurantsParseRoute()` and pass in an array of the relevant URL segments. These segments are ordered in the same way as we set them in `RestaurantsBuildRoute()`. We initialize an array, `$vars`, to hold the variables we return. Before setting the elements of `$vars`, we use `isset()` to make sure that the variables in `$segments` actually exist. Then we set the `task` and `id` elements of this array to the first and the second elements of `$segments` respectively.

Finally, we return `$vars`, which Joomla! in turn sets as request variables. This way, the entire routing process is transparent to the rest of the code. All of the request variables you would normally expect to be present under a conventional script call will be there.

Save `router.php` and try clicking on some of the links and pay attention to the location bar in your browser. You should now notice URLs like `http://www. oursite.com/reviews/view/1` or `http://www.oursite.com/index.php/ reviews/view/1`. If the URLs look like `http://www.oursite.com/component/ reviews/view/1`, this just means that you followed a non-SEF URL. Now this will clear up as you navigate around.

Adding comments

Most visitors will take our word for it when we say that a restaurant is great (or that it isn't). However, there may be a few who disagree. Why not give them the opportunity to leave comments about their experiences with the restaurant? We'll need a place to store these comments, so enter the following SQL command into your database console:

```
CREATE TABLE `jos_reviews_comments` (
  `id` int(11) NOT NULL auto_increment,
  `review_id` int(11) NOT NULL,
  `user_id` int(11) NOT NULL,
  `full_name` varchar(50) NOT NULL,
  `comment_date` datetime NOT NULL,
  `comment_text` text NOT NULL,
  PRIMARY KEY  (`id`)
  )
```

If you're using phpMyAdmin, pull up the following screen and enter **jos_reviews_comments** as the table name and **6** in the **Number of fields** section:

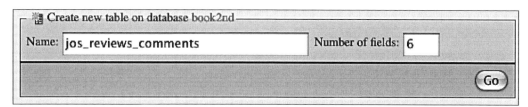

After clicking **Go**, a grid is displayed. Fill in the details so that it looks like the following screen:

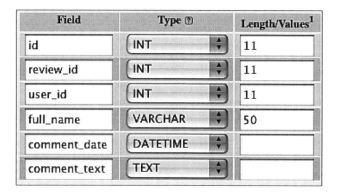

Make sure that you make the field **id** into an automatically-incremented primary key:

We also want to add another database class to handle the basic functions for this new table. Because we already have the class for the reviews themselves in `/administrator/components/com_restaurants/tables`, we will add the second one here as well. Create a file named `comment.php` and add the following `TableComment` class to it, making sure that each column in the table is represented as a member variable:

```php
<?php
defined('_JEXEC') or die('Restricted access');
class TableComment extends JTable
{
  var $id = null;
  var $review_id = null;
  var $user_id = null;
  var $full_name = null;
  var $comment_date = null;
  var $comment_text = null;
  function __construct(&$db)
  {
    parent::__construct( '#__reviews_comments', 'id', $db );
  }
}
```

Now that we've created a place to hold the comments, a form should be added so that people can enter these comments. Until now, the views in the component have had the same structure—a folder containing `view.html.php` and the folder `tmpl`. The `tmpl` folder is in place so that the major elements of the view can be separated further. Because the form we are about to add can be thought of as an accessory to the main view, we will add it to a separate file and call it from the main template.

Create a file named `default_comment_form.php` and save this file to the `/components/com_restaurants/views/single/tmpl` folder. Add the following code to this file:

```php
<?php defined( '_JEXEC' ) or die( 'Restricted access' ); ?>
<form action="index.php" method="post">

<div><strong>Name:</strong></div>
<div><input class="text_area" type="text" name=
          "full_name" id="full_name" value=
```

```
                "<?php echo $this->name; ?>" /></div>
<div><strong>Comment:</strong></div>
<div><textarea class="text_area" cols="40" rows=
            "4" name="comment_text" id=
            "comment_text"></textarea></div>

<input type="hidden" name="review_id" value=
            "<?php  echo $this->review->id; ?>" />

<input type="hidden" name="task" value="comment" />

<input type="hidden" name="option" value="<?php echo $option; ?>" />

<input type="submit" class="button" id="button" value="Submit" />

</form>
```

This form points to index.php and has several hidden variables that will help Joomla! load the correct piece of our code when someone adds a comment. We use option to get back to the com_restaurants component, task to tell the component that we want to add a comment, and review_id to identify the review that the commenter is commenting on. There is one variable on the form that is currently not set-this is, $this->name. If the visitor is logged into our site, we want to use the name that they have already entered to pre-fill this input. To do this, open up the /components/com_restaurants/views/single/view.html.php file, and add the highlighted code inside display():

```
$backlink = JRoute::_('index.php?option=com_restaurants');

$user =& JFactory::getUser();

$this->assignRef('review', $review);
$this->assignRef('smoking', $smoking);
$this->assignRef('date', $date);
$this->assignRef('backlink', $backlink);
$this->assignRef('name', $user->name);

parent::display($tpl);
```

The call to JFactory::getUser() returns Joomla!'s current user object. This contains most of the fields found in the **jos_users** table, along with some related functions that can be used for authorization. When the current user is a visitor who is not logged into the site, the function will return a user object with blank fields. Because we are only interested in the name of the user for the form, we assign this value to the view.

Before loading the review again to see the comment form, the main template file needs to be adjusted to load the form. Add the following code to the end of the `/components/com_restaurants/views/single/tmpl/default.php` file:

```php
<?php echo $this->loadTemplate('comment_form'); ?>
```

Now when you load the link for **The Daily Dish**, the screen should look similar to this:

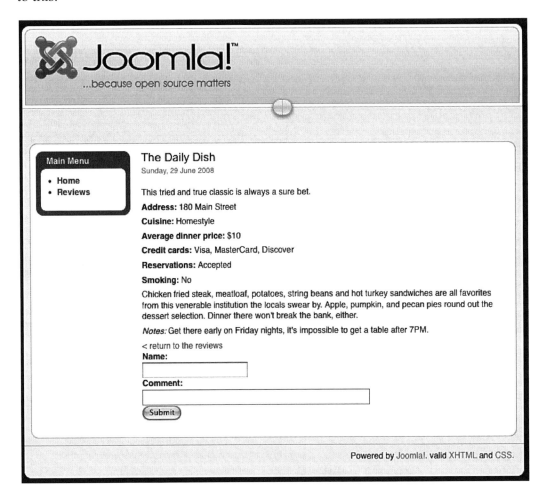

You may notice that even though we added code to automatically fill in the **Name** field of the form, this field is currently blank, as we have not logged in to the frontend of Joomla!. To log into the frontend, we will need to add a module with a form where a username and password can be entered. To do this, go to the backend of Joomla! and go to **Extensions | Module Manager**, then click **New**. A large list of module choices will appear.

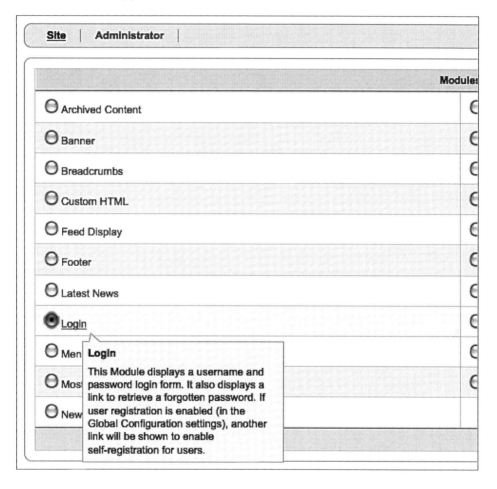

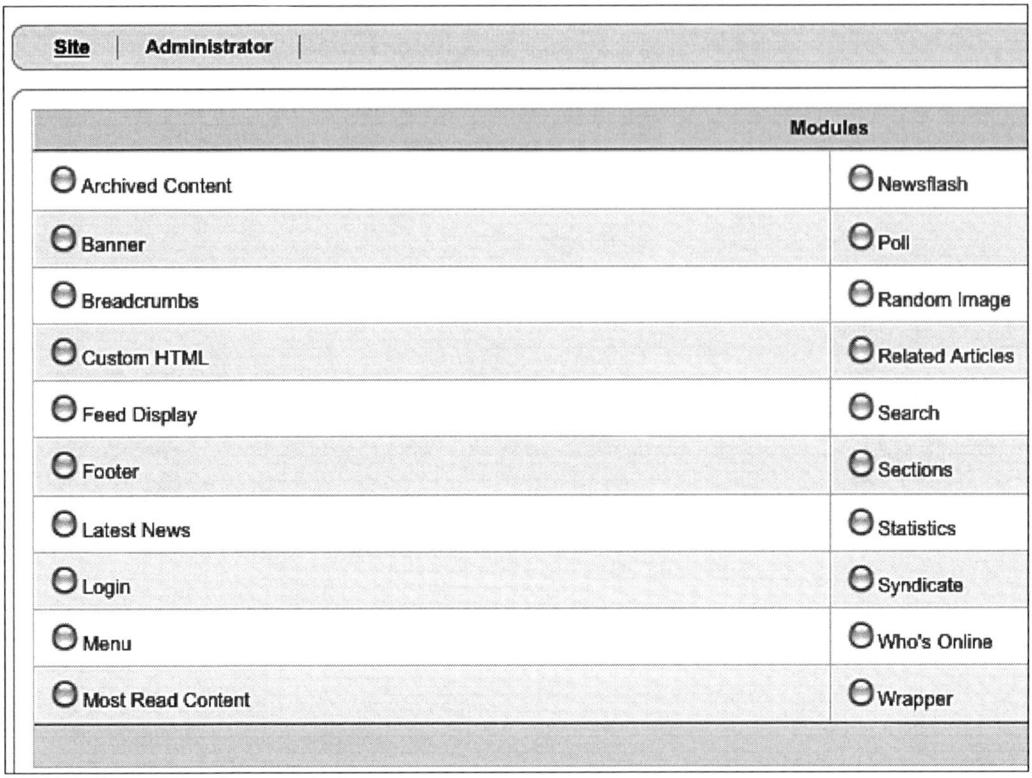

Select **Login** from this list. Enter the text **Login** in the field **Title,** and then click **Save**. Go back to **The Daily Dish** in the frontend and reload the page. A login form should now appear on the left. You can use your **admin** username from the backend to log into this form. When you do so, the page reloads and the **Name** field is pre-filled with **Administrator**.

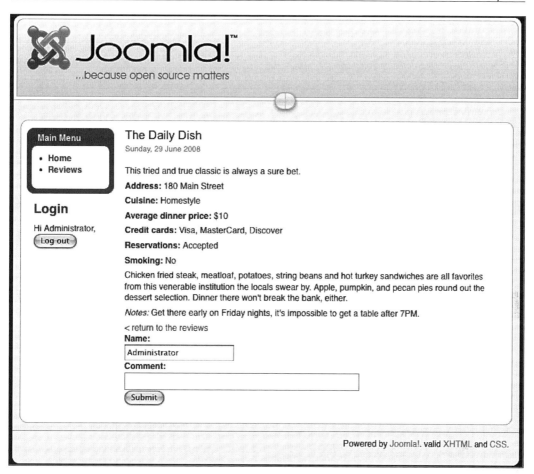

Before we attempt to fill in and submit the comment form, we need to add the code that will process the input and insert it into the database. In the form that was added to `default_comments_form.php`, `task` was set to **comment**. Because a controller is already available in `/components/com_restaurants/restaurants.php`, this can be used to handle the task **comment** with a `comment()` function. Add the following code to the controller in the `restaurants.php` file:

```
function comment()
{
    JTable::addIncludePath(JPATH_COMPONENT_ADMINISTRATOR . DS .
    'tables');
    $row =& JTable::getInstance('comment', 'Table');

    $row->review_id = JRequest::getInt('review_id', 0);
```

```
    $row->comment_date = date( 'Y-m-d H:i:s' );

    $user =& JFactory::getUser();

    if($user->id)
    {
        $row->user_id = $user->id;
    }

    $row->full_name = JRequest::getString('full_name', '');
    $row->comment_text = JRequest::getString('comment_text', '');

    if (!$row->store())
    {
        JError::raiseError(500, $row->getError());
    }
$this->setRedirect(JRoute::_('index.php?option=com_restaurants&id=' .
$row->review_id . '&view=single'), 'Comment Added.');
}
```

First, we use the addIncludePath() function to pull in our table classes from the backend of the component. The constant JPATH_COMPONENT_ADMINISTRATOR is automatically set to the absolute path to administrator/components/com_restaurants. So adding DS and the string 'tables' gets us to the table directory. Next, the table object is pulled in and assigned to $row.

At this point, we could use the bind() member function of $row and pass in JRequest::get('post') just as we did in the backend with the reviews table. However, this form is available to the general public and within the reach of malicious hackers. You must always take extra caution in these circumstances. In this case, we will use different member functions of JRequest to enforce specific variable types.

Because **review_id** is an integer key field in the database, the getInt() member function of JRequest is used. This retrieves **review_id** from our HTTP request, but allows the value through only if it is truly an integer. After this, PHP's date() function is used to set $row->comment_date to the current date and time, in the MySQL datetime format.

We then get a reference to the current user object to get the user's ID so that we can set $row->user_id with it. At the moment, we're allowing both logged-in and anonymous comments, but recording this now will give us the flexibility to track the registered users later. When the visitor is not logged in, $user will be empty and the user_id column will consequently default to 0.

The fields, **full_name** and **comment_text** are freeform text entry fields. We want to let through as much data as we safely can, but do not want to let users add their own HTML. If we let HTML through, hackers could use this to control the markup on the page, ultimately embedding JavaScript that could be used to launch Cross-Site Scripting attacks. Retrieving these variables through `JRequest::getString()` strips out any HTML and returns any remaining text.

Finally, the `store()` member function of `$row` is called. If this function call fails, an HTTP 500 error is raised through `JError::raiseError()`, with the reason for failure retrieved from `$row->getError()`. If all is well, the controller is set to redirect back to the review that the user was viewing when they made the comment. The link to the review is passed through `JRoute::_()` to ensure that the proper SEF URL is built.

Displaying comments

After saving the code files, you will be able to submit the form and return to the review. However, nothing will appear to happen as we do not have the code in place to display the comments. On other web sites, you will often see that the content is directly followed by comments, which are also followed by a form for adding more comments.

We will follow the same style in our example. To support this change in the view, we first need to create a model to load the comments. Open the `single.php` file in the `/components/com_restaurants/models` folder, and add the following code:

```php
<?php
defined( '_JEXEC' ) or die( 'Restricted access' );
jimport('joomla.application.component.model');
class RestaurantsModelSingle extends JModel
{
    var $_comments = null;

    function &getComments()
    {
        $id = JRequest::getInt('id', 0);

        if (empty($this->_comments)) {
            $query = "SELECT full_name, comment_date,
             comment_text FROM #__reviews_comments WHERE review_id =
             '{$id}'";
            $this->_comments = $this->_getList($query);
        }
        return $this->_comments;
    }
}
```

Note that this time the function is named getComments() instead of getData().
Using getData() here would be a bit misleading, as the primary data we are using
for the single view is the row from the database for the restaurant review. The
function extracts **id** from the request then checks to see if $this->_comments
has not already been filled. If it has not, it the function proceeds to select the
full_name, **comment_date**, and **comment_text** fields for the review from the
jos_reviews_comments table.

To use the comments, we need to assign them to the template. Make the highlighted
changes to view.html.php in your single view folder:

```
$user =& JFactory::getUser();

$comments =& $this->get('Comments');

$this->assignRef('review', $review);
$this->assignRef('smoking', $smoking);
$this->assignRef('date', $date);
$this->assignRef('backlink', $backlink);
$this->assignRef('name', $user->name);
$this->assignRef('comments', $comments);


parent::display($tpl);
```

Instead of calling $this->get('Data'), we call $this->get('Comments'). Joomla!
automatically assembles the correct function name to use based on what is passed
into get(). With the comments assigned to the template, all that's left to do is to
display them. As with the comment form, the displayed comments are an addition
to the main view. We will put the output code for the comments in a separate file.
Create a file named default_comments.php in the views/single/tmpl folder, and
add this code to the following new file:

```
<?php
defined( '_JEXEC' ) or die( 'Restricted access' );
foreach ($this->comments as $comment)
{
    ?>
    <p> </p>
    <p><strong><?php echo htmlspecialchars($comment->full_name);
     ?></strong>
    <em><?php echo JHTML::Date($comment->comment_date); ?></em></p>
    <p><?php echo htmlspecialchars($comment->comment_text); ?></p>
    <?php
}
```

After making sure that it is being called from within Joomla!, this code cycles through the comments that were assigned to the template in `view.html.php`, outputting the full name, comment body, and comment date. The values for **full_name** and **comment_text** are passed through `htmlspecialchars()` to ensure that the final markup is valid HTML.

If you were to now load a review containing comments, you would not see them, because the comments layout has not been assigned to the main layout. In the `views/single/tmpl/default.php` file, add this layout, by making the highlighted code change shown here:

```
<p><?php echo htmlspecialchars($this->review->review); ?></p>
<p><em>Notes:</em> <?php echo htmlspecialchars($this->review->notes);
    ?></p>
<a href="<?php echo htmlspecialchars($this->backlink);
    ?>">&lt; return to the reviews</a>
<?php
echo $this->loadTemplate('comments');
echo $this->loadTemplate('comment_form');
```

Once you've added a comment or two, refresh the review detail page and you should see a screen like the following:

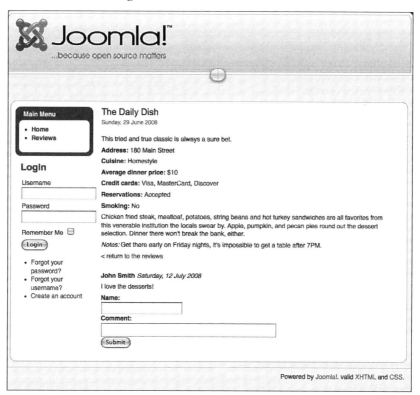

Summary

Our review site is developing nicely!. Our reviewers' curiosities are being satisfied, and they're beginning to get excited over the concept of being able to publish their reviews consistently. We've also added some user interaction so that our visitors can agree or disagree with the reviewers, and feel that they're part of the site. The links to our reviews are now more readable and are ready to be crawled by search engines. This frontend is a starting point from which we can add more features to make the site more enticing.

5
JTable, JHTML, and JUser

With a full backend and frontend in place for reviews, traffic to the site is growing and our critics are busy eating at more restaurants. This gives us some time to explore some features of Joomla! that have not yet made it into the **Restaurant Reviews** component. We can use these features to help us manage data, generate common HTML elements, and determine the status of the current user. This will take us through the following tasks:

- Overriding JTable methods
- Adding ordered records
- Recording traffic
- Checking out and checking in records
- Getting user information
- Generating elements with JHTML
- Setting ordering

Overriding JTable methods

Because the **Restaurant Reviews** component is now in use and in a stable state, we will leave it alone for the moment. Instead of using the **jos_reviews** table, we will create a new component with its own table. This component will manage the profiles of the critics and also allow us to try different methods without worrying about the user interface or the data. You can write this component in a completely separate installation of Joomla! if you desire, but it is perfectly safe to write it within the existing one.

Before writing the component, we need to set up the MySQL database table that will hold the critic profiles. If you are using the command line interface for MySQL, this query can be entered to create the database table (assuming your database prefix is **jos_**):

```
create table jos_critic (
    `id` int(11) auto_increment,
    `name` varchar(255),
    `favorite_food` varchar(255),
    `bio` text,
    `checked_out` tinyint(1),
    `checked_out_time` datetime,
    `editor` varchar(255),
    `hits` int(11) unsigned default 0,
    `access` int(11) unsigned,
    `groupname` varchar(255),
    `ordering` int(11),
    primary key(id)
);
```

If you are using phpMyAdmin instead, navigate to the database of your Joomla! installation, then scroll to the bottom of the right frame, make the following entries, and then click **Go**:

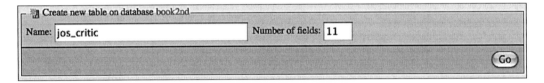

Then add the following fields:

Field	Type ⓘ	Length/Values[1]
id	INT	11
name	VARCHAR	255
favorite_food	VARCHAR	255
bio	TEXT	
checked_out	TINYINT	1
checked_out_tii	VARCHAR	
editor	VARCHAR	255
hits	INT	11
access	INT	11
groupname	VARCHAR	255
ordering	INT	11

Also, make sure that the **id** field is set to **auto_increment** as a primary key:

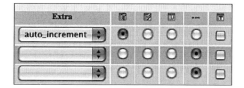

With the database table in place, we can now begin writing the component that will interact with this table. In the `components` folder of your Joomla! installation, create a folder named `com_critic`. Within this folder, create another one called `tables`. This folder will hold a file named `critic.php`.

> In Chapter 3, the `tables` folder for the **Restaurant Reviews** component was placed in `/administrator/components/com_restaurants` instead of `/components/com_restaurants`. Joomla! is flexible enough to let you place the `tables` folder wherever you desire, but the preferred place is the backend of your component. We are placing this folder in the frontend to make it easier for us to access the examples.

The code in `tables/critic.php` will look very similar to the code written in Chapter 3. Each column in the database will be represented by a member variable of the `TableCritic` class. The constructor will identify the table we wish to work with and its primary key. Add this code to the file:

```php
<?php
defined( '_JEXEC' ) or die( 'Restricted access' );
class TableCritic extends JTable
{
    var $id = null;
    var $name = null;
    var $favorite_food = null;
    var $bio = null;
    var $checked_out = null;
    var $checked_out_time = null;
    var $editor = null;
    var $hits = null;
    var $access = null;
    var $groupname = null;
    var $ordering = null;

    function __construct( &$db )
    {
        parent::__construct( '#__critic', 'id', $db );
    }
}
```

As with all PHP files in Joomla!, we use `defined('_JEXEC')` to make sure that the file is not being called directly. The `TableCritic` class is then declared as an extension of `JTable`. To use this class, we will create some frontend code that stores records. Add another `critic.php` file, but place this one directly underneath `com_critic`. Because we will be doing several different tests with `JTable`, this file will contain a controller with task functions for each test. Use this code in the `/components/com_critic/critic.php` file to create the controller:

```php
<?php
defined( '_JEXEC' ) or die( 'Restricted access' );
JTable::addIncludePath(JPATH_COMPONENT . DS . 'tables');
jimport('joomla.application.component.controller');
class CriticController extends JController
{
    function addNewCritic()
    {
        $data = array(
            'favorite_food' => 'Pad Thai',
            'bio' => 'John began criticizing food in kindergarden'
                . ' and has not stopped since. His accomplishments'
                . ' include earning "2005 Critic of the Year" from'
                . ' Digest Digest.'
            );
        $row =& JTable::getInstance('critic', 'Table');
        $row->bind($data);
        $row->store();
    }
}
$controller = new CriticController();
$controller->execute(JRequest::getCmd('task'));
```

After checking to make sure that we are within Joomla!, the `addIncludePath()` member function of `JTable` is used to include all of the files within the `tables` folder of the current component. The `jimport()` function is used to load the core controller code, then the `CriticController` class is defined as an extension of `JController`.

This class has `addNewCritic()` as its sole function at the moment. This function is very similar to the `save()` function used in Chapter 3, but instead of pulling the variables for the record from the HTTP request, they are hard coded into the `$data` array. (This saves us from having to create a form just to demonstrate the features of `JTable`.)

The data is bound to an instance of `TableCritic` and then stored in the database. After the `CriticController` definition, it is instantiated as a new object and stored in `$controller`. The `task` variable is pulled from the request. So far, only a value of `addNewCritic` would do anything useful.

Adding a check() function

Before executing this code, take a closer look at the data that addNewCritic() would enter into the database. Although it includes the favorite food and a short biography of the critic, one crucial piece of information is missing—the name of the critic. It would be helpful to add some code to ensure that the **Name** field is not left blank. Joomla! has a standard way of doing this by using a check() member function in the JTable class. Code for checking the data integrity is centralized there, making it easy for you to validate the data regardless of where you are using the JTable object.

Go back to tables/critic.php and add this check() function, which tests the value of the name column:

```php
function check()
{
    if (trim($this->name) == '')
    {
        return false;
    }
    return true;
}
```

Because name is a member variable of the TableCritic class, we can access its value by using $this->name. The value is passed through PHP's trim() function to remove any extra spaces (for instance, in case someone leaned on the *spacebar* and then hit *tab*). If the result of trim() is an empty string, false is returned. Otherwise, the record meets the criteria and true is returned.

This function is not called automatically. We must add it to the code where we are attempting to enter data, for it to be of any use. Go to the /components/ com_critic/critic.php file, and add this highlighted code:

```php
$row->bind($data);

if (!$row->check())
{
JError::raiseError(500, 'Please add a name for the critic' );
return;
}

$row->store();
```

This code will prevent us from adding a row to the **jos_critic** table that does not have a value for name. When the check() member function of TableCritic returns false, the raiseError() member function of JError is called with two parameters—the HTTP status number and the message to display with the status. If you attempt to execute the addNewCritic task now by going to index.php?option=com_critic&task=addNewCritic, you will get this screen:

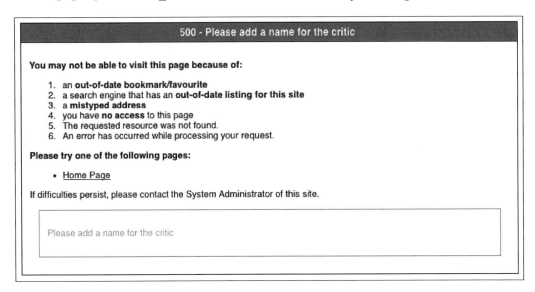

To fix this, add the highlighted data to the array in the addNewCritic() function:

```
$data = array(
    'name' => 'John Worthington',
    'favorite_food' => 'Pad Thai',
```

If you run the code again, by refreshing the page, you should receive a standard Joomla! page in the frontend with no output in the component area. However, the query did run and the database records for **jos_critic** will look like this when you browse them in phpMyAdmin:

←T→	id	name	favorite_food	bio	checked_out	checked_out_time
□ ✎ ✕	1	John Worthington	Pad Thai	John began criticizing food in kindergarden and ha...	*NULL*	*NULL*

Overriding the bind() function

The `bind()` function is a useful shortcut for populating the member variables of our `JTable` classes by using an array rather than setting each one manually. In many cases, it is sufficient to pass in the values you have and accept default values for all the rest. In others, you may want to define the default value within the `bind()` function so that you do not have to test it later. This can be done by adding a `bind()` function to the `TableCritic` class that overrides the one in `JTable`. Add the following `bind()` function to the `TableCritic` in `tables/critic.php` file:

```
function bind($vars, $ignore = array())
{
    parent::bind($vars, $ignore);
    if (trim($this->groupname) == '') {
        $this->groupname = 'Public';
    }
    return true;
}
```

Now when the `bind()` function is called in `/components/com_critic/critic.php`, the version in `TableCritic` will be used instead of the one in `JTable`. Because the original `bind()` function takes two parameters, we define our override function with the same two parameters as well. The first one is an array of data to match to the member variables of our class. The second one is optional—if you want the `bind()` function to ignore any of the variables in the first array, you can pass in a list of their keys.

Before any code setting defaults are called, the original `JTable` version of `bind()` is called. We are not interested in fundamentally changing the operation of the `bind()` function; we only want to add some features to it. Calling the original function allows us to re-use the code without copying and pasting it into our new version. Once the data is loaded, we test the value of `$this->groupname` passed through `trim()`. If this is an empty string, it is set to **Public**. Finally, **true** is returned.

To test this new version of `bind()`, add another function to the controller in `/components/com_critic/critic.php` to add a different record. This function will be called `addAnotherCritic()` and will consist of the following code:

```
function addAnotherCritic()
{
    $data = array(
        'name' => 'Sarah Highworthy',
        'favorite_food' => 'Coq au vin',
        'bio' => 'Sarah has an affinity for French food, but also'
            . ' appreciates barbecue from the United States.'
```

```
                    . ' She previously edited the newsletter dedicated'
                    . ' to game and poultry called "Off The Bone"'
            );
        $row =& JTable::getInstance('critic', 'Table');
        $row->bind($data);

        if (!$row->check())
        {
            JError::raiseError(500, 'Please add a name for the critic' );
            return;
        }
        $row->store();
    }
```

To execute this code, go to `index.php?option=com_critic&task=addAnother Critic` in the frontend. As with `addNewCritic()`, you will not see any output in the component area, but should see a standard frontend page with no errors. The contents of the **jos_critic** table will look like this now:

←T→			id	name	favorite_food	bio	checked_out	checked_out_time	editor	hits	access	groupname
⊟	✎	✕	1	John Worthington	Pad Thai	John began criticizing food in kindergarden and ha...	*NULL*	*NULL*	*NULL*	*NULL*	*NULL*	*NULL*
⊟	✎	✕	2	Sarah Highworthy	Coq au vin	Sarah has an affinity for French food, but also ap...	*NULL*	*NULL*	*NULL*	*NULL*	*NULL*	Public

Adding ordered records

There are many circumstances where you will want to enforce a specific ordering for your database records. In our case, certain critics may request to be placed at the top of the list due to their seniority. The `JTable` class has built-in functions that help you move records up and down within a list and add new ones in the correct place.

When we added the **jos_critic** table to the database, an **ordering** column was added. Because records are now added without values for this column, we need to go back and add this information now. For the record with **id** set to **1**, change the **ordering** column to **1**, and change **ordering** to **2** for record **2**. If you are using the MySQL command line client, this query will do it automatically:

```
UPDATE jos_critic SET ordering = id;
```

In phpMyAdmin, click the **Browse** tab after selecting the **jos_critic** table, then edit both records individually. Click on the pencil icon to the left of the data columns, then add the appropriate value in the **ordering** field and click **Go**:

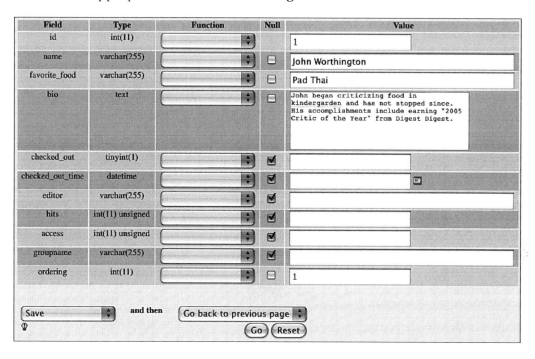

Now that the existing records are in order, another one can be added at the end. Before adding another function to the controller to add another record, go back to the `tables/critic.php` file, and make the highlighted adjustment to the `bind()` function override:

```
if (trim($this->groupname) == '')
{
    $this->groupname = 'Public';
}

if (!$this->id)
{
    $this->ordering = $this->getNextOrder();
}
return true;
```

Instead of using a handwritten query to get the highest value in the ordering column, we can use the getNextOrder() function of JTable, which does it for us automatically. Before setting the ordering member variable, we first make sure that **id** is not set. If **id** is set, we can assume that this is an update instead of an addition, and that any changes to the **ordering** field will be determined by the passed in data. Otherwise, we set **ordering** to the next number in the sequence.

Now that bind() has been adjusted to account for ordering, add the following addOrderedCritic() function to the controller in the /components/com_critic/ critic.php file:

```
function addOrderedCritic()
{
    $data = array(
        'name' => 'Karen Anderson',
        'favorite_food' => 'Lasagna',
        'bio' => 'Karen is a seasoned critic of seasonings.'
            . ' She always knows when something is too'
            . ' salty, too bitter, overdressed, or otherwise'
            . ' unappetizing to discerning palates.'
        );

    $row =& JTable::getInstance('critic', 'Table');
    $row->bind($data);

    if (!$row->check())
    {
        JError::raiseError(500, 'Please add a name for the critic' );
        return;
    }
    $row->store();
}
```

Save the file, then go to index.php?option=com_critic&task=addOrderedCritic in the frontend. The component area of the template will be blank, but the rest of the screen should be normal, and without errors, notices, or warnings. The database table listing in phpMyAdmin will look like this:

		id	name	favorite_food	bio	checked_out	checked_out_time	editor	hits	access	groupname	ordering
	✎ ✗	1	John Worthington	Pad Thai	John began criticizing food in kindergarden and ha...	*NULL*	*NULL*	*NULL*	*NULL*	*NULL*	*NULL*	1
	✎ ✗	2	Sarah Highworthy	Coq au vin	Sarah has an affinity for French food, but also ap...	*NULL*	*NULL*	*NULL*	*NULL*	*NULL*	Public	2
	✎ ✗	3	Karen Anderson	Lasagna	Karen is a seasoned critic of seasonings. She alwa...	*NULL*	*NULL*	*NULL*	*NULL*	*NULL*	Public	3

At the moment, the values in the **id** column of **jos_critic** are identical to the ones in **ordering**. You could almost get away using the **id** column in place of ordering, but that would mean that a record would not be able to move in the list once it has been added to the table. Changing **id** field values would be unworkable—you would have no reliable way of referring to a specific record in the database at any given time.

Because the **ordering** field is in place with appropriate values, we can add a couple of functions to the controller that will allow us to change it. The following moveUp() and moveDown() functions allow us to specify the **id** for a row in the URL and move the row one place:

```
function moveUp()
{
    $id = JRequest::getInt('id', 0);
    $row =& JTable::getInstance('critic', 'Table');
    $row->load($id);
    $row->move(-1);
}

function moveDown()
{
    $id = JRequest::getInt('id', 0);
    $row =& JTable::getInstance('critic', 'Table');
    $row->load($id);
    $row->move(1);
}
```

If you look carefully, you will notice that the only difference between these two functions is the parameter that is passed into the move() member function of $row. This determines the direction in which the record has moved in the order. In both cases, **id** is extracted from the request and verified to be an integer. An instance of TableCritic is then stored in $row. The database record is then retrieved using load() and the **id** from the request.

> Lower numbers in the **ordering** column infer higher placement in the record ordering. Calling $row->move(-1) moves a record one place higher.

With these task functions now in place, go to `index.php?option=com_critic&tas k=moveDown&id=1` then go to `index.php?option=com_critic&task=moveUp&id=3`. Your **ordering** column in phpMyAdmin should look like this now:

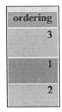

When the `moveDown()` function executed, **ordering** on record #1 was set to **2**, then #2 was set to **1** automatically. When `moveUp()` executed, #3 was set to **2**, then #1 was set to **3** automatically. Had we done this by hand, it would have involved writing a lot of laborious SQL. The functions in `JTable` handle all of this for us instead. If we try to call `index.php?option=com_critic&task=moveDown&id=1` or `index. php?option=com_critic&task=moveUp&id=2`, the **ordering** column will stay the same. The `JTable::move()` function will not allow us to go higher than the number of records in the set, or lower than 1.

Recording traffic

As we display records on the publicly-accessible Internet, it is often desirable to keep track of how many times a specific record has been accessed. The `hit()` member function of `JTable` can do this, assuming that your table has a column named **hits**. To demonstrate this, add a function named `showCritic()` with the following code to the controller in the `/components/com_critic/critic.php` file:

```
function showCritic()
{
    $id = JRequest::getInt('id', 0);
    $row =& JTable::getInstance('critic', 'Table');
    $row->load($id);
    $row->hit($id);

    ?>
    <p><strong><?php echo $row->name; ?></strong></p>
    <p>Favorite food: <?php echo $row->favorite_food; ?></p>
    <p><?php echo $row->bio; ?></p>
    <?php
}
```

The function first extracts **id** from the request and makes sure that it is an integer. After this, a reference to a `TableCritic` object is assigned to `$row`. The `load()` member function of `$row` is called to pull up the record corresponding to `$id`. Then the `hit()` function is called with the same `$id` immediately afterwards. Finally, a few fields of the record are displayed on screen in HTML. If you go to `index.php?option=com_critic&task=showCritic&id=1`, your screen should now look like this:

John Worthington

Favorite food: Pad Thai

John began criticizing food in kindergarden and has not stopped since. His accomplishments include earning "2005 Critic of the Year" from Digest Digest.

Also, your **hits** column in **jos_critics** will now show **1** hit for record #1:

			id	name	favorite_food	bio	checked_out	checked_out_time	editor	hits
☐	✎	✕	1	John Worthington	Pad Thai	John began criticizing food in kindergarden and ha...	NULL	NULL	NULL	1
☐	✎	✕	2	Sarah Highworthy	Coq au vin	Sarah has an affinity for French food, but also ap...	NULL	NULL	NULL	0
☐	✎	✕	3	Karen Anderson	Lasagna	Karen is a seasoned critic of seasonings. She alwa...	NULL	NULL	NULL	0

Checking out and checking in records

Joomla! allows multiple users to be logged into the website at once. Some of these users will have privileges for editing existing records in the database. When multiple users attempt to edit the same record in the database conflicts can occur. Consider the following scenario—two administrators log into the website and pull up the same record for editing within a few minutes of each other. The first user is making heavy edits and will not be saving the record for at least 20 minutes. The second user pops in, makes a small edit, and saves the record right away. When the first user finally saves the record, it ends up overwriting the second user's work.

To avoid all this, Joomla! has a system that you can use for checking in and checking out records so that only one person can at a time work on a given record. For the system to work correctly, your database table needs to have the columns **checked_out** and **checked_out_time**, as **jos_critic** does. The **checked_out** column keeps track of the ID of the user currently working on the record. The **checked_out_time** column keeps track of the date and time when the record was checked out. This is useful to know in case someone appears be editing the record for hours on end. Sometimes, users forget to check the record back in before closing their browser. The record will remain locked until you unlock it manually.

To fully demonstrate how the system works, you will need to be logged in to the frontend of the system. If you do not already have a login form in the frontend, one can be added as a module by going to **Extensions | Module Manager**, clicking **New**, selecting **Login** from the list, adding a **Title**, and clicking **Save**. With the module in place, log in to the frontend with any username registered on your Joomla! installation.

First, add the `checkOutCritic()` task function to the controller in the `/components/com_critic/critic.php` file, by using the following code:

```
function checkOutCritic()
{
    $user =& JFactory::getUser();
    $id = JRequest::getInt('id', 0);
    $row =& JTable::getInstance('critic', 'Table');
    $row->load($id);
    $row->checkout($user->id);
    echo " The record for {$row->name} is now checked out by
      {$user->name}";
}
```

This function first gets a reference to the current user object and assigns it to `$user`. Next, **id** is extracted from the request and `$row` is set to an instance of the `TableCritic` class. The `load()` method is used to select the record from the database that matches `$id`. With this object loaded and ready, the `checkout()` method is called and the `id` field of the `$user` object is passed in. Finally, a status message is displayed with the name of the user and the name of the record. The output that appears when you follow `index.php?option=com_critic&task=checkOutCritic&id=1` should appear similar to this:

> The record for John Worthington is now checked out by Alex

The time and user id are also reflected in the **jos_critic** table:

			id	name	favorite_food	bio	checked_out	checked_out_time
	🖉	✕	1	John Worthington	Pad Thai	John began criticizing food in kindergarden and ha...	63	2008-10-24 15:35:19
	🖉	✕	2	Sarah Highworthy	Coq au vin	Sarah has an affinity for French food, but also ap...	*NULL*	*NULL*
	🖉	✕	3	Karen Anderson	Lasagna	Karen is a seasoned critic of seasonings. She alwa...	*NULL*	*NULL*

> Remember that you must be logged in for `checkOutCritic()` to work properly. Otherwise, the record will not appear as checked out by any of the users.

Checking in records involves similar code. Add the `checkInCritic()` with this code to the controller:

```
function checkInCritic()
{
    $id = JRequest::getInt('id', 0);
    $row =& JTable::getInstance('critic', 'Table');
    $row->load($id);
    $row->checkin($id);
    echo "The record for {$row->name} is now checked in.";
}
```

The differences between `checkInCritic()` and `checkOutCritic()` are that `checkin()` is called instead of `checkout()` and the status message is different. Going to `index.php?option=com_critic&task=checkInCritic&id=1` will result in a screen like this :

> The record for John Worthington is now checked in.

> Note that it is not necessary to use the `load()` member function before using `checkout()` or `checkin()`. These examples load the data first, so that a precise status message can be displayed at the end.

Getting user information

When we checked out a record in the previous section, we used the `getUser()` function from the `JFactory` class to get a reference to the current user object. We only used the **id** and the **name** properties of this object, but more are available, along with some member functions. To show more of the properties available, add the following task function `userInfo()` to the controller in the `/components/com_critic/critic.php` file:

```php
function userInfo()
{
    $user =& JFactory::getUser();
    ?>
    <p>Name: <?php echo $user->name; ?></p>
    <p>Username: <?php echo $user->username; ?></p>
    <p>Email: <?php echo $user->email; ?></p>
    <p>User Type: <?php echo $user->usertype; ?></p>
    <p>User Group ID: <?php echo $user->gid; ?></p>
    <p>Register Date: <?php echo JHTML::_('date',
     $user->registerDate); ?></p>
    <p>Last Visit Date: <?php echo JHTML::_('date',
     $user->lastvisitDate); ?></p>
    <p>Block: <?php echo $user->block; ?></p>
    <p>Send Email: <?php echo $user->sendEmail; ?></p>
    <p>Guest: <?php echo $user->guest; ?></p>
    <?php
}
```

If you now go to `index.php?option=com_critic&task=userInfo` in the frontend, you should get a screen similar to this one:

Name: Alex
Username: alex
Email: alex@test.com
User Type: Registered
User Group ID: 18
Register Date: Monday, 01 September 2008
Last Visit Date: Wednesday, 03 September 2008
Block: 0
Send Email: 0
Guest: 0

These fields represent some of the more useful ones available in the `JUser` object that is returned by `JFactory::getUser()`. The `name`, `username`, and `email` properties are typed in when the user is initially created. The `usertype` is also selected upon creation. The properties `block` and `sendEmail` act as Boolean values for whether the user is blocked or wants to receive email, respectively. Other properties displayed on this screen are automatically generated by Joomla!.

When you are writing code that depends on user information, it is important to make sure that the user is actually logged in. This is where the `guest` property becomes useful. When no user is logged into the system, `guest` will be set to 1; otherwise it is set to 0. To test this, add the following function to the controller in the `/components/com_critic/critic.php` file:

```
function guestOrUser()
{
    $user =& JFactory::getUser();
    if ($user->guest) {
        echo "Welcome visitor!";
    }
    else
    {
        echo "Welcome {$user->name}!";
    }
}
```

This function gets a reference to the user object, then tests whether the value of `$user->guest` is non-zero. When you go to `index.php?option=com_critic&task=guestOrUser` while logged into the site, you should get a welcome message with your name. When you log out, you will simply be greeted as a visitor.

Generating elements with JHTML

Creating commonly-used UI elements such as lists and option buttons is automated through the use of the JHTML class. Functions within this class are designed to take an array of database results and turn them into the elements you desire. This eliminates the need for creating a loop to cycle over the results and incrementally build a string with the HTML element—Joomla! does it for you.

Because there are already three critics listed in the database, they can be used to demonstrate how lists are generated through JHTML. Add this task function `generateLists()` to the controller in the `/components/com_critic/critic.php` file:

```php
function generateLists()
{
    $db =& JFactory::getDBO();
    $db->setQuery('SELECT id,
     name FROM #__critic ORDER BY ordering');
    $rows = $db->loadObjectList();

    echo '<p>' . JHTML::_('select.genericlist', $rows, 'critics',
     '', 'id', 'name') . '</p>';
    echo '<p>' . JHTML::_('select.genericlist', $rows, 'critics',
     'size="5"', 'id', 'name') . '</p>';
    echo '<p>' . JHTML::_('select.genericlist', $rows, 'critics[]',
     'size="5" multiple="multiple"', 'id', 'name') . '</p>';
    echo '<p>' . JHTML::_('select.radiolist', $rows, 'critics', '',
     'id', 'name') . '</p>';
}
```

This function first gets a reference to the current database object, then selects the **id** and **name** columns from the **jos_critic** table. Records are sorted by the **ordering** field we populated earlier. After loading the results into an array, JHTML is called four times to generate four different HTML elements.

The `_()` function is used as Joomla! loads only the necessary HTML element rendering functions at runtime. The first parameter determines the element to be generated, while the second is the data to be used. This is followed by the HTML name of the element and any attributes to be added. Finally, the column names in the rows to be used for values and labels (**id** and **name**) are identified in the remaining two parameters.

To see how these elements appear on the screen, go to `index.php?option=com_critic&task=generateLists` in the frontend. After making some selections, your screen should look similar to the following:

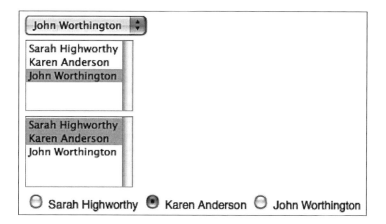

The first three calls use `select.genericlist` to generate `<select>` elements. The first call is rendered as a drop-down as no HTML attributes were passed in. The second one is exactly the same as the first, except that `size="5"` was added to the attributes parameter. You can select only one item from this list. As far as the incoming data is concerned, this is equivalent to the first call. The third call is the same as the second call, but also has `multiple="multiple"` added to allow the selection of more than one value. The name of this element has `[]` added to the end, to tell PHP to treat the incoming value as an array.

The final call to `JHTML::_()` specifies `select.radiolist` as the type. The same data, name, attributes, and columns are passed in here as in the first `select.genericlist`; the only difference being that a radio button is generated instead.

In addition to lists based on data from the database, JHTML can generate elements based on predetermined sets of values. For certain interfaces, such as control panels, elements for selecting **Yes** and **No** are very common. For some controls, you may also need to provide a range of values to pick from. Here, the `generateYesNoAndIntegers()` function demonstrates calls for generating these. Add the following code to the controller in the `critic.php` file:

```
function generateYesNoAndIntegers()
{
    echo '<p>' . JHTML::_('select.booleanlist', 'yesorno', '', 1)
        . '</p>';
    echo '<p>' . JHTML::_('select.integerlist', 1, 50, 1, 'pick1')
        . '</p>';
    echo '<p>' . JHTML::_('select.integerlist', 50, 100, 10,
        'pick10') . '</p>';
}
```

Loading `index.php?option=com_critic&task=generateYesNoAndIntegers` will yield a screen like this:

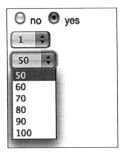

The first call to `JHTML::_()` loads the `select.booleanlist` function, passing in `yes` or `no` as the name, no additional HTML attributes, and a selected value of `1` for **yes** (`0` for **no** is assumed if the third parameter is not given). The last two calls to `_()` generate `select.integerlist`, which automatically generates a list of numbers based on the parameters passed in. For the first one, the list starts at 1, ends at 50, and each option increases by 1. This list is named `pick1`. The second list is named `pick10`, starts at 50, ends at 100, and each option increases by 10.

Pre-filled lists

Some lists can be generated by JHTML with little information being passed into the `_()` function. Contents for lists of images and registered users are automatically loaded when the `list.images` and `list.users` elements are called. Add the function `autoLists()` below to the `/components/com_critic/critic.php` file:

```
function autoLists()
{
    echo '<p>' . JHTML::_('list.users', 'users', '') . '</p>';
    echo '<p>' . JHTML::_('list.images', 'selectanimage') . '</p>';
    echo '<p>' . JHTML::_('list.images', 'selectanimage',
    'clock.jpg') . '</p>';
    echo '<p>' . JHTML::_('list.images', 'selectanimage', '', '',
    'images/stories/fruit') . '</p>';
}
```

When `index.php?option=com_critic&task=autoLists` is loaded in the frontend, the screen should look like the following:

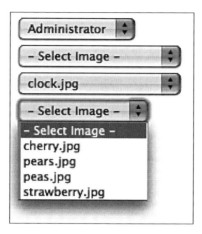

The first list includes all of the users who are registered in the system. This list is named `users`, as specified in the first parameter after `list.users`. The function requires that you pass in the ID of a user as well, but passing in a null string will simply yield the list. Passing in `true` as a third parameter will also add an option labeled **No User**.

The last three lists are for image folders. If you just pass in the HTML name that you want to use for the list, you get the first of these three—a list of the images within the `/images/stories` directory. Next, the same call is made, only with the image `clock.jpg` specified in the second parameter; this marks it as selected. Finally, the third call passes in two null strings after the list name; this skips the default image and the optional JavaScript that can be added to the drop-down. The last parameter is a path to use for the list; this is relative to the Joomla! root.

Running content plug-ins

When content items are loaded through the `com_content` component, Joomla! automatically runs the output through plug-ins in the **content** group. These plug-ins do things such as highlight inline source code, and cloak email addresses from spammers. However, Joomla! does not automatically run these plug-ins on output from components that you code. If you want these plug-ins to be used, JHTML has a function that will take a string and run it through all of the content plug-ins. To test this function, add the `usePlugins()` function to the controller in the `/components/com_critic/critic.php` file:

```
function usePlugins()
{
    $content = 'support@packtpub.com';
    echo '<p>' . $content . '</p>';
    echo '<p>' . JHTML::_('content.prepare', $content) . '</p>';
}
```

When you go to `index.php?option=com_critic&task=usePlugins` in the frontend, you should see one plain-text email address and one that is a link:

> support@packtpub.com
>
> support@packtpub.com

The first time that the email address is output, it is simply concatenated with paragraph tags in an `echo` statement. For the second time, it is passed through the `content.prepare` function. If you have the email cloaking plug-in turned on, it should find the email address in the content. This will be turned into JavaScript code that will reassemble itself into an anchor tag when the page is loaded.

 If your component has a lot of content that should be run through content plug-ins, avoid calling `JHTML::_('content.prepare')` multiple times. This will slow down performance as Joomla! will execute each plug-in every time the function is called. Instead, you should assemble your content first, and then run it through the function all at once.

Using JHTML in the backend

Joomla!'s backend can use JHTML classes just as easily as the frontend can. There are a few elements that are better used for backend interfaces, especially when records are displayed in a list. Core components use JHTML to generate UI elements related to the checked-in status, access level, and ordering of records.

To demonstrate this, a simple backend needs to be created. Create a new folder named `com_critic` under the `/administrator/components` folder. Within this new folder, create a file called `critic.php`, and add the following code to it:

```php
<?php
defined( '_JEXEC' ) or die( 'Restricted access' );
jimport( 'joomla.application.component.controller' );

class CriticController extends JController
{
    function display($tpl = null)
    {
```

```php
        $view = JRequest::getVar('view', '');
        if ($view == '')
        {
            JRequest::setVar('view', 'critics');
        }
        parent::display($tpl);
    }
}
$controller = new CriticController();
$controller->execute( JRequest::getCmd( 'task' ) );
$controller->redirect();
```

Just as we created a controller in Chapters 3 and 4 for the **Restaurant Reviews** component, we will do the same here. This controller does not currently have any task functions and simply overrides the display() function to set the default view. To add this view, create a folder named views under the com_critic folder, and a folder named critics within the views folder. This new folder should contain a file named view.html.php and a folder named tmpl. Add this code to the view.html.php file:

```php
<?php
defined( '_JEXEC' ) or die( 'Restricted access' );
jimport( 'joomla.application.component.view');

class CriticViewCritics extends JView
{
    function display($tpl = null)
    {
        $db =& JFactory::getDBO();
        $db->setQuery('SELECT * FROM #__critic');
        $rows = $db->loadObjectList();
        $this->assignRef('rows', $rows);
        parent::display($tpl);
    }
}
```

Instead of creating a model for the query, we have simply chosen to load the data here and assign it to the view. If this component were to become much more complex, it would be wiser to add this to a model instead. However, this is only being used to demonstrate a few features of JHTML, so we will leave it in the current state. To complete the view, create the default.php file in the tmpl folder, and enter this code into it:

```php
<?php defined( '_JEXEC' ) or die( 'Restricted access' ); ?>
<form action="index.php?option=com_critic" method=
            "post" name="adminForm">
    <table class="adminlist">
        <thead>
```

```
    <tr>
    <th><input type="checkbox" name="toggle" value=
    "" onclick="checkAll(<?php echo count( $this->rows );
     ?>);" /></th>
    <th>Name</th>
    <th>Favorite Food</th>
    <th>Bio</th>
    <th>Ordering</th>
    <th>Hits</th>
    <th>Access</th>
    </tr>
</thead>
<tbody>
<?php
$i = 0;
foreach ($this->rows as &$row)
{
    $checked = JHTML::_('grid.checkedout', $row, $i);
    $access = JHTML::_('grid.access', $row, $i);
    ?>
    <tr>
        <td><?php echo $checked ?></td>
        <td><?php echo $row->name ?></td>
        <td><?php echo $row->favorite_food ?></td>
        <td><?php echo $row->bio ?></td>
        <td><?php echo $row->ordering ?></td>
        <td><?php echo $row->hits ?></td>
        <td><?php echo $access ?></td>
    </tr>
<?php
$i++;
}
?>
</tbody>
</table>
<input type="hidden" name="option" value="com_critic" />
<input type="hidden" name="task" value="" />
<input type="hidden" name="boxchecked" value="0" />
<?php echo JHTML::_( 'form.token' ); ?>
</form>
```

This layout file is similar to the one used for **Restaurant Reviews** in Chapter 3. In this example, a call to JHTML::_('grid.access'); is made. This call returns a link displaying the current access level. Clicking on this link adds a task to the form and submits it in the same way that clicking a toolbar button does.

Before loading the component in the backend, check to make sure that all of the files are in place. Your final file and folder structure for /administrator/components/ com_critic should look like this:

With the files in place and saved, go to /administrator/index.php?option=com_ critic in your Web browser. You should see a screen showing the critics, along with the **Access** field:

	Ordering	Hits	Access
ə Year" from Digest Digest.	3	2	Public
ter dedicated to game and poultry	1	0	Public
unappetizing to discerning	2	0	Public

Setting access

If you click on one of these links now, nothing will happen as there are no functions in the controller to handle the task set by the link. This link can set any one of these three different tasks—accessregistered, accessspecial, and accesspublic. To handle these tasks, we could create a different function for each. However, all of them would essentially do the same thing—load the row for the record, set the permission level, then save the record and redirect the browser back to the main screen. Instead, we will add one function to the controller to handle all of the three tasks. Make the following highlighted changes to /administrator/components/ com_critic/critic.php:

```php
<?php
defined( '_JEXEC' ) or die( 'Restricted access' );
jimport( 'joomla.application.component.controller' );
```

```
JTable::addIncludePath(JPATH_COMPONENT_SITE . DS . 'tables');


class CriticController extends JController
{
    function display($tpl = null)
    {
        $view = JRequest::getVar('view', '');
        if ($view == '')
        {
            JRequest::setVar('view', 'critics');
        }
        parent::display($tpl);
    }
    function setAccess()
     {
     JRequest::checkToken() or jexit( 'Invalid Token' );
     $cid = JRequest::getVar('cid', array(0));
     $id = (int) $cid[0];
     $row =& JTable::getInstance('critic', 'Table');
     $row->load($id);

     switch ($this->getTask()) {
         case 'accesspublic':
             $row->access = 0;
             $row->groupname = 'Public';
             break;

         case 'accessregistered':
             $row->access = 1;
             $row->groupname = 'Registered';
             break;

         default:
             $row->access = 2;
             $row->groupname = 'Special';
             break;
     }
     $row->store();
     $this->setRedirect('index.php?option=com_critic');
  }
}
```

```
$controller = new CriticController();
$controller->registerTask('accessregistered', 'setAccess');
$controller->registerTask('accessspecial', 'setAccess');
$controller->registerTask('accesspublic', 'setAccess');
$controller->execute( JRequest::getCmd( 'task' ) );
$controller->redirect();
```

Before we can load records from the **jos_critic** table, we need to tell JTable to look in the frontend of the component for the table classes. This is done with JTable::addIncludePath(JPATH_COMPONENT_SITE . DS . 'tables');. Within the controller, the setAccess() function has been created to handle changing the access level. Because we are modifying data, the function first checks for the anti-CSRF form token. Next, the record ID is extracted from the request; this is then used to load the record from the database.

After the row has been loaded, a switch() statement is used to determine which task was called from the interface. In each case, both access and groupname are set for the row, with **0**, **1**, and **2** corresponding to **Public**, **Registered**, and **Special**, respectively. Once these fields are set, the record is saved and the user is redirected back to the list of critics.

Finally, just after the CriticController object is created, the registerTask() member function is called three times, to register the accessregistered, accessspecial, and accesspublic tasks with the setAccess() method.

With this function in place, try clicking on the **Public** link again. When the page reloads, it should turn red and say **Registered**, as shown here:

	Ordering	Hits	Access
m Digest Digest.	3	2	Registered
ted to game and	1	0	Public
ing to discerning	2	0	Public

If you click the link again, it will turn black and read **Special**. Clicking the link once more will change it back to **Public**. As the **access** column in the record changes value, the link generated by JHTML::_('grid.access') changes between the accessregistered, accessspecial, and accesspublic tasks. It will automatically select the next task in the rotation.

These functions only set the **access** and **groupname** fields in your database table. They do not inherently restrict access to that data. It is up to your component to determine whether the current user is a part of a group that has access to the record.

Setting ordering

Several of Joomla!'s core components allow you to order records in a list by clicking on arrows in the **Ordering** column. We can accomplish the same by using Joomla!'s JPagination class, and the move() member function of JTable. Before doing this, we should start displaying the records in the correct order. Make the highlighted adjustment to the query in the /administrator/components/com_critic/views/critics/view.html.php file:

```
$db =& JFactory::getDBO();
$db->setQuery('SELECT * FROM #__critic ORDER BY ordering');
$rows = $db->loadObjectList();
```

Save the file, and then reload /administrator/index.php?option=com_critic in the browser. Your screen should now have the records sorted by the **Ordering** column and should look similar to the following:

	Ordering	Hits	Access
the United States. She previously edited	1	0	Public
ing is too salty, too bitter, overdressed,	2	0	Public
s accomplishments include earning	3	2	Public

Next, we need to bring in the `JPagination` class that will help us generate the up and down arrows on the list screen. Again, in the `views/critics/view.html.php` file, add the following highlighted code:

```
$rows = $db->loadObjectList();

jimport('joomla.html.pagination');
$rowcount = count($rows);
$pageOrd = new JPagination($rowcount , 0, $rowcount );

$this->assignRef('rows', $rows);
$this->assignRef('pageOrd', $pageOrd);
$this->assign('rowcount', $rowcount);

parent::display($tpl);
```

The `JPagination` class is brought in with the call to `jimport('joomla.html.pagination');`. This class works primarily with creating the navigation used on list screens with multiple pages, so it needs a few parameters relating to the size of the list. A count of the rows is taken and then passed into the `JPagination` constructor as the first and third parameters. The first parameter is the total number of records in the list. The second and third are the record numbers where the current page begins and ends. Because we are only using one page in this instance, **0** is used for the start value and the total number of rows is used for the end.

Finally, the `$pageOrd` object and the total number of rows are assigned to the template. To use the object and output the ordering arrows, the following highlighted adjustment must be made to `views/critics/tmpl/default.php`:

```
<td><?php echo $row->bio ?></td>
<td class="order">
  <span><?php echo $this->pageOrd->orderUpIcon( $i ); ?></span>
  <span><?php echo $this->pageOrd->orderDownIcon( $i,
    $this->rowcount ); ?></span>
</td>
<td><?php echo $row->hits ?></td>
```

Save all of your files, and then load /administrator/index.php?option=com_ critic in your browser. You will now see ordering arrows such as these:

	Ordering	Hits	Access
ited the	▼	0	Public
d, or	▲ ▼	0	Public
2005	▲	2	Public

If you click on the arrows now, they will not have any effect on the ordering of the records and the page will simply load again. This is because clicking on the arrows sets task to orderup or orderdown, then submits the form. To handle these tasks, we will create a single function in the controller called order(), similar to the way setAccess() was created. Add the following code for the order() function to the controller in the /administrator/components/com_critic/critic.php file:

```
function order()
{
    JRequest::checkToken() or jexit( 'Invalid Token' );
    $cid = JRequest::getVar('cid', array(0));
    $id = (int) $cid[0];
    $row =& JTable::getInstance('critic', 'Table');
    $row->load($id);
    if ($this->getTask() == 'orderdown')
    {
        $dir = 1;
    }
    else
    {
        $dir = -1;
    }
    $row->move($dir);
    $this->setRedirect('index.php?option=com_critic');
}
```

The order() function first checks to make sure that the request has a legitimate request token, as we are making modifications to the database. Next, the ID of the checked record is extracted from the request. (The checkbox of the record is automatically checked just before the form is submitted). This ID is used to load the corresponding **jos_critic** record from the database.

Before reordering the records, the direction in which to move is determined. A call to `$this->getTask()` lets us know which task was called, so that `$dir` can be set appropriately. The `move()` member function of the record is then called with `$dir` passed in. Finally, the user is redirected back to the main screen.

Because we want two different tasks to use `order()`, we must register them with the controller. The following highlighted adjustments to the `/administrator/components/com_critic/critic.php` file will take care of this:

```
$controller->registerTask('accessspecial', 'setAccess');
$controller->registerTask('accesspublic', 'setAccess');
$controller->registerTask('orderup', 'order');
$controller->registerTask('orderdown', 'order');
$controller->execute( JRequest::getCmd( 'task' ) );
$controller->redirect();
```

Now the arrows are finally ready for use. As you click the up and down arrows in the **Ordering** column, the records will change places.

	Ordering	Hits	Access
sly edited the	▼	0	Public
hing "2005	▲ ▼	2	Public
dressed, or	▲	0	Public

Summary

Joomla! provides you with numerous functions and classes that can save you time and effort when carrying out routine tasks. The `JTable` class has pre-built methods for handling record management, as long as the appropriate columns are in place. Getting the `JUser` object will provide you with everything you need to know about the user who is currently logged in (or will tell you if the user is only a guest). Common user interface elements in both the frontend and backend can be generated through the suite of tools provided by `JHTML`. Finally, the backend interface elements necessary for ordering records are easily output using methods from the `JParameter` class.

6
Module Development

We now have an efficient system for managing reviews and taking in comments.
However, visitors have to go to the component to see the reviews. The front page of
our site will probably have a few articles introducing the site, but it would be nice
if we could pull the content directly from the reviews and display this there as well.
This is where modules can help. You can use them to fetch data and display it almost
anywhere on the page. In this chapter, we will cover the following topics on
module development:

- Registering the module in the database
- Creating and configuring a basic module
- Getting and setting parameters
- Centralizing data access and output using helper classes
- Selecting display options using layouts
- Displaying the latest reviews
- Displaying a random review

Registering the module in the database

As with the component, we will have to register the module in the database so that
it can be referenced in the backend and used effectively. Entering a record into the
jos_modules table will take care of this. Open your database console and enter the
following query:

```
INSERT INTO jos_modules (title, ordering,
         position, published, module, showtitle, params)
         VALUES ('Restaurant Reviews', 1, 'left', 1,
         'mod_reviews', 1, 'layout=default\nitems=3\nrandom=1');
```

If you're using phpMyAdmin, enter the fields as shown in the following screenshot:

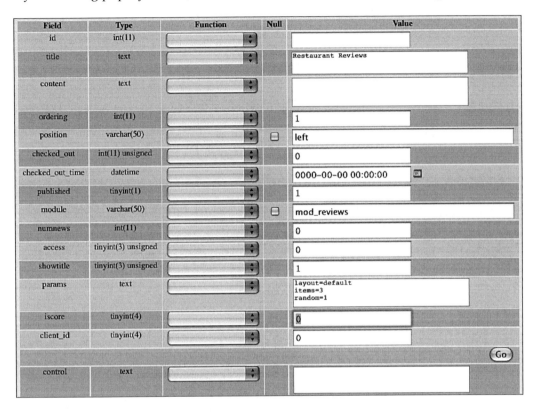

If you refresh the frontend immediately after entering the record in **jos_modules**, you'll notice that the module doesn't appear, even though the **published** column is set to **1**. To fix this, go to **Extensions | Module Manager** in the backend and click the **Restaurants Reviews** link. Under **Menu Assignment**, select **All** and then click **Save**.

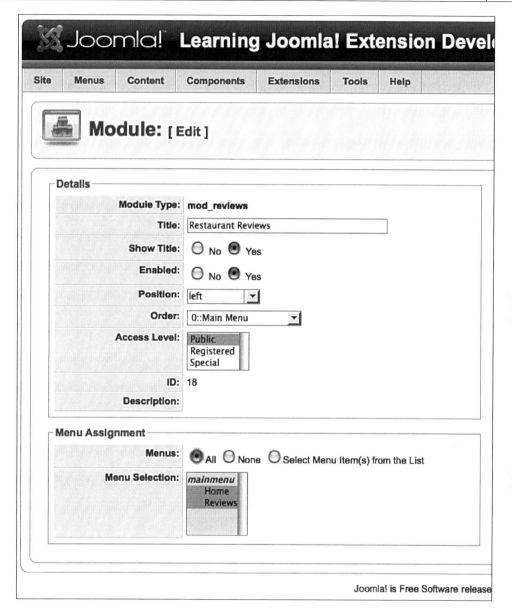

In the frontend, the left-hand side of your front page should now look like this:

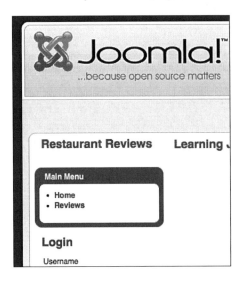

Even though we have not yet added any PHP code, Joomla! displays the module title we specified in the database. The ordering of the module is defaulted to **0**, so the title of this module is displayed on top of all of the other titles published to the left position.

Creating and configuring a basic module

Modules are both simple and flexible. You can create a module that simply outputs static text, or one that queries remote databases for things like weather reports. Although you can create rather complex modules, they're best suited to displaying data and simple forms. You would typically not use a module for complex record or session management—you can do this through a component or plug-in instead.

To create the module for our reviews, we will have to create a folder called `mod_reviews` under the existing/`modules` folder. We will also need to create the `mod_reviews.php` file inside the `mod_reviews` folder. To start with, we'll create a basic module that displays links to the most recent reviews. In the `mod_reviews.php` file, add the following code:

```php
<?php
defined('_JEXEC') or die('Restricted access');
$items = $params->get('items', 1);
$db =& JFactory::getDBO();
$query = "SELECT id, name FROM #__reviews WHERE
```

```
                     published = '1' ORDER BY review_date DESC";
$db->setQuery( $query, 0, $items );
$rows = $db->loadObjectList();
foreach($rows as $row)
{
   echo '<a href="' . JRoute::_('index.php?option=com_restaurants&id='
   . $row->id . '&view=single') . '">' . $row->name . '</a><br />';
}
```

When you save the file and refresh the home page, your module should look similar to the following:

When the module is loaded, the $params object is pulled into scope and can be used to get and set the parameters. When we added the row into **jos_modules**, the **params** column contained three values—one for **items** (set to **3**), one for **style** (set to **simple**), and another for **random** (set to **1**). We set $items to the parameter **items** using the get() member function, defaulting it to **1** if no value exists.

 If desired, you can use the member function set($name, $value) to override or add a parameter for your module.

After getting a database object reference, we write a query to select the **id** and **name** from **jos_reviews** and sort the results in reverse-chronological order of the published date. We use the second and third parameters of setQuery() to generate a **LIMIT** clause that is automatically added to the query. This ensures that the correct syntax is used for the database type. Once the query is built, we load all of the relevant database rows, go through them, and generate a link to each review.

Recruiting some helpers

We would like to have our module do more than just display links to the reviews. It would be helpful to include a summary of the review along with each link, and have the opportunity to display a random review. However, the way we currently have it coded is not sufficient to handle different scenarios efficiently. To fix this, we will centralize the data functions into a helper class. Create a file called `helper.php` in the `/modules/mod_reviews` folder and add the following code to this new file:

```php
<?php
defined( '_JEXEC' ) or die( 'Restricted access' );

class modReviewsHelper
{
    function getReviews(&$params)
    {
        $items = $params->get('items', 1);
        $db =& JFactory::getDBO();
        $query = "SELECT id, name, quicktake FROM #__reviews WHERE
         published = '1' ORDER BY review_date DESC";
        $db->setQuery( $query, 0, $items );
        $rows = $db->loadObjectList();

        foreach ($rows as &$row)
        {
        $row->link = modReviewsHelper::makeReviewLink($row);
        }
    return $rows;
    }

    function makeReviewLink(&$review)
    {
    $link = JRoute::_("index.php?option=com_restaurants&view=
            single&id=" . $review->id);
        return $link;
    }
}
```

The `getReviews()` function performs the same database actions as the original module, except that it returns the rows instead of going through them. This way, we separate the database functionality from the display logic. Also, the database query now includes the **Quicktake** column. This is the field in the component that is used for short descriptions of the restaurants. It will also be useful for longer review display formats.

The `getReviews()` function calls `makeReviewLink()` to create links to single reviews, and then assigns them to each review object in the result list. To create a link, we pass `index.php?option=com_restaurants&view=single&id=` and the review **id** into `JRoute::_()`, to make our links search-engine-friendly. Finally, we return the link.

Trying some different layouts

The helper class does not produce any output itself, but instead behaves in a way similar to the data models used in our component. Layout files in this module will act the same way as layouts do in component views, containing the actual markup to be output.

The first layout we create will be named `_review`. This layout file will do one thing—output a fully-formatted anchor tag that uses the name of the review it links to as the link text. With this layout in place, we will be able to construct additional layouts without re-coding the anchor tag display logic.

To create this file, create a `tmpl` folder under the existing `/modules/mod_reviews` folder, create a new file named `_review.php` inside the `tmpl` folder, and then add the following lines of code to this new file:

```php
<?php defined('_JEXEC') or die('Restricted access'); ?>
<a href="<?php echo $review->link ?>"><?php echo $review->name; ?></a>
```

The underscore at the beginning of `_review` is a convention to remind us that the layout is for internal use; it is not offered as a choice to the administrator. In addition to this internal layout, we can create other layouts for different display options. To start with, we will create one named `default.php`. Create a `default.php` file in the `/modules/mod_reviews/tmpl` folder, and add the following code to this new file:

```php
<?php defined( '_JEXEC' ) or die( 'Restricted access' );
foreach ($list as $review)
{
    ?>
    <p>
        <?php require(JModuleHelper::getLayoutPath('mod_reviews',
            '_review')); ?>
    </p>
    <?php
}
```

Note that this layout cycles through a list of reviews, wrapping a call to the _review layout in paragraph tags. Using the same method, we will also create a bulleted layout. Create a `bulleted.php` file in `/modules/mod_reviews/tmpl` and add the following code to this new file, to create the links as a bulleted list:

```php
<?php defined( '_JEXEC' ) or die( 'Restricted access' ); ?>
<ul>
<?php
foreach ($list as $review) {
    ?>
    <li>
        <?php require(JModuleHelper::getLayoutPath('mod_reviews',
            '_review')); ?>
    </li>
    <?php
}
?>
</ul>
```

The bulleted layout uses the same basic logic as the default layout; the only difference is that it wraps the results in an unordered list. Both options ultimately load the _review layout via the `getLayoutPath()` member function of `JModuleHelper`, ensuring that the link generation is consistent across layouts.

We now have two different display options and a helper class, but none of this code is yet accessible by the module. Open the `mod_reviews.php` file and replace the contents of this file with the following code:

```php
<?php
defined('_JEXEC') or die('Restricted access');

require_once (dirname(__FILE__).DS.'helper.php');

$list = modReviewsHelper::getReviews($params);

$layout = 'default';
$path = JModuleHelper::getLayoutPath('mod_reviews', $layout);

if (file_exists($path))
    {
        require($path);
    }
```

The first `require()` call pulls in the file for the helper class we just wrote. The constant `__FILE__` is a PHP shortcut to the full absolute path and file name of the currently-executing PHP file. Passing it through `dirname()` strips off the filename so that the only path is used. Then DS and `'helper.php'` are concatenated so that `helper.php` is loaded.

Next, we pull in a sorted set of recent reviews using the getReviews() member function of the helper class. The $params object is passed into the function. This object is automatically created by Joomla! when the module is loaded. It is pre-populated based on the values of the **params** column in the **jos_modules** table for the current module.

Finally, we use the getLayoutPath() member function of JModuleHelper to pull in a display layout from our module. The $layout variable has been set to 'default' and is passed in as the second parameter of getLayoutPath(). If no second parameter is passed into getLayoutPath(), a default value is assumed.

Save all of the open files and refresh the front page in your browser. The module should look the same as shown in the last screenshot. Now, go back to the mod_reviews.php file and edit the call to getLayoutPath() so that the bulleted layout is called instead of default:

```
$list = modReviewsHelper::getReviews($params);
$layout = 'bulleted';
$path = JModuleHelper::getLayoutPath('mod_reviews', $layout);
```

Save all of the files and refresh your browser. The module should now appear similar to the following:

It would be nice if we could display a small introduction for the review along with each link. Take the code in the existing default.php file in the tmpl folder and copy it into a new file of detail.php, and then make the highlighted addition:

```
<?php defined( '_JEXEC' ) or die( 'Restricted access' );
foreach ($list as $review) {
    ?>
    <p>
        <?php require(JModuleHelper::getLayoutPath('mod_reviews',
            '_review')); ?>
    <p><?php echo htmlspecialchars($review->quicktake); ?></p>
    </p>
    <?php
}
```

As with the change to the bulleted layout, `mod_reviews.php` will also need to be modified. Change the value of `$layout` to `detail`:

```
$list = modReviewsHelper::getReviews($params);
$layout = 'detail';
$path = JModuleHelper::getLayoutPath('mod_reviews', $layout);
```

Save all of the open files and refresh your browser. If you entered something in the **Quicktake** field in the backend when editing your reviews, you should see something like the following:

Mixing it up

Our module is great at highlighting the latest opinions for our diners, but our frequent visitors may want to see the past reviews. Let's fix that with some adjustments to the `helper` function that retrieves the reviews. Go to the `getReviews()` function in the `/modules/mod_reviews/helper.php` file and make the code changes highlighted below:

```
$items = $params->get('items', 1);
$random = $params->get('random', 0);

$db =& JFactory::getDBO();

$query = "SELECT id, name, quicktake FROM #__reviews WHERE  published
        = '1' ORDER BY review_date DESC";

if ($random)
{
    $db->setQuery( $query );
}
else
{
```

```
$db->setQuery( $query, 0, $items );
}

$rows = $db->loadObjectList();

if ($random)
{
 shuffle($rows);
 $rows = array_slice($rows, 0, $items);
}

foreach ($rows as &$row)
{
    $row->link = modReviewsHelper::makeReviewLink($row);
}
return $rows;
```

First, the value of the **random** parameter is extracted and stored in $random. When we originally went to the database to register this module, we set **random** to **1** in the params field, so this is what $random will be set to. If no value can be found in for the **random** parameter, it defaults to the second parameter passed into the get() function (in this case, **0**).

The same database query is used, but the limiting effect we use needs to be handled differently when random reviews are turned on. To randomize properly, we need to pull all of the records out of the database, mix them, and then limit by the number of $items. Therefore, when $random is not set to **0**, the $query is passed in with no limits specified. Otherwise, the previous call to setQuery() that includes the limits is used.

After retrieving an array of results, we check again to see if $random is set to **0**. If so, the $rows array is passed into PHP's shuffle() function. This function randomizes all of the elements in the array. Of these randomized reviews, we want to list no more than the number specified in $items. To do this, array_slice() is used to return the elements from the $rows array, starting from **0** and counting up to $items.

Save the file and refresh your browser. Then refresh it repeatedly. With any luck, the reviews should appear in a random order. At the moment, the items parameter for `mod_reviews` is set to **3**. If you have fewer than three reviews in the database this is okay—`array_slice()` will stop once it reaches the end of the array. Because this example has only two reviews, you will not see different reviews, but they should eventually swap places:

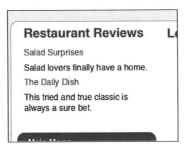

Summary

Now that this module is in place, we are able to draw visitors in with the content we've already entered. When updates are made to the reviews, they'll automatically be reflected in the module. We've implemented a helper class to centralize some of our data access and display functions. Several different layouts have been added so that we have multiple choices for display. This module can be used anywhere on the site, and will show our visitors the variety of restaurants that we've reviewed.

Expanding the Project

Our components and modules are doing a good job of managing the reviews and taking in comments. However, there are a lot of modifications that we could make in order to give our reviewers greater control over the display. Also, now that we have comments, we need a way of moderating them. We will make the following modifications and additions in this chapter:

- Publishing and deleting records
- Adding an Apply task
- Paginating results in list screens
- Requiring fields
- Performing searches
- Migrating toolbars to views
- Managing comments

Publishing records

When we first built out the backend for managing the reviews, the **Publish** and **Unpublish** buttons were added. However, if you try to use these buttons right now, they have no effect. Logic must be added to the controller to handle the publish and unpublish tasks. Let's start with the publish task. Edit the /administrator/ components/com_restaurants/restaurants.php file, and add the following function to the RestaurantsController class:

```
function publish()
{
    global $option;
    $cid = JRequest::getVar('cid', array());
    $row =& JTable::getInstance('review', 'Table');
```

```
if (!$row->publish($cid))
{
    JError::raiseError(500, $row->getError() );
}
$s = '';
if (count($cid) > 1)
{
    $s = 's';
}
$this->setRedirect('index.php?option=' . $option,
  'Review' . $s . ' published.');
}
```

This function first pulls the $option variable from global scope and extracts the **cid** request variable. Next, an instance of TableReview is fetched and stored in $row. If we were saving a complete TableReview record, this is the point where we would call the bind() member function and follow this with a call to the store(). JTable provides a publish() function that can be used instead. This function assumes that the database table has a column named **published** (which **jos_reviews** does). It accepts an array of IDs that match the primary key of the records you would like to publish.

If publish() fails, the database error is returned from getError() and is raised. Otherwise, the administrator is redirected back to the list of reviews with a message stating that the reviews have been published. This message has been pluralized by counting the number of IDs in $cid. Note that doing the pluralization is not strictly necessary, but it is a cleaner way of displaying the message than writing **Review(s) Published**.

Save the file, then go to Joomla!'s backend and navigate to **Components | Restaurant Reviews**. If all of the reviews are currently published, you may want to edit one and set **Published** to **No** so that you can see the new function in action.

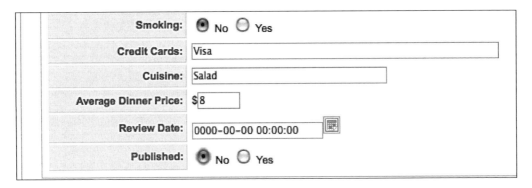

Once you have a review that is ready for publishing, select the checkbox to the left of the review title and click the **Publish** button. If the request is successful, you will be on the list of reviews again, but the success message will be at the top:

Unpublishing reviews

To add the functionality for publishing reviews, we only needed to add a function to the controller to handle the `publish` task. You could also handle the `unpublish` task with another controller function. Before diving in and coding this function, think about what the `publish()` function is doing—extracting the IDs, setting the **published** column to **1** for those records, then redirecting back to the list screen.

An `unpublish()` function would do exactly the same thing, only it would set the **published** column to **0**. Wouldn't it be nice to use the same code with a few slight modifications, instead of writing a whole new function? Fortunately, Joomla!'s controllers natively support this scenario. Edit the `/administrator/components/com_restaurants/restaurants.php` file and add the following highlighted line:

```
$controller = new RestaurantsController();
$controller->registerTask('unpublish', 'publish');
$controller->execute( $task );
$controller->redirect();
```

Whenever the task is set to `unpublish`, the controller will execute the `publish()` function instead of looking for `unpublish()` or calling `display()` by default. It is important to have all calls to `registerTask()` placed before the call to `execute()`. Otherwise, the controller will try to match `$task` to a function before the additional tasks have been registered, and as a result the default function will be called.

How can I reset the default function for the controller?

If you do not want `display()` to be called by default when an unknown task is passed into `execute()`, call the `registerDefaultTask()` member function, passing in the function that you want to use as your default function. For instance, if your controller object is named `$controller` and you call `$controller->registerDefaultTask('process')` before calling `$controller->execute($task)`, the controller will default to the `process()` function if the task name doesn't match any of the other functions.

With the `unpublish` task now registered to the `publish()` function, there are some modifications to make before it can work as intended. Go back to the `restaurants.php` file and make the highlighted changes and additions to `publish()`:

```php
function publish()
{
    global $option;
    $cid = JRequest::getVar('cid', array());
    $row =& JTable::getInstance('review', 'Table');

    $publish = 1;

    if($this->getTask() == 'unpublish')
    {
        $publish = 0;
    }
    if(!$row->publish($cid, $publish))
    {
        JError::raiseError(500, $row->getError() );
    }
    $s = '';
    if (count($cid) > 1)
    {
        $s = 's';
    }
    $msg = 'Review' . $s;

    if ($this->getTask() == 'unpublish')
```

```
    {
        $msg .= ' unpublished';
    }
else
    {
        $msg .= ' published';
    }
    $this->setRedirect('index.php?option=' . $option, $msg);
}
```

Because the `publish()` function is now doing double-duty, we need to know what the value of `$task` is, so that we can act accordingly. The member function `getTask()` can be used to retrieve this value. Towards the beginning of the amended `publish()` function, the `$publish` variable is now being set to **1** straight away. If `getTask()` returns `unpublish`, this variable gets set to **0** instead.

Just after this logic, the call to `$row->publish()` has been modified so that `$publish` is the second parameter. If the second parameter is omitted as before, `publish()` assumes the value of this to be **1**. The `publish()` function will set the **published** column of the table to whatever value gets passed in as the second parameter. In this case, it will be either **1** for `published` or **0** for `unpublished`.

Finally, the messages that are passed back to the list screen now need to account for whether we are publishing records or unpublishing them. The `$msg` variable is started using a part of the same logic that was used before. Then, an appropriate verb is added to the message based on whether or not `getTask()` returns `unpublished`. Instead of building the message within the call to `setRedirect()`, `$msg` is passed in.

Select one or more of the records in the list of reviews and click **Unpublish**. Your screen will be similar to this one:

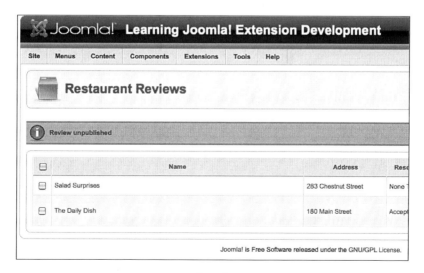

Before moving on, there is a security issue that must be addressed. Earlier on, we added logic to the `save()` function and the `single` view to make sure that the request was authentic and defend the site against CSRF attacks. This was done because `save()` makes changes to the database. Because `publish()` now also makes database modifications, the same logic must be added to this function, as well as to the list screen where the request originates. Edit the `restaurants.php` file, and add the highlighted line to the `publish()` function:

```php
function publish()
{
 JRequest::checkToken() or jexit( 'Invalid Token' );

    global $option;
```

Then go to the `/administrator/components/com_restaurants/views/all/tmpl/default.php` file and add the form token to the list screen:

```php
</table>
<?php echo JHTML::_( 'form.token' ); ?>
<input type="hidden" name="option" value="<?php echo $option;?>" />
<input type="hidden" name="task" value="" />
```

Before publishing or unpublishing any more records, refresh the list screen by going to **Components | Restaurant Reviews**. Then test the publishing and unpublishing buttons. You shouldn't notice any difference in the user interface, but you should see the form token if you look at the HTML source.

Deleting records

Sometimes our restaurant critics will want to remove their old drafts, and reviews of restaurants that have closed. Once again, adding a function to the `RestaurantsController` class in `/administrator/components/com_restaurants/restaurants.php` will power the **Delete** button in the toolbar seen in the `all` view. Open that file and add the following `remove()` function:

```php
function remove()
{
    JRequest::checkToken() or jexit( 'Invalid Token' );
    global $option;

    $cid = JRequest::getVar('cid', array(0));
    $row =& JTable::getInstance('review', 'Table');

    foreach ($cid as $id)
    {
        $id = (int) $id;
```

```
        if (!$row->delete($id))
        {
            JError::raiseError(500, $row->getError() );
        }
    }
    $s = '';

    if (count($cid) > 1)
    {
        $s = 's';
    }
    $this->setRedirect('index.php?option=' . $option,
      'Review' . $s . ' deleted.');
}
```

Notice that although the name of the `JToolBarHelper` member function that generates the **Delete** button is `deleteList()`, the button is passing in the task `remove` when it is clicked. Because of this, the name of the function that gets added to the controller is `remove()`. Because this function is making modifications to the database, the request must be checked for the anti-CSRF token by using `JRequest::checkToken()`. If the request is valid, the function continues by getting the array of checkboxes and an instance of the `TableReview` class.

Unlike the `publish()` member function of `JTable`, the `delete()` function only accepts one ID at a time. Because of this, the `$cid` array is cycled through. Each `$id` is cast as an integer to ensure that the code only attempts to delete rows using numeric IDs. If the `delete()` member function fails, `JError::raiseError()` is used to return the error message from the database. As with the `RestaurantsController::publish()` function, the number of IDs in `$cid` are counted, and an appropriately pluralized status message is generated as the user is redirected back to the `all` view.

Save the `restaurants.php` file and go back to **Components | Restaurant Reviews** in the backend. If you do not want to delete one of the existing reviews, click **New** and create a few quick test reviews:

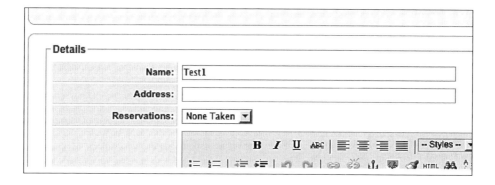

After creating several test articles, you should be back at the `all` view. Select some of these articles and then click the **Delete** button. You should get the following message displayed above the list:

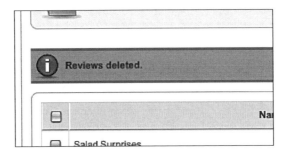

When you deleted these records, you may have noticed that the component did so immediately, without confirming whether not this is what you actually wanted to do. This could be very dangerous; someone could select one of the checkboxes and click the **Delete** button when they really meant to click the **Edit** button. To remedy this, a confirmation message must be added to the code for the **Delete** button. Make the highlighted change to the toolbar code at the top of the `restaurants.php` file:

```
JToolBarHelper::editList();
JToolBarHelper::deleteList('Are you sure you want to delete reviews?');
JToolBarHelper::addNew();
```

After saving the `restaurants.php` file, reload the screen so that the JavaScript gets updated. Then select one or more reviews and click the **Delete** button. You should get an alert like this one:

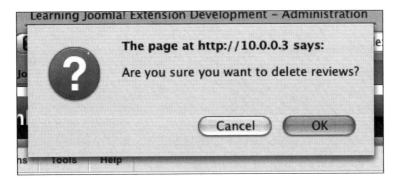

If you click **Cancel**, the alert will go away and you will return to the screen. If you click **OK**, the form will be submitted and the review will be deleted.

Adding Apply

There's still one more toolbar button in our backend that needs to be powered by code in the controller—the **Apply** button in the `single` view. **Apply** works just like **Save**, only the user gets redirected back to the `single` view for the review after the record has been saved to the database. Just as we did for the `unpublish` task, we can register the `apply` task to the `save()` function, and then make a few small modifications. In the `restaurants.php` file, make the highlighted addition to register the `apply` task:

```
$controller = new RestaurantsController();
$controller->registerTask('unpublish', 'publish');
$controller->registerTask('apply', 'save');
$controller->execute( $task );
```

Now, if you edit a file and click **Apply**, the controller will act as if you had clicked **Save**. To get it to behave the way we want, we just need to redirect the user back to where the review can be edited. Make the highlighted change at the end of the `save()` function in the `RestaurantsController` in the `restaurants.php` file:

```
if (!$row->store())
{
    JError::raiseError(500, $row->getError() );
}

if ($this->getTask() == 'apply')
{
    $this->setRedirect('index.php?option=
    ' . $option . '&task=edit&cid[]=
    ' . $row->id, 'Changes Applied');
}
else
{
    $this->setRedirect('index.php?option=
    ' . $option, 'Review Saved');
}
```

As with the `publish()` function, the `getTask()` member function is used to determine which task was originally submitted. If `apply` was used, the `setRedirect()` function sends the user back to the screen with `edit` as the task. It also sets the first element of **cid** to the ID of the review that was just saved (found in `$row->id`) using `cid[]` in the URL. This simulates the action of someone selecting one of the checkboxes for the reviews and clicking **Edit** from the `all` view.

To test this function, open one of the reviews for editing, make a change, and then click the **Apply** button. The review should appear again with the following message:

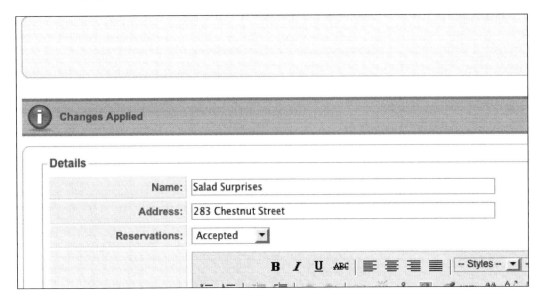

Requiring specific fields

When the restaurant critics are entering reviews into the system, there are a few fields on the form in the single view that they should always complete. As a minimum, we have decided that each review needs a **Name**, **Address**, and a **Quicktake**. Without these fields, a review is effectively useless. To enforce these requirements, we need to add some JavaScript that will intercept the events when the **Save** and **Apply** buttons are clicked, and check that these fields have been specified.

The JavaScript that we will add should test the value of each required field, then throw an alert and stop the form from submitting when any one of them is blank. The backend of Joomla! is configured so that whenever one of the toolbar buttons is clicked, it attempts to execute the `submitbutton()` JavaScript function (if one exists). Let's add one of these functions to the top of the `single` view. Go to `/administrator/components/com_restaurants/views/single/tmpl/default.php` and add the highlighted code:

```
JHTML::_('behavior.calendar');
$editor =& JFactory::getEditor();
?>
<script language="javascript" type="text/javascript">
function submitbutton(pressbutton)
```

```
{
    if (pressbutton == 'save' || pressbutton == 'apply')
    {
    var quicktake = <?php echo $editor->getContent( 'quicktake' ); ?>
        if (document.adminForm.name.value == '')
        {
            alert("Please enter the name of the restaurant.");
        }
    else if (document.adminForm.address.value == '')
        {
            alert("Please enter the street address of
              the restaurant.");
        }
    else if (quicktake == '' && document.adminForm.quicktake.value
              == '')
        {
            alert("Please enter a quicktake summary of
              the restaurant.");
        }
    else
        {
            submitform(pressbutton);
        }
    }
    else
    {
        submitform(pressbutton);
    }
}
</script>
    <form action="index.php" method="post" name=
    "adminForm" id="adminForm">
```

When one of the toolbar buttons is clicked in Joomla!'s backend, the submitbutton() function is executed and the task is passed in as pressbutton. On this screen, we only need to check the fields when the user is attempting to save the record to the database; this currently happens only for the save and apply tasks. If the user clicks the **Cancel** button, the condition fails, submitform(pressbutton) is executed from the else clause, and the form submission goes through. If the task is save or apply, the code checks the **Name**, **Address**, and **Quicktake** fields one by one. Because the name of the form is adminForm, we can use JavaScript DOM to drill down to the values for each of our fields.

This works fine for **Name** and **Address**, but **Quicktake** is a special case. Because the **Quicktake** field is being filled out from a JavaScript-based WYSIWYG editor and not necessarily a true form input, we need to use the Joomla! framework to add code to help us get the value. Before writing the JavaScript portion, we use the `getEditor()` function of the `JFactory` class to get a reference to the current editor object. This is stored in `$editor`. Once we're inside the JavaScript, we declare `quicktake` as a variable, and escape back into PHP so that we can output what the `getContent()` member function of `$editor` returns. This function will return JavaScript code based on the selected WYSIWYG editor. We pass the name of the field we want to get the contents of, into `getContent()`.

If any of these three fields are blank, an appropriate alert is shown and the form is not submitted. Note that these conditions are checked one at a time; if all three are blank and **Save** is clicked, only the first alert will display. If only the first field is subsequently filled in and the **Save** button is clicked again, the fields will be re-checked and the second one will fail. This cycle will repeat every time **Save** is clicked until the user has filled in all of the required fields.

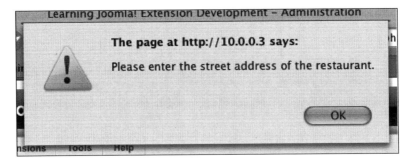

 Note that the last condition of the JavaScript checks both `quicktake` and `document.adminForm.quicktake.value`. When an existing record is loaded, the WYSIWYG HTML editor does not necessarily load in the form input contents automatically. However, the form element `quicktake` will be completed and will be available for testing. Adding the code to check both the editor and the form input ensures that is not left blank, while still allowing the user to save unmodified data.

Once all of the required fields are completed, `submitform(pressbutton)` will be called and the form will be submitted normally.

Shouldn't we check the data in PHP before saving?

In addition to adding user interface checks to the form in JavaScript, we should be adding logic to our `TableReview` class to make sure that the values are non-blank before saving them into the database. Our data model is very simple at the moment, and having blank values for these fields won't cause serious issues. The only people who have the ability to add records to this table are authenticated administrators. Because the backend does not work with JavaScript turned off, it is reasonable to assume that our check will suffice for now. However, it is best to also validate the data format in PHP, in addition to the malicious data stripping that happens in `JTable::bind()`. To learn how this can be done, refer to Chapter 5 of this book.

Using pagination to break up long lists

As the restaurant critics add more reviews to the system, the all view will become very long and readers will have to do a lot of scrolling. To make this screen more manageable, we will paginate the list of results so that only a certain number of reviews appear on the screen at a time; this is similar to the way search engines display several pages of results.

Before writing more code, make sure there are at least six reviews in the database; adding reviews with titles, addresses, and quicktakes such as 'Test1' will be fine. This will ensure that there are enough reviews to paginate.

At the moment, the `all` view is being fed with database results from the model in the `/administrator/components/models/all.php` file. This model will need to be modified to handle pagination. The `getData()` function will now have to return only the rows to be displayed on the current page. A function for generating the pagination will also be needed. Finally, the pagination function will need to know the total number of records so that the correct number of links to pages can be generated.

Adding this feature will involve an almost entire rewrite of the `all` model, so let's add this code one piece at a time. First, some additional member variables will be needed to hold the total number of records as well as a special pagination object. Add the highlighted member variables to `RestaurantsModelAll`:

```
var $_data = null;
var $_pagination = null;
var $_total = null;
```

Why are there underscores in front of the variable names?

Because these variables will only be used within the object, and will only be available through member functions, an underscore is a reminder that these are private variables. In PHP 5, the need for this convention can be avoided by using the private keyword, which enforces encapsulation.

The same query will be used by both getData() and getTotal(). This query may change in the future if search functionality is added for the backend interface. Because searches would change this query, migrate the existing SQL in getData() to a new function called buildSearch():

```
function buildSearch()
{
    return "SELECT * FROM #__reviews";
}
```

Before building the pagination function, the function that returns the total number of records to paginate must be available. Add a new function called getTotal(), as follows:

```
function getTotal()
{
    if (!$this->_total)
    {
        $query = $this->buildSearch();
        $this->_total = $this->_getListCount($query);
    }
    return $this->_total;
}
```

The getTotal() function first checks to see if the model has already retrieved the total and stored it as a private variable. If it has not, the buildSearch() function is called to get the query, which is then passed into the member function _getListCount(). The result is stored in the $_total member variable. Finally, the $_total member variable is returned.

Everything needed for generating the pagination object is now available. Joomla! has a special pagination class called JPagination that keeps track of which "page" the user is on and generates the HTML elements for the user interface. This class can be loaded by calling jimport('joomla.html.pagination'). Once it is loaded, you can create a JPagination object instance to handle your list. Add the getPagination() function, shown below:

```
function &getPagination()
{
if(!$this->_pagination)
```

```
    {
        jimport('joomla.html.pagination');
        global $mainframe;
        $this->_pagination = new JPagination($this->getTotal(),
          JRequest::getVar('limitstart', 0), JRequest::getVar('limit',
          $mainframe->getCfg('list_limit')));
    }
    return $this->_pagination;
}
```

Before attempting to generate a pagination object, the function first checks to see if one has already been assigned to the $_pagination member variable. If not, it continues to load the JPagination class, and pulls the $mainframe object from the global scope. Next, $this->_pagination is declared as a new instance of JPagination. The total number of records to paginate (retrieved from getTotal()) is passed in as the first parameter. The second parameter is the record number to start with for the beginning of the current page. The pagination HTML automatically generates links and form variables with limitstart set, so this is extracted from the HTTP request.

The final parameter is the number of records to display on a single page. This can be adjusted through the generated HTML controls, but we want to have a default value for the first time that the users hit the screen. In Joomla!'s **Global Configuration**, the **Site** tab has a control for **List Length** that administrators can set to their liking. This value can be retrieved by passing list_limit into the getCfg() member function of the $mainframe object.

Finally, the getData() function must be rewritten to only select the records to be displayed on the current page. Make the highlighted changes to getData():

```
function &getData()
{
 $pagination =& $this->getPagination();

    if (empty($this->_data))
    {
     $query = $this->buildSearch();
     $this->_data = $this->_getList($query,
       $pagination->limitstart, $pagination->limit);
    }
    return $this->_data;
}
```

The pagination object is retrieved and stored in $pagination by calling the getPagination() member function. If you attempt to grab $this->_pagination directly without calling getPagination(), it will fail as the pagination object instance is not created until getPagination() is called. If records are not already in $_data, the buildSearch() member function is called to get the SQL for retrieving the records, which is stored in $query. Finally, the $_data member variable is set to the results of the _getList() member function. As before, the query is the first parameter. The second and third parameters are the beginning record for the page and the total number of records to display on the page, respectively. These are available directly from the $pagination object; the getData() function does not need to be concerned with where the values came from.

If you save the model and refresh the **Components | Restaurant Reviews** page, you most likely will not see a difference (unless you have more than twenty reviews). This is because the pagination HTML must still be added to the all view. Open the /administrator/components/com_restaurants/views/all/view.html.php file, and make the highlighted additions to the display() member function:

```php
function display($tpl = null)
{
    $rows =& $this->get('data');
    $pagination =& $this->get('pagination');

    $this->assignRef('rows', $rows);
    $this->assignRef('pagination', $pagination);

    parent::display($tpl);
}
```

When $this->get('pagination') is called, RestaurantsModelAll::getPagination() is executed. Notice that this function is also executed in the model itself. When getPagination() is called this second time, it will reuse the object already in memory instead of generating a new one. The object is then assigned to the template in the same way as the data is. Because there will be HTML output, the template also needs to be adjusted. Open tmpl/default.php and make the following addition:

```php
    }
  ?>
<tfoot>
  <tr>
      <td colspan="7"><?php echo $this->
      pagination->getListFooter(); ?></td>
  </tr>
</tfoot>
  </table>
```

To take advantage of the stylesheet for the backend, the table row is wrapped in a `<tfoot>` element just above the closing `</table>` tag. This single row has a single cell that spans all seven columns of the table. It is important to keep the `colspan` consistent with the number of columns in the table as the stylesheet centers this cell. Because pagination was assigned to the template, it is called as a member variable and its member function `getListFooter()` is executed. This function automatically generates the appropriate HTML depending on where the user is in the list.

Refresh the page and you should see a dropdown at the bottom of the list:

Test2	None Taken	
Test3	None Taken	
Test4	None Taken	
Test5	None Taken	
Display # 20 ▼		

Unless you have more than twenty reviews in the system, your screen will look very similar to the previous one. The list limit in Joomla!'s **Global Configuration** defaults to **20**, which is probably enough for the reviews we have entered so far. To see the pagination in action, select **5** from the dropdown. The form should automatically be submitted, and you will see a series of links:

Name	Address	Reservations	Cu
	283 Chestnut Street	Accepted	Salad
	180 Main Street	Accepted	Homes
	Test1	None Taken	
	Test2	None Taken	
	Test3	None Taken	
Display # 5 ▼ ⊘ Start ⊘ Prev 1 2 Next ⊘ End ⊘ Page 1 of 2			

Clicking on either the **2** link or the **Next** link will take you to the second page of results:

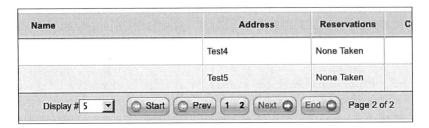

Searching

Although pagination will help our restaurant critics to navigate through the records in consistent chunks, sometimes they will have a specific review in mind or will want to narrow down the display to a certain set of reviews. Adding search capabilities to our component will help the reviewers find specific reviews quickly. The changes that were made to the `all` model for pagination will make adding the search feature a little easier.

Adjusting the model

The model will now need to keep track of the search term for multiple calls. Also, as the query will no longer be a static string, this should be cached as well. Add the following private variables to the `all` model:

```
var $_total = null;
var $_search = null;
var $_query = null;
```

Next, the model will need a function that prepares the search term and returns it. This function needs to do three things—get the search term from the session (rather than the request), set it to lowercase, and store it in the `$_search` member variable. Add the following `getSearch()` function to the `RestaurantModelAll` controller:

```
function getSearch()
{
    if (!$this->_search)
    {
        global $mainframe, $option;
        $search = $mainframe->getUserStateFromRequest
        ( "$option.search", 'search', '', 'string' );
        $this->_search = JString::strtolower($search);
    }
    return $this->_search;
}
```

After checking to see whether the $_search member variable is already set, $mainframe and $option are pulled in from global scope. Instead of using a member function of JRequest to get the value for search, the getUserStateFromRequest() member function of $mainframe is used. This function will pull search from the HTTP request if it is not already a session variable or if the request changed the value of search. Otherwise, it will return the value stored in the session variable. This makes it possible for you to edit a review and then be returned back to your search without having to pass the search variable around from view to view.

The last piece of the model that needs to be adjusted is the buildSearch() function. At the moment, it simply returns a string. Now that our model will allow for actual searches with terms, some query logic is needed instead. Replace the existing buildSearch() function with the one below:

```
function buildSearch()
{
    if (!$this->_query)
    {
        $search = $this->getSearch();
        $this->_query = "SELECT * FROM #__reviews";

        if ($search != '')
        {
            $fields = array('name', 'address', 'quicktake', 'review',
             'notes', 'cuisine');
            $where = array();
            $search = $this->_db->getEscaped( $search, true );

            foreach ($fields as $field)
            {
            $where[] = $field . " LIKE '%{$search}%'";
            }
            $this->_query .= ' WHERE ' . implode(' OR ', $where);
        }
    }
    return $this->_query;
}
```

The function first checks to see if the $_query member variable is set. If not, it starts building the query. The search term is retrieved from the getSearch() member function and stored in $search. Next, the $_query member variable is set with the same query that was used in the old function. This is used as a base for the rest of the query; if no search term is set, the original query will be used. If a search term is set, the function builds a WHERE clause. The $fields array contains a list of table columns to search. Before cycling through this array, the $search variable is passed into the getEscaped() member function of the database object reference in JModel. This function makes $search safe to use in the query. In LIKE clauses, the characters % and _ have special meaning. When you pass true as the second parameter to getEscaped(), it automatically escapes these characters as well.

With the $search variable ready for the database, the $fields array is cycled through and LIKE clauses are added to the $where array. Because we want to see if the string in $search appears anywhere within the column, we surround the term with % characters. After the loop has completed, the WHERE clause is concatenated to the end of the $_query private member variable. PHP's implode() function is called to join up all of the LIKE clauses and separate them by OR so that if any field matches the search term, the row is returned in the results.

Adjusting the view

If you go to **Components | Restaurant Reviews** now and add &search=dish onto the end of the URL, you might get a screen similar to the following (assuming you have a review containing the string **dish**):

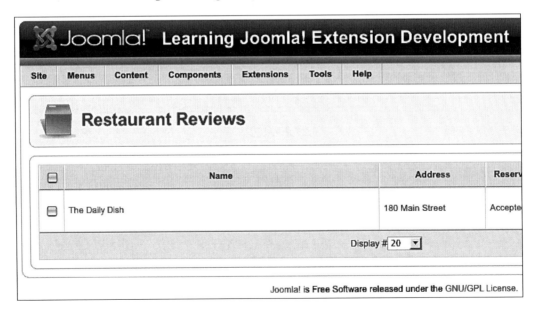

It's good to know that the code for building the WHERE clause works, but this will not be acceptable to our restaurant reviewers. They will be using the form and will not be paying any attention to the URL. To fix this, there are a few quick adjustments that we need to make to the all view. First, we need to add a form input where the reviewers can enter the desired search term. Open the /administrator/ components/com_restaurants/views/all/tmpl/default.php file, and add the highlighted code below:

```
    <form action="index.php" method="post" name="adminForm">
 <table>
    <tr>
        <td align="left">
        Search:
        <input type="text" name="search" value=
        "<?php echo $this->search ?>" id="search" />
        <button type="submit">Go</button>
        </td>
    </tr>
 </table>
    <table class="adminlist">
      <thead>
```

This HTML is straightforward—there's a small table with an input field for the search term and then a button to submit the form. However, there's one part where we escape into PHP and output $this->search. The value for $this->search has not been set yet, so open views/all/view.html.php and add the highlighted code:

```
    $rows =& $this->get('data');
    $pagination =& $this->get('pagination');
    $search = $this->get('search');

    $this->assignRef('rows', $rows);
    $this->assignRef('pagination', $pagination);
    $this->assign('search', $search);
```

To get the search term, the model's `getSearch()` function is reused when we call `$this->get('search')`. Because the value of `$search` will be a small string, it is assigned to the template by value using `$this->assign()`. Once the code is in place, save all of the files and go to **Components | Restaurant Reviews** (making sure you do not use the URL from before, which contains `&search=dish`). The search form should now appear, as shown in this example:

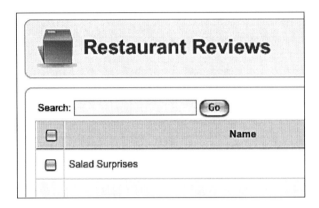

Now type in a search string that you know is contained in more than one review (but not all of them) and click **Go**. The `all` view will now filter out all of the items that do not contain your search term. If you have more than five reviews that do match the search term, there is a test that you can do to make sure that the pagination and search features are working together correctly. Set the dropdown for **Display #** to **5** and your screen should look similar to this one:

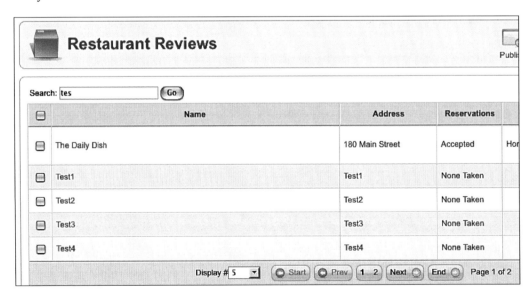

When you click **Next**, the search term should stay in the **Search** input field and you should see the next screen of results:

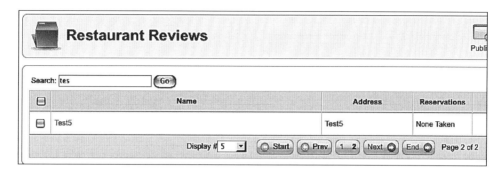

Migrating toolbars to views

When we first built out the backend, we added toolbars to the top of the restaurants.php file and decided which one to display by using a switch() statement. This was okay for testing, but it will make maintenance a bit unpleasant. Now that we have views in place, we can place our toolbars directly in them. Take the toolbar code from the default: case in restaurants.php and add it to views/all/tmpl/default.php:

```php
<?php
defined( '_JEXEC' ) or die( 'Restricted access' );

    JToolBarHelper::title( JText::_( 'Restaurant Reviews' ),
            'generic.png' );
    JToolBarHelper::publishList();
    JToolBarHelper::unpublishList();
    JToolBarHelper::editList();
    JToolBarHelper::deleteList('Are you sure you want
      to delete reviews?');
    JToolBarHelper::addNew();
?>
<form action="index.php" method="post" name="adminForm">
```

Next, do the same for the edit and add tasks on the single view. Cut the toolbar code and paste it into views/single/tmpl/default.php:

```php
JHTML::_('behavior.calendar');
$editor =& JFactory::getEditor();
```

```
    JToolBarHelper::save();
    JToolBarHelper::apply();
  JToolBarHelper::cancel();
  ?>
  <script language="javascript" type="text/javascript">
```

While we are here, there are a few adjustments that we can make to smooth out the interface. This view is used for both editing and adding reviews, but there is currently no visual feedback to remind you which of these tasks is being done. Also, some people prefer to change the **Cancel** button to a **Close** button when editing a record. The highlighted changes below will solve both of these:

```
if ($this->row->id)
{
    JToolBarHelper::title( JText::_( 'Edit Restaurant Review' ),
        'addedit.png' );
}
else
{
    JToolBarHelper::title( JText::_( 'Add Restaurant Review' ),
        'addedit.png' );
}


    JToolBarHelper::save();
    JToolBarHelper::apply();
if ($this->row->id)
{
    JToolBarHelper::cancel( 'cancel', 'Close' );
}
else
{
    JToolBarHelper::cancel();
}
```

Because the row is assigned to the view, the value of **id** can be tested at `$this->row->id`. If it is non-zero and non-null, the title is set to **Edit Restaurant Review**; otherwise, it is set to **Add Restaurant Review**. At the bottom of the list, we test **id** again. If it exists, we call `JToolBarHelper::cancel()`, but we pass in the task `cancel` and the label **Close**. Notice that the same function is called both times and the same request is made—only the label is changing.

Before continuing, be sure to entirely remove the `switch()` statement from the top of `restaurants.php`. Now when you edit an existing review, you should see the following toolbar:

The toolbar will look like this when you add a review:

Managing comments

Back in Chapter 4, we added a feature to the site which allows visitors to add their comments to reviews on the site. Unfortunately, websites offering comments are frequently abused. We need to build a backend manager where comments can be removed or edited.

Before we start adding models, views, and controller methods, let's stop to think about how we want to organize the new code. At the moment, the controller handles everything related to managing the records in the **jos_reviews** table. We could add methods to the current controller for managing the **jos_reviews_comments** table as well.

This approach would require us to come up with task names that would not conflict with the existing ones; for instance, we would have to add `saveComment()` so as not to conflict with `save()`. This would also require that all of the new toolbar buttons have tasks to match the ones we are adding. This is entirely possible—for most buttons, you simply pass the new task you want to use as the first parameter to the corresponding member function of `JToolBarHelper`.

However, this approach would be a bit messy. If we ever wanted to add another type of record to the component, we would have to add yet more functions to the same controller. Soon, we would have a lot of completely unrelated functions sitting side by side.

Fortunately, there is a better way. We can create a second controller for the comments and then modify the `restaurants.php` file to pick the one we want. Similar to the way we currently pass the `view` parameter into our requests, we will pass in a value for `controller` to tell the code which controller to use.

To separate the code properly, we need to move the current controller for the reviews out of the `restaurants.php` file. Inside the `/administrator/components/com_restaurants` folder, create a new folder named `controllers`. Copy the file `restaurants.php` to `controllers/reviews.php` and place it in this new folder. Remove the highlighted code from `controllers/reviews.php`:

```
defined( '_JEXEC' ) or die( 'Restricted access' );

JTable::addIncludePath(JPATH_COMPONENT.DS.'tables');

jimport('joomla.application.component.controller');

........
........
    }
}

$controller = new RestaurantsController();
$controller->registerTask('unpublish', 'publish');
$controller->registerTask('apply', 'save');
$controller->execute( $task );
$controller->redirect();
```

You may have noticed that we just removed two calls to `registerTask()`, which bind task values to other functions. These must be replaced. However, because the class will no longer be instantiated in this file, we need to find a different way of calling `registerTask()`. To do this, we will add a `__construct()` function to the controller that will make these calls for us. Add the following `__construct()` function to the controller:

```
function __construct($config = array())
    {
        parent::__construct($config);
        $this->registerTask('unpublish', 'publish');
        $this->registerTask('apply', 'save');
    }
```

It is important to call `parent::__construct($config)` as this is a function defined by `JController` to be run when the object is created. This call to the parent function must be made before the calls to `registerTask()`; `JController::__construct()` takes inventory of all of the functions that can be registered with tasks.

What is the __construct() method?

The __construct() member function is a "magic method" in PHP that gets automatically called when the object is instantiated. This is extremely helpful when you want to add setup code for your class. The companion function to __construct() is __destruct(), called just before the object is destroyed and removed from memory. This is useful for shutdown code such as closing open files, network streams, and database connections. You can learn more about these and other magic methods at http://www.php.net/oop5.magic.

Finally, because we will have multiple controllers, the class name RestaurantsController will no longer be appropriate. Change the class name of the controller from RestaurantsController to RestaurantsControllerReviews:

```
jimport('joomla.application.component.controller');

class RestaurantsControllerReviews extends JController
{
```

Once you are done with the changes to controllers/reviews.php, go back to the/administrator/components/com_restaurants/restaurants.php file, and delete everything beneath the line JTable::addIncludePath(JPATH_COMPONENT. DS.'tables'). Your file will now look like this:

```
<?php
defined( '_JEXEC' ) or die( 'Restricted access' );

JTable::addIncludePath(JPATH_COMPONENT.DS.'tables');
```

If we were to go to the backend right now, it would not show anything, as we have moved the controller and nothing is currently loading it. To fix this, we need to extract the value of controller from the request, make sure the requested controller is valid (or default to reviews), and then execute the correct controller. Add the code below to the end of the restaurants.php file:

```
$controller = JRequest::getCmd('controller', 'reviews');
switch ($controller)
{
    default:
        $controller = 'reviews';

    case 'reviews':
    case 'comments':
        require_once(
          JPATH_COMPONENT.DS.'controllers'.DS.$controller.'.php' );
        $controllerName = 'RestaurantsController'.$controller;
```

```
$controller = new $controllerName();
$controller->execute( JRequest::getCmd('task') );
$controller->redirect();
break;
}
```

The code first extracts the controller name from the request using `JRequest::`
`getCmd()`. This function ensures that the value consists only of letters, numbers, and
underscores. The code then proceeds into a large `switch()` statement. This `switch()`
is designed in such a way that the value for `$controller` will only ever be `reviews`
or `comments`. The use of `switch()` is not as important as making sure that the valid
values for `$controller` are white-listed.

If `$controller` is not set to `reviews` or `comments`, it is immediately set to `reviews`
as the `default` case. There is no `break` statement on the default `case`, so it will fall
through to the rest of the code under the line `case 'comments':`. Using the value
of `$controller`, an appropriate controller file is loaded. Next, the name of the
controller class is assembled and stored in `$controllerName`. The `$controller`
variable is then used to hold a new controller object that is instantiated using
`$controllerName`. The `execute()` member function is called with the current `task`
passed in. Finally, if the controller sets a redirect, the `redirect()` member function
forwards the browser.

Once you save all of the files, the component should be functioning as it was before,
only it is now ready for our comment management code. Fundamentally, the
code for managing comments is not much different from the code for managing
reviews. We will still create a model, some views, and a controller to tie everything
together. Start by adding the model. Create a new file named `comments.php` in
the `/administrator/components/com_restaurants/models` folder and add the
following code to this new file:

```php
<?php
defined( '_JEXEC' ) or die( 'Restricted access' );

jimport('joomla.application.component.model');

class RestaurantsModelComments extends JModel
{
    var $_data = null;
    var $_pagination = null;
    var $_total = null;
    var $_search = null;
    var $_query = null;

    function &getData()
```

```
    {
        $pagination =& $this->getPagination();

        if (empty($this->_data))
        {
        $query = $this->buildSearch();
        $this->_data = $this->_getList($query,
         $pagination->limitstart, $pagination->limit);
        }
        return $this->_data;
    }

    function &getPagination()
    {
        if(!$this->_pagination)
        {
        jimport('joomla.html.pagination');
        global $mainframe;
        $this->_pagination = new JPagination($this->getTotal(),
         JRequest::getVar('limitstart', 0), JRequest::getVar('limit',
         $mainframe->getCfg('list_limit')));
        }
        return $this->_pagination;
    }

    function getTotal()
    {
        if (!$this->_total)
        {
        $query = $this->buildSearch();
        $this->_total = $this->_getListCount($query);
        }
        return $this->_total;
    }

    function buildSearch()
    {
        if (!$this->_query)
        {
        $search = $this->getSearch();
        $this->_query = "SELECT c.*,
         r.name as restaurant FROM #__reviews_comments AS c LEFT
        JOIN #__reviews AS r ON r.id = c.review_id";
        if ($search != '')
        {
            $search = $this->_db->getEscaped( $search, true );
            $this->_query .= " WHERE c.full_name LIKE '%{
            $search}%' OR c.comment_text LIKE '%{$search}%' OR r.name
             LIKE '%{$search}%'";
        }
            $this->_query .= ' ORDER BY c.comment_date DESC';
        }
```

```
        return $this->_query;
    }

    function getSearch()
    {
        if (!$this->_search)
        {
        global $mainframe, $option;
        $search = $mainframe->getUserStateFromRequest(
          "$option.comments.search", 'search', '', 'string' );
        $this->_search = JString::strtolower($search);
        }

        return $this->_search;
    }
}
```

The getData(), getPagination(), and getTotal() functions are identical to the ones found in the all model that we created earlier. The buildSearch() function joins in the **jos_reviews** table so that the name of the restaurant that the comment is attached to can be pulled out in the same query. It also facilitates searching on the name of the comment author, the comment text, and the name of the restaurant. The comments are sorted in reverse-chronological order so that the most recent ones are always easy to find.

There is only one small difference in the getSearch() function—the name of the session variable is ultimately set to com_restaurants.commens.search (once $option is interpreted). This allows a user to have different search terms for the reviews and comments screens recalled when they navigate back to them. If a user searches for "John" in the comments screen, then "Dish" in the reviews screen, the search will still be set to "John" when they go back to the comments screen.

With the model in place, there are two views we need to add—one for listing all comments and one editing specific comments. The view comments will be used for all comments, while the view comment will be used for individual ones. Create a folder named comments in the existing /administrator/components/com_restaurants/ views folder, and create a new file named view.html.php inside containing the following code:

```
<?php
defined( '_JEXEC' ) or die( 'Restricted access' );

jimport( 'joomla.application.component.view');

class RestaurantsViewComments extends JView
{
    function display($tpl = null)
```

```
    {
        $rows =& $this->get('data');
        $pagination =& $this->get('pagination');
        $search =& $this->get('search');

        $this->assignRef('rows', $rows);
        $this->assignRef('pagination', $pagination);
        $this->assign('search', $search);

        parent::display($tpl);
    }
}
```

Next, create a folder named tmpl within the existing views/comments folder. Create a file named default.php inside the tmpl folder, and containing this code:

```php
<?php
defined( '_JEXEC' ) or die( 'Restricted access' );

JToolBarHelper::title( JText::_( 'Comments' ), 'generic.png' );
JToolBarHelper::editList();
JToolBarHelper::deleteList('Are you sure you want
        to delete comments?');
?>
<form action="index.php" method="post" name="adminForm">
<table>
    <tr>
        <td align="left">
        Search:
        <input type="text" name="search" value=
            "<?php echo $this->search ?>" id="search" />
        <button type="submit">Go</button>
        </td>
    </tr>
</table>
<table class="adminlist">
  <thead>
    <tr>
        <th width="20">
        <input type="checkbox" name="toggle" value="" onclick=
            "checkAll(<?php echo count( $this->rows ); ?>);" />
        </th>
        <th class="title">Restaurant Name</th>
        <th width="15%">Commenter</th>
```

```php
            <th width="20%">Comment Date</th>
            <th width="30%">Comment</th>
        </tr>
    </thead>
    <?php
    jimport('joomla.filter.output');
    $k = 0;
    for ($i=0, $n=count( $this->rows ); $i < $n; $i++)
      {
      $row = &$this->rows[$i];
      $checked = JHTML::_('grid.id', $i, $row->id );
      $link = JFilterOutput::ampReplace( 'index.php?option=
      ' . $option . '&task=edit&controller=comments&cid[]='. $row->id );
        ?>
        <tr class="<?php echo "row$k"; ?>">
            <td><?php echo $checked; ?></td>
            <td><a href="<?php echo $link; ?>">
                <?php echo $row->restaurant; ?></a></td>
            <td><?php echo $row->full_name; ?></td>
            <td><?php echo JHTML::Date($row->comment_date); ?></td>
            <td><?php echo JString::substr($row->comment_text,
                0, 149); ?></td>
        </tr>
        <?php
        $k = 1 - $k;
      }
      ?>
    <tfoot>
      <td colspan="5"><?php echo $this->pagination->getListFooter();
        ?></td>
    </tfoot>
    </table>
    <?php echo JHTML::_( 'form.token' ); ?>
    <input type="hidden" name="option" value="<?php echo $option;?>" />
    <input type="hidden" name="controller" value="comments" />
    <input type="hidden" name="task" value="" />
    <input type="hidden" name="boxchecked" value="0" />
    </form>
```

This template lists the comments in much the same manner as the `all` view lists reviews. Because comments are more easily identified when you can read them, they are included in the listings. However, some visitors will write very long comments, so `JString::substr()` returns the first 150 characters. The `JString` member function is used instead of PHP's built-in substring function as it is aware of UTF-8 characters, while the native `substr()` in current versions of PHP is not. Finally, the form has the hidden input field `controller` preset to `comments`. This will ensure that the `RestaurantsControllerComments` controller is used.

Create another folder named `comment` inside the `views` folder. The `view.html.php` file in this new folder should have this code:

```php
<?php
defined( '_JEXEC' ) or die( 'Restricted access' );

jimport( 'joomla.application.component.view');

class RestaurantsViewComment extends JView
{
    function display($tpl = null)
    {
        $row =& JTable::getInstance('Comment', 'Table');
        $cid = JRequest::getVar( 'cid', array(0), '', 'array' );
        $id = $cid[0];
        $row->load($id);
        $this->assignRef('row', $row);

        parent::display($tpl);
    }
}
```

Now, create a `tmpl` folder under the `views/comment` folder, create a file named `default.php` in it, and fill the new file with the following code:

```php
<?php defined( '_JEXEC' ) or die( 'Restricted access' );

JHTML::_('behavior.calendar');

JToolBarHelper::title( JText::_( 'Edit Comment' ), 'generic.png' );
JToolBarHelper::save();
JToolBarHelper::cancel( 'cancel', 'Close' );

?>
<form action="index.php" method="post" name="adminForm"
id="adminForm">
  <fieldset class="adminform">
    <legend>Comment</legend>
    <table class="admintable">
    <tr>
      <td width="100" align="right" class="key">
        Name:
      </td>
      <td>
        <input class="text_area" type="text" name=
        "full_name" id="full_name" size="50" maxlength=
        "250" value="<?php echo $this->row->full_name;?>" />
      </td>
```

```
        </tr>
        <tr>
          <td width="100" align="right" class="key">
            Comment:
          </td>
          <td>
            <textarea class="text_area" cols="20" rows="4"
            name="comment_text" id="comment_text" style=
            "width:500px"><?php echo $this->row->comment_text;
            ?></textarea>
          </td>
        </tr>
        <tr>
          <td width="100" align="right" class="key">
            Comment Date:
          </td>
          <td>
            <?php echo JHTML::_('calendar', $this->row->comment_date,
            'comment_date', 'comment_date'); ?>
          </td>
        </tr>
        </table>
    </fieldset>
    <?php echo JHTML::_( 'form.token' ); ?>
    <input type="hidden" name="id" value="<?php echo $this->row->id;
        ?>" />
    <input type="hidden" name="option" value="<?php echo $option;
        ?>" />
    <input type="hidden" name="controller" value="comments" />
    <input type="hidden" name="task" value="" />
</form>
```

Finally, we need to add a controller so that everything is tied together. Create a file named `comments.php` in the `/administrator/components/com_restaurants/controllers` folder, and fill it with the following code:

```php
<?php
defined( '_JEXEC' ) or die( 'Restricted access' );

jimport('joomla.application.component.controller');

class RestaurantsControllerComments extends JController
{
    function save()
    {
        JRequest::checkToken() or jexit( 'Invalid Token' );
```

```
    global $option;
    $row =& JTable::getInstance('comment', 'Table');

    if (!$row->bind(JRequest::get('post')))
    {
        JError::raiseError(500, $row->getError() );
    }

    if (!$row->store())
    {
        JError::raiseError(500, $row->getError() );
    }

    $this->setRedirect('index.php?option=
        ' . $option . '&controller=comments', 'Comment Saved');
}

function remove()
{
    JRequest::checkToken() or jexit( 'Invalid Token' );
    global $option;
    $cid = JRequest::getVar('cid', array(0));

    $row =& JTable::getInstance('comment', 'Table');

    foreach ($cid as $id)
    {
        $id = (int) $id;

        if (!$row->delete($id))
        {
            JError::raiseError(500, $row->getError() );
        }
    }

    $s = '';

    if (count($cid) > 1)
    {
        $s = 's';
    }

    $this->setRedirect('index.php?option=
        ' . $option . '&controller=comments',
        'Comment' . $s . ' deleted.');
}

function display()
```

```
        {
            $view = JRequest::getVar('view');

            if (!$view)
            {
                switch ($this->getTask())
                {
                case 'edit':
                    JRequest::setVar('view', 'comment');
                    break;

                default:
                    JRequest::setVar('view', 'comments');
                    break;
                }
            }

            parent::display();
        }
    }
```

The save() and remove() functions are very basic. The save() function does not need any field adjustments as this interface does not allow for new comments—you can only edit or remove existing ones. Instead of writing an edit() function, we are letting the controller default to display(); then we check the task to see if we need to pull the comment view for the edit task.

Save all of the files and go to index.php?option=com_restaurants&controller= comments. If you have several comments added to articles, your screen should look similar to this one:

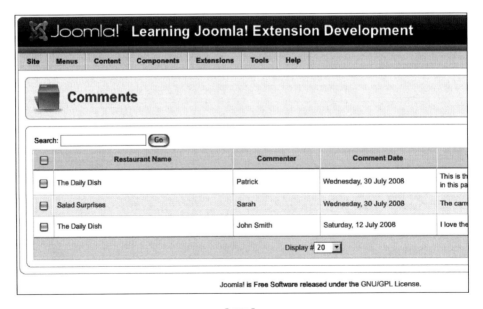

As we can see in the following screenshot, searching for the term **dish** will pull up only the comments for the review for **The Daily Dish** restaurant:

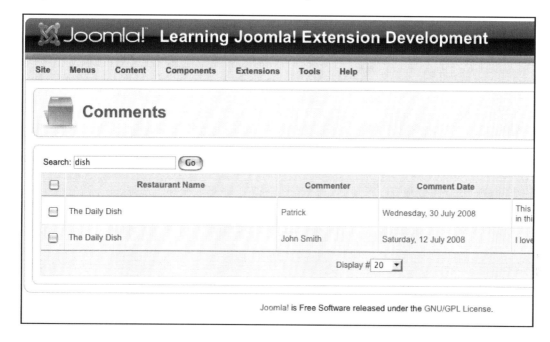

Clicking on the title of a reviewed article will pull up the `comment` view, for editing:

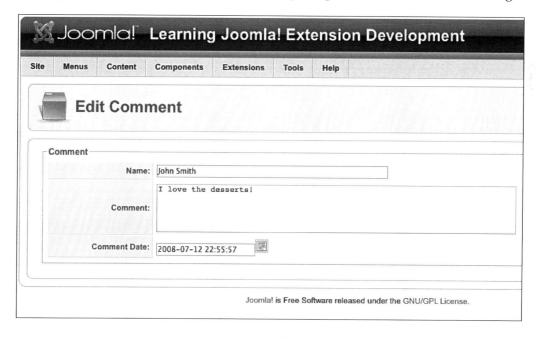

When you click **Close**, you are returned back to the search results for **dish**, automatically.

Linking the comments controller

Although we were able to get to this part of the component by going to `index.php?option=com_restaurants&controller=comments`, this will not be acceptable to the reviewers. To add a link that they can find, we need to go back to the database to add a menu item underneath the **Restaurant Reviews** link in the **Components** menu.

To create this insert query, we need to get the id for the current backend component link. If you're using a command-line SQL client and your database table prefix is **jos_**, enter the following query:

```
SELECT id FROM jos_components WHERE link = `option=com_restaurants`;
```

If you are using phpMyAdmin, browse the **jos_components** table until you find the row for **Restaurant Reviews** and note the value in the id column.

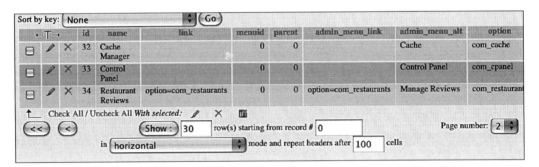

Once you have a value for **id**, enter the following query in your SQL client, substituting **34** with the **id** in your system, if necessary:

```
INSERT INTO jos_components (name, parent, admin_menu_link,
    admin_menu_alt, ordering, params) VALUES ('Manage Comments', 34,
    'option=com_restaurants&controller=comments', 'Manage Comments', 1,
    '');
```

If you're using phpMyAdmin, an insert screen for **jos_components** should look like the following:

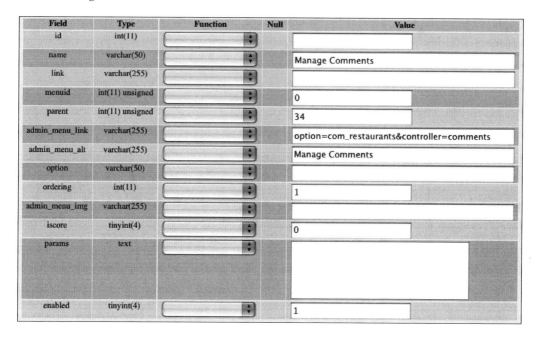

Field	Type	Function	Null	Value
id	int(11)			
name	varchar(50)			Manage Comments
link	varchar(255)			
menuid	int(11) unsigned			0
parent	int(11) unsigned			34
admin_menu_link	varchar(255)			option=com_restaurants&controller=comments
admin_menu_alt	varchar(255)			Manage Comments
option	varchar(50)			
ordering	int(11)			1
admin_menu_img	varchar(255)			
iscore	tinyint(4)			0
params	text			
enabled	tinyint(4)			1

When you refresh the backend and move the cursor over the menu options, you should notice a new submenu link, along with a link above the component display:

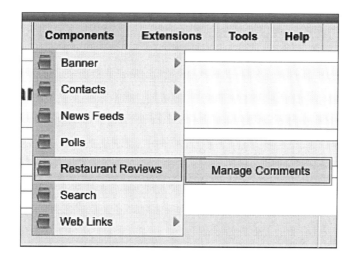

Although this is helpful for getting users to the **Comments** screen, the **Restaurant Reviews** link is now a parent item that automatically pops out the submenu when you hover the mouse over it. You can still click the **Restaurant Reviews** menu item and ignore **Manage Comments**, but some of our users may not catch on to this. To solve the problem, we can create another link to the **Restaurant Reviews** screen that is a child of the original one. Use the component id from above in place of **34,** and run this SQL query:

```
INSERT INTO jos_components (name, parent, admin_menu_link,
   admin_menu_alt, ordering, params) VALUES ('Manage Reviews', 34,
   'option=com_restaurants&controller=reviews', 'Manage Reviews', 2, '');
```

If you are using phpMyAdmin, your screen for inserting the row into the database should look like this:

Field	Type	Function	Null	Value
id	int(11)			
name	varchar(50)			Manage Reviews
link	varchar(255)			
menuid	int(11) unsigned			0
parent	int(11) unsigned			34
admin_menu_link	varchar(255)			option=com_restaurants&controller=reviews
admin_menu_alt	varchar(255)			Manage Reviews
option	varchar(50)			
ordering	int(11)			2
admin_menu_img	varchar(255)			
iscore	tinyint(4)			0
params	text			
enabled	tinyint(4)			1

When the query is finished running, reload the backend of Joomla!, move the mouse over the **Components** link, then mouse over the **Restaurant Reviews** link. Your screen should now show options for both managing comments and managing reviews:

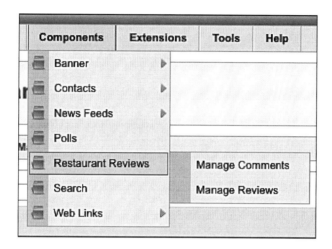

Summary

As our site is growing, we have now added more of the features that the reviewers will need in the future. Form validation will prevent our reviewer from adding incomplete records. Searches and pagination will help them to quickly find existing reviews for editing. Toolbars are now complete, context-sensitive, and tied into the views they serve. Finally, comment moderation allows the reviewers to remove offensive or off-topic comments.

8
Using JavaScript Effects

As our critics continue to write reviews and moderate comments, we will take some time to look into options for improving the user interface and adding new functions. Modern websites use JavaScript-driven effects to aid navigation, reduce on-screen clutter, and provide interactive features that are not possible with static HTML. Joomla! has several built-in elements that you can use without writing a single line of JavaScript. The MooTools framework powers many elements seen throughout the Joomla! backend UI; these can be reused in both the frontend and the backend. We will learn to use JavaScript effects through these topics:

- Modal boxes
- Tool tips
- Sliding panes
- Customizing Google Maps
- Using jQuery

Modal boxes

There will be some times when you will want to highlight a piece of information without making visitors load a completely separate webpage. The "lightbox" effect is now frequently used across the web as a way of doing this. When you click on a link where this effect is applied, the webpage is grayed out and a small window with the required content floats on top of the page. Users are prevented from clicking elsewhere on the page until the window is closed. This window is referred to as a modal box.

To demonstrate the use of modal boxes (along with the other examples in this chapter), we will create a component separate from "Restaurant Reviews". Go to the components folder of your Joomla! installation and create a folder named com_js. Within this folder, create a file named js.php with the following code:

```php
<?php
defined( '_JEXEC' ) or die( 'Restricted access' );

jimport('joomla.application.component.controller');

class JsController extends JController
{
    function modalBox()
    {
        JHTML::_('behavior.modal', 'a.popup');
?>
        <a href="index.php?option=com_js&amp;task=insideModal&amp;
        format=raw" class="popup">Read the daily menu.</a>
        <?php
    }

    function insideModal()
    {
?>
        <h1>Today's Menu</h1>
        <ul>
            <li>Crispy chicken nuggets with ginger dressing</li>
            <li>Swordfish in bean curd sauce</li>
            <li>Stir-fried vegetables over white rice</li>
        </ul>
        <?php
    }
}

$controller = new JsController();
$controller->execute(JRequest::getCmd('task'));
```

After checking to make sure that the request to execute js.php is coming from within Joomla!, the controller code is loaded from the Joomla! framework. JsController is then declared as an extension of JController. After the class is defined, $controller is set as a new instance of JsController and the execute() member function is called, with the current task passed in.

The controller contains two functions—`modalBox()` and `insideModal()`. The `modalBox()` function is intended to be displayed as a standard page in Joomla!, while `insideModal()` has the HTML content that will fill the modal window. Inside `modalBox()`, there is a call to `JHTML::_('behavior.modal', 'a.popup');`. Calling `JHTML::_('behavior.modal')` tells the Joomla! framework to load the JavaScript necessary for powering modal boxes. The parameter `'a.popup'` tells the JavaScript powering the modal box that we want to add this effect to all anchor tags that have a class of `popup`.

An anchor tag is output after the `JHMTL::_()` call. This link points back to the `com_js` component and sets the task to `insideModal`. Unlike most links in Joomla!, this one specifies the desired format of the output. Setting `format` to `raw` ensures that Joomla! does not attempt to load the template or any of the modules when generating the output; we only want the HTML intended for the window to be loaded.

If you go to `index.php?option=com_js&task=modalBox` now, you should see a screen similar to the following one:

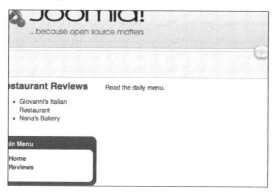

When you click on the **Read the daily menu** link, a window will appear on the screen like this:

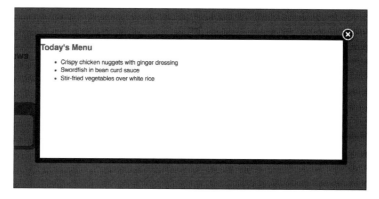

Notice that although JavaScript powers this effect, we did not write a single line of it. The call to the JHTML class did this for us. To see the JavaScript that JHTML generated, use your browser's **View Source** function. Within the `<head>` tags of the HTML source, you should see a portion of code similar to the following:

```
<link rel="stylesheet" href="/media/system/css/modal.css" type=
"text/css" />
<script type="text/javascript" src=
"/media/system/js/mootools.js"></script>
<script type="text/javascript" src=
"/media/system/js/modal.js"></script>
<script type="text/javascript">
        window.addEvent('domready', function(){
            SqueezeBox.initialize({});

            $$('a.popup').each(function(el) {
                el.addEvent('click', function(e) {
                    new Event(e).stop();
                    SqueezeBox.fromElement(el);
                });
            });
        });
</script>
```

Joomla! makes frequent use of the MooTools JavaScript framework, and the code powering the modal box is no exception. After loading some CSS for formatting the appearance of the box, MooTools itself is loaded. The modal box JavaScript is loaded once MooTools is available. These files are static and are distributed with Joomla!.

The third `<script>` tag includes the JavaScript dynamically generated by Joomla! for our specific modal box. All of the code is enclosed within a call to `window.addEvent()`. This JavaScript function is added to the `window` object by MooTools and allows us to add event handlers. In this case, we are adding a handler to the `domready` event so that the code waits until the DOM is fully loaded.

On the highlighted line of the code, notice the string `a.popup`. This is the same selector we passed in as the second parameter of JHTML::_(). We can pass in any desired class selector here, but in this case we only want to attach the event to anchor tags with a class of `popup`. The rest of the code cycles through all of the `a.popup` elements in the HTML document and applies the MooTools `SqueezeBox` plug-in to each of them.

Configuring the modal box

Although the current use of JHTML::_() pulls in the desired behavior, we would like to make some adjustments. The default window for the modal is rather large for the content we are displaying. A way of controlling the height and width would be helpful.

Fortunately, there is a way of configuring the modal box. The call to JHTML::_(' behavior.modal') takes a multidimensional array containing settings as an additional parameter. Make the highlighted adjustments to the modalBox() function in the /components/com_js/js.php file:

```php
function modalBox()
{
    $params = array(
        'size' => array(
            'x' => 350,
            'y' => 250
            )
        );

    JHTML::_('behavior.modal', 'a.popup', $params);

    ?>
    <a href="index.php?option=com_js&amp;task=insideModal&amp;format=
     raw" class="popup">Read the daily menu.</a>
    <?php
}
```

The $params array has one element for the size setting. This element is an array with the width and height values we want to use; these are represented as x and y respectively. This specific array above sets the width to 350 pixels and the height to 250 pixels. The $params array is now loaded with our desired configuration, so we pass it in as the third parameter of JHTML::_().

Save js.php and reload index.php?option=com_js&task=modalBox in the browser. After clicking on the **Read the daily menu** link, the modal box should appear as shown below as shown below:

The JavaScript generated by Joomla! has also changed. Use your browser's **View Source** function to pull up the HTML code of the page. Then look for the block of `<script>` declarations in the `<head>` section where the modal box is defined. The code should look similar to this:

```
<link rel="stylesheet" href="/media/system/css/modal.css" type=
"text/css" />
<script type="text/javascript" src=
"/media/system/js/mootools.js"></script>
<script type="text/javascript" src=
"/media/system/js/modal.js"></script>
<script type="text/javascript">

        window.addEvent('domready', function() {

            SqueezeBox.initialize({ size: { x: 350, y: 250}});

            $$('a.popup').each(function(el) {
                el.addEvent('click', function(e) {
                    new Event(e).stop();
                    SqueezeBox.fromElement(el);
                });
            });
        });
</script>
```

The generated JavaScript is almost exactly the same as it was before, except for the highlighted line. In the first example, above an empty object was passed into `SqueezeBox.initialize()`. In this example, the `$params` array we passed into `JHTML::_()` has been transformed by Joomla! into a JavaScript object. This object is now passed into `SqueezeBox.initialize()` to configure the `SqueezeBox` plug-in.

The raw format and MVC

In this example, two functions in the controller are used—one to generate the main page and one to fill the modal box with HTML content. However, complex components will be written using views as well. Instead of using a separate controller function for displaying the modal box HTML, a view can be used.

To start, create a `views` folder in the existing `/components/com_js` folder. Within this new folder, create another folder named `modalcontent`. For a typical view, you would create a file in this folder named `view.html.php`. This view is a little different; we will be setting the format to `raw` so we can get only the HTML code for the contents and not an entire Joomla! page with the template. To handle the `raw` format, create the file `view.raw.php` instead. Fill this file with the following code:

```
<?php
defined( '_JEXEC' ) or die( 'Restricted access' );

jimport( 'joomla.application.component.view');

class JsViewModalcontent extends JView
{
}
```

This code might seem a little odd at first glance. Each view in Joomla! must be represented by an object that is an extension of `JView`. By default, if the `display()` function is not overridden in the child object, `JView::display()` will be called instead. This function will load `tmpl/default.php` (unless the layout parameter is set to something other than `default`). Because this example does not load anything from the database or act on the custom variables passed to it, it is desirable to allow Joomla! to execute the default `JView::display()` function. The file `default.php` must exist in the `views/modalcontent/tmpl` folder, though. Create the folder `tmpl`, and then create a file named `default.php`, and fill it with the following code:

```
<?php defined( '_JEXEC' ) or die( 'Restricted access' ); ?>
<h1>Tomorrow's Menu</h1>
<ul>
    <li>Crispy beef nuggets with ginger dressing</li>
    <li>Catfish in bean curd sauce</li>
    <li>Steamed vegetables over white rice</li>
</ul>
```

As with other layout files in Joomla! views, and with all `.php` files, we first check to make sure the call is coming from within Joomla!. Then, the static HTML content is output. To demonstrate the use of this view instead of a controller function, create a slightly modified version of the `modalBox()`, in `/components/com_js/js.php`, and name it `modalBoxMVC()`:

```
function modalBoxMVC()
{
    $params = array(
        'size' => array(
            'x' => 350,
            'y' => 250
            )
        );

    JHTML::_('behavior.modal', 'a.popup', $params);

    ?>
    <a href="index.php?option=com_js&amp;view=modalcontent&amp;
     format=raw" class="popup">Read tomorrow's menu.</a>
    <?php
}
```

Save all of the open files, and then load `index.php?option=com_js&task=modalBoxMVC` in your browser and click on the **Read tomorrow's menu.** link. Your screen should look like the example shown below:

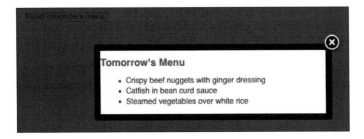

Tool tips

Another effect used across the web is the tool tip. Tool tips are used to add messages that are displayed near the mouse pointer when you hover over specific elements on the screen. This is helpful for adding definitions of things without taking up space on the page. Adding a tool tip in Joomla! is even simpler than adding modal boxes—you don't need to make a separate call to display the content. In the `/components/com_js/js.php` file, add the following function to the controller:

```
function toolTipTest()
{
    JHTML::_('behavior.tooltip');
    ?>
        <span class="hasTip" title="Click here to go to the
        home page"><a href="index.php">Homepage</a></span>
    <?php
}
```

As with the modal box, we call JHTML::_() to pull in the MooTools framework. This time, `behavior.tooltip` is passed as the parameter. After this, an anchor tag is output, to create a link. This anchor tag is wrapped in a `<span>` that has two attributes—`class` and `title`. The class attribute is set to `hasTip`; this is the default class the tool tip JavaScript looks for when setting up the effect. The `title` attribute determines the text to be displayed when you move the mouse over the link.

After saving `js.php`, load `index.php?option=com_js&task=toolTipTest` and move your mouse over the **Homepage** link. The tool tip should appear, similar to this example:

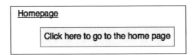

If you want to use a class other than `hasTip` for your elements with tool tips, you can override it in `JHTML::_()`. For example, to use the class `mytip` insted, make the highlighted modifications to the function `toolTipTest()` in `/components/com_js/js.php` file:

```
function toolTipTest()
{
    JHTML::_('behavior.tooltip', '.mytip');
    ?>
        <span class="mytip" title="Click here to go to the
        home page"><a href="index.php">Homepage</a></span>
    <?php
}
```

When you save `js.php` and reload `index.php?option=com_js&task=toolTipTest`, the functionality will be the same as before, but the class will be `mytip`.

Sliding panes

Throughout the backend of Joomla!, there are several screens containing sliding panes full of options. This is done to save space on the screen, and to make specific settings easier to find. The CSS that creates the "tabbed" visual effect is automatically included in the backend. To use the siding panes, you only need to bring in the JavaScript and make some calls to a `JPane` object.

To test the panes, create a component in the backend at `/administrator/components/com_js`. Add the file `js.php` to this folder, and fill it with the following code:

```
<?php
defined( '_JEXEC' ) or die( 'Restricted access' );

jimport('joomla.application.component.controller');

class JsController extends JController
{
    function showPanes()
    {
        jimport('joomla.html.pane');

        ?>
        <div class="col width-45">
        <?php

        $pane = &JPane::getInstance('sliders');

        echo $pane->startPane('menu-pane');
        echo $pane->startPanel('Name', 'info-name');
```

```
        echo '<p>John Worthington</p>';
        echo $pane->endPanel();
        echo $pane->startPanel('Favorite Food', 'info-food');
        echo '<p>Pad Thai</p>';
        echo $pane->endPanel();
        echo $pane->startPanel('Bio', 'info-bio');
        echo '<p>John began criticizing food in kindergarden and has
         not stopped since. His accomplishments include earning "2005
         Critic of the Year" from Digest Digest.</p>';
        echo $pane->endPanel();
        echo $pane->endPane();

        ?>
        </div>
        <?php
    }
}
$controller = new JsController();
$controller->execute(JRequest::getCmd('task'));
```

As with the frontend of the component, the backend checks to make sure the file is called within Joomla!, and then defines a controller and executes it. The showPanes() function starts with a call to jimport('joomla.html.pane'); to load the JPane class. The <div> tag has classes of col and width-45; these are defined in the backend CSS to display a column that takes 45% of the available screen width.

Within the <div>, $pane is set using the getInstance() member function of JPane. The string 'sliders' is passed into getInstance() as JPane is capable of handling other similar effects using the same function calls. Once $pane is set, the member functions startPane(), endPane(), startPanel(), and endPanel() are called in sequence. The startPane() and endPane() functions are used to enclose all of the slider's panels. startPane() also requires a parameter that defines the HTML id used on the <div> that encloses the panels. Each panel is then defined using startPanel(), followed by the content for the panel, and ending with endPanel(). The startPanel() function accepts a title to be displayed as the first parameter and an HTML id for the panel as the second.

To see the JPane slider in action, save js.php and load administrator/index. php?option=com_js&task=showPanes in your browser. You should get the following screen:

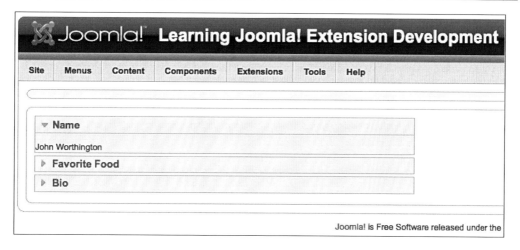

As you click on a different heading, the panel for that heading will expand as the previous one slides up. No matter what you click, one and only one pane is always visible. If you want to allow every panel to be closed, make the highlighted modification within showPanes():

```php
<?php

$pane = &JPane::getInstance('sliders',
  array('allowAllClose' => true));

echo $pane->startPane('menu-pane');
```

As with the modal box, the array that is passed in gets transformed into a JavaScript object that is output when Joomla! writes the JavaScript powering the panes. This array defines the 'allowAllClose' setting as true.

Through JPane::getInstance(), the sliding panes can quickly be turned into a tabbed interface. Change 'sliders' to 'tabs' by making the highlighted change:

```php
<?php

$pane = &JPane::getInstance('tabs');

echo $pane->startPane('menu-pane');
```

After saving `js.php`, reload `administrator/index.php?option=com_js&task=showPanes` in your browser. You should now have a tabbed interface that looks like the following example:

The sliders can be used in the frontend as well as the backend of Joomla!. To use the sliders in the frontend, open the file `/components/com_js/js.php`, and add the following function to the controller:

```
function frontendPanes()
{
    jimport('joomla.html.pane');

    $pane = &JPane::getInstance('sliders');

    echo $pane->startPane('menu-pane');
    echo $pane->startPanel('Name', 'info-name');
    echo '<p>John Worthington</p>';
    echo $pane->endPanel();
    echo $pane->startPanel('Favorite Food', 'info-food');
    echo '<p>Pad Thai</p>';
    echo $pane->endPanel();
    echo $pane->startPanel('Bio', 'info-bio');
    echo '<p>John began criticizing food in kindergarden and has not
        stopped since. His accomplishments include earning "2005 Critic
        of the Year" from Digest Digest.</p>';
    echo $pane->endPanel();
    echo $pane->endPane();
}
```

The code works in exactly the same way as it does in the backend, only we are not wrapping the sliders in a `<div>` this time. The frontend does not have the CSS that the backend does, so the display will be different, but the functionality will be the same. Save `js.php`, and load `index.php?option=com_js&task=frontendPanes` in your browser. Your screen should now look like this:

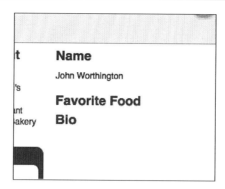

Customizing Google Maps

Although modal boxes and sliding panes are useful, MooTools can help with other JavaScript tasks. Google Maps has a comprehensive API for interacting with maps on your website. MooTools can be used to load the Google Maps engine at the correct time. It can also act as a bridge between the map and other HTML elements on your site.

To get started, you will first need to get an API key to use Google Maps on your domain. You can sign up for a free key at `http://code.google.com/apis/maps/signup.html`. Even if you are working on your local computer, you still need the key. For instance, if the base URL of your Joomla installation is `http://localhost/joomla`, you will enter `localhost` as the domain for your API key.

Once you have an API key ready, create the file `basicmap.js` in `/components /com_js`, and fill it with the following code:

```
window.addEvent('domready', function() {
    if (GBrowserIsCompatible()) {

        var map = new GMap2($('map_canvas'));
        map.setCenter(new GLatLng(38.89, -77.04), 12);

        window.onunload=function(){
            GUnload();
        };

    }
});
```

The entire script is wrapped within a call to the MooTools-specific `addEvent()` member function of `window`, just like the `SqueezeBox` script for the modal box, earlier. Because we want this code to execute once the DOM is ready, the first parameter is the event name `'domready'`. The second parameter is an anonymous function containing our code.

What does the call to `function()` do?

Using `function()` in JavaScript is a way of creating an anonymous function. This way, you can create functions that are used in only one place (such as event handlers) without cluttering the namespace with a needless function name. Also, the code within the anonymous function operates within its own scope; this is referred to as a closure. Closures are very frequently used in modern JavaScript frameworks, for event handling and other distinct tasks.

Once inside of the function, `GBrowserIsCompatible()` is used to determine if the browser is capable of running Google Maps. If it is, a new instance of `GMap2()` is declared and bound to the HTML element that has an id of `'map_canvas'` and is stored into `map`. The call to `$('map_canvas')` is a MooTools shortcut for `document.GetElementById()`.

Next, the `setCenter()` member function of `map` is called to tell Google Maps where to center the map and how far to zoom in. The first parameter is a `GLatLng()` object, which is used to set the specific latitude and longitude of the map's center. The other parameter determines the zoom level, which is set to 12 in this case. Finally, the `window.onunload` event is set to a function that calls `GUnload()`. When the user navigates away from the page, this function removes Google Maps from memory, to prevent memory leaks.

With our JavaScript in place, it is now time to add a function to the controller in `/components/com_js/js.php` that will load it along with some HTML. Add the following `basicMap()` function to this file:

```
function basicMap()
{
    $key = 'DoNotUseThisKeyGetOneFromCodeDotGoogleDotCom';

    JHTML::_('behavior.mootools');

    $document =& JFactory::getDocument();
    $document->addScript('http://maps.google.com/maps?file=api&v=
        2&key=' . $key);
    $document->addScript(
        JURI::base() . 'components/com_js/basicmap.js');

    ?>
    <div id="map_canvas" style="width: 500px; height: 300px"></div>
    <?php
}
```

The `basicMap()` function starts off by setting `$key` to the API key received from Google. You should replace this value with the one you receive at `http://code.google.com/apis/maps/signup.html`. Next, `JHTML::_('behavior.mootools');` is called to load MooTools into the `<head>` tag of the HTML document. This is followed by getting a reference to the current document object through the `getDocument()` member function of `JFactory`. The `addScript()` member function is called twice—once to load in the Google Maps API (using our key), then again to load our `basicmap.js` script. (The Google Maps API calls in all of the functions and class definitions beginning with a capital 'G'.)

Finally, a `<div>` with an id of `'map_canvas'` is sent to the browser. Once this function is in place and `js.php` has been saved, load `index.php?option=com_js&task=basicMap` in the browser. Your map should look like this:

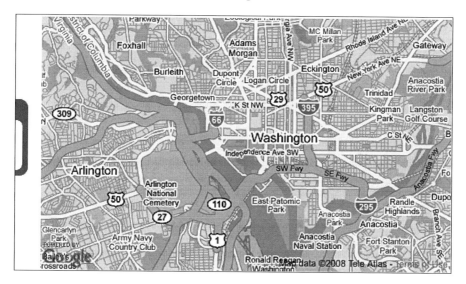

We can make this map slightly more interesting by adding a marker to a specific address. To do so, add the highlighted code below to the `basicmap.js` file:

```
window.addEvent('domready', function() {
    if (GBrowserIsCompatible()){
        var map = new GMap2($('map_canvas'));
        map.setCenter(new GLatLng(38.89, -77.04), 12);

        var whitehouse = new GClientGeocoder();
        whitehouse.getLatLng('1600 Pennsylvania Ave NW',
          function(latlng){
            marker = new GMarker( latlng );
            marker.bindInfoWindowHtml('<strong>The White
              House</strong>');
```

```
            map.addOverlay(marker);
        });

        window.onunload=function(){
        GUnload();
        };

    }
});
```

This code sets `whitehouse` as an instance of the `GClientGeocoder` class. Next, the `getLatLng()` member function of `GClientGeocoder` is called. The first parameter is the street address to be looked up. The second parameter is an anonymous function where the `GLatLng` object is passed once the address lookup is complete. Within this function, `marker` is set as a new `GMarker` object, which takes the passed-in `latlng` object as a parameter. The `bindInfoWindowHTML()` member function of `GMarker` is called to add an HTML message to appear in a balloon above the marker. Finally, the maker is passed into the `addOverlay()` member function of `GMap2`, to place it on the map.

Save `basicmap.js` and then reload `index.php?option=com_js&task=basicMap`. You should now see the same map, only with a red pin. When you click on the red pin, your map should look like this:

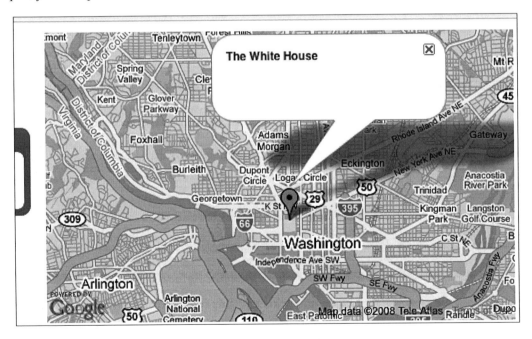

Interactive maps

These two different maps show the basic functionality of getting Google Maps on your own website. These maps are very basic; you could easily create them at maps. google.com then embed them in a standard Joomla! article with the HTML code they provide you. However, you would not have the opportunity to add functions that interact with the other elements on your page. To do that, we will create some more HTML code and then write some MooTools-powered JavaScript to bridge our content with Google Maps.

Open the /components/com_js/js.php file and add the following selectMap() function to the controller:

```
function selectMap()
{
    $key = 'DoNotUseThisKeyGetOneFromCodeDotGoogleDotCom';

    JHTML::_('behavior.mootools');

    $document =& JFactory::getDocument();
    $document->addScript('http://maps.google.com/maps?file=api&v
    =2&key=' . $key);
    $document->addScript(
    JURI::base() . 'components/com_js/selectmap.js');

    ?>
    <div id="map_canvas" style="width: 500px; height: 300px"></div>
    <select id="map_selections">
        <option value="">(select...)</option>
        <option value="1200 K Street NW">Salad Surprises</option>
        <option value="1221 Connecticut Avenue NW">The Daily
         Dish</option>
        <option value="701 H Street NW">Sushi and Sashimi</option>
    </select>
    <?php
}
```

This function is almost identical to basicMap() except for two things— selectmap.js is being added instead of basicmap.js, and a <select> element has been added beneath the <div>. The <select> element has an id that will be used in the JavaScript. The options of the <select> are restaurants, with different addresses as values. The JavaScript code will bind a function to the onChange event so that the marker will move as different restaurants are selected.

To add this JavaScript, create a file named `selectmap.js` in the `/components/com_js` folder, and fill it with the following code:

```
window.addEvent('domready', function() {
    if (GBrowserIsCompatible()) {

        var map = new GMap2($('map_canvas'));
        map.setCenter(new GLatLng(38.89, -77.04), 12);

        var restaurant = new GClientGeocoder();

        $('map_selections').addEvent('change', function(){
            if(this.value != '')
            {
                name = this.options[this.selectedIndex].text;
                restaurant.getLatLng(this.value, function(latlng){
                    map_marker = new GMarker( latlng );
                    map.clearOverlays();
                    map.addOverlay(map_marker);
                    map_marker.openInfoWindowHtml('<strong>' + name +
'</strong>');
                });
            }
        });

        window.onunload=function(){
            GUnload();
        };

    }
});
```

This script is similar to the one used for the first two maps, until we get past the call to `map.setCenter()`. The variable `restaurant` is first set as an instance of the `GClientGeocoder()` class. However, member functions are not called on it right away, as it was done in the previous example. This is because we want to wait for the `<select>` element to change before we do anything. The call to `$('map_selections')` finds the `<select>` element, and then `addEvent()` is used to assign a function to the `onChange` event; the string `'change'` is passed as the first parameter.

The function passed in as the second parameter first checks to make sure that the element's value is not null by checking `this.value`. If the value is not null, this function proceeds by getting the option's text and storing it in `name`. Then the `getLatLng()` member function of `GClientGeocoder` is called on `restaurant`. The street address is passed in as the first parameter. Once the latitude and longitude of the address is found, the anonymous function in the second parameter accepts the `GLatLng` object that is returned, using it to set `map_marker` as a new `GMarker` object.

Before adding the marker to the map, the `clearOverlays()` function of the map object is called to remove any previously-placed marker. Then, the marker is passed into the `addOverlay()` function to be placed on the map. Although the marker is now set on the map, we can still interact with it. The `openInfoWindowHtml()` member function of `GMarker` allows us to do this and pass in some HTML with the name of the restaurant.

With the controller function and JavaScript in place and saved, load `index.php?option=com_js&task=selectMap` in your browser. The map should load again, this time with a dropdown box at the bottom. Select one of the restaurants, and then switch to another. If you select **Sushi and Sashimi** from the list, your map should look similar to the following:

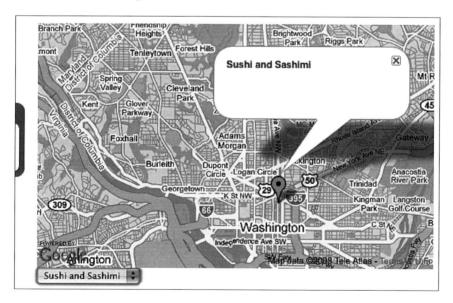

These examples scratch the surface of what is possible with the Google Maps API. You can manage layers, add shapes, use custom icons instead of the standard pins, and use many other features to build sophisticated custom maps. For more information, go to `http://code.google.com/apis/maps/documentation/index.html` where you can read more about the available features.

Using jQuery

Another popular JavaScript framework is jQuery. The jQuery framework has functionality that is similar to MooTools, but uses a different style of code. Although they are separate projects, extra care must be taken when using them together. By default, both frameworks automatically reserve $ to have a special meaning in JavaScript. If you do not take steps to avoid this behavior, one library will overwrite the other's assignments and the scripts will fail.

Fortunately, jQuery has strategies that you can use to avoid this conflict. There are three things that you must do to keep jQuery and MooTools out of each other's way:

- Load jQuery only after MooTools has been loaded
- Call `jQuery.noConflict()` to return control of $ to MooTools
- Reference jQuery directly in your scripts instead of using $

Writing jQuery code

Before avoiding conflicts with MooTools, start by writing some jQuery without MooTools being present. First, go to `jquery.com`, download the latest version of jQuery, and then place it in the `/components/com_js` directory; the production version of the script will be fine. Then, create a file named `jquery-test.js` in the `/components/com_js` folder, and fill this new file with the following code:

```
$(document).ready(function() {
    $('#message_box').click(function() {
        $(this).addClass('contentheading');
    });
});
```

This is a simple application of jQuery — when the DOM is fully loaded in the browser, the code within the first call to `function()` executes. The code `$('#message_box')` finds the element in the DOM that has an id of `'message_box'`, and uses `click()` to assign an `onClick` JavaScript event to it. Finally, the `addClass()` method is used to add the CSS class `'contentheading'` to the element.

With `jquery-test.js` in place, open the `/components/com_js/js.php` file, and add the following function task to the controller:

```
function useJquery()
{
    $document =& JFactory::getDocument();
    $document->addScript(
      JURI::base() . 'components/com_js/jquery-1.2.6.min.js');
    $document->addScript(
```

```
        JURI::base() . 'components/com_js/jquery-test.js');

    ?>
    <p id="message_box">This is a message</p>
    <?php
}
```

First, a reference to the document object is stored in $document by using the getDocument() member function of JFactory. Next, the addScript() member function is used to add the jQuery framework and our test script. Finally, a paragraph tag with the id 'message_box', and containing a short message, is output. Load index.php?option=com_js&task=useJquery in your browser, and click on the **This is a message** link. Your screen should now look similar to this:

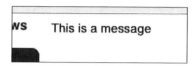

Using jQuery with MooTools

The code that we just wrote works fine on its own, but will fail right now if we attempt to also use a MooTools-driven effect. To remedy this, we need to make an adjustment to our script and invoke jQuery's noConflict mode. Open the file/components/com_js/js.php and add the following function to the controller:

```
function useJqueryAndMooTools()
{
    JHTML::_('behavior.tooltip');

    $document =& JFactory::getDocument();
    $document->addScript(
     JURI::base() . 'components/com_js/jquery-1.2.6.min.js');

    $document->addCustomTag('<script type="text/javascript">
     jQuery.noConflict();
     </script>');

    $document->addScript(
     JURI::base() . 'components/com_js/jquery-test.js');

    ?>
    <p id="message_box">This is a message</p>
    <span class="hasTip" title="Click here to go to the home page">
        <a href="index.php">Homepage</a>
    </span>
    <?php
}
```

The highlighted portions of useJqueryAndMooTools() are the added pieces that differentiate it from useJquery(). The call to JHTML::_('behavior.tooltip'); loads the code necessary for the tooltip, including MooTools. Because MooTools is now being loaded, we use the addCustomHeadTag() member function of the document object to make a quick call to jQuery.noConflict(); so that $ is left for MooTools. Finally, an anchor tag wrapped in a <span> element has been added with the tooltip information.

If you save js.php and load index.php?option=com_js&task=useJqueryAndMooTools now, you will get an error; we have not yet adjusted jquery-test.js to account for the call to jQuery.noConflict();. Open jquery-test.js and make the highlighted adjustment:

```
jQuery(document).ready(function($) {
    $('#message_box').click(function() {
        $(this).addClass('contentheading');
    });
});
```

Because the $ shortcut is no longer available, we must call the jQuery function by name. However, we can regain control of the $ shortcut within our jQuery code. This is because the call to function() allows us to pass a reference to the jQuery function into the local scope, with any desired name. Because $ has been specified as the parameter of function(), the rest of the code can use it without further modification.

Load index.php?option=com_js&task=useJqueryAndMooTools in your browser, click on the **This is a message** link, then move and the mouse over the **Homepage** link. Your screen should look similar to this:

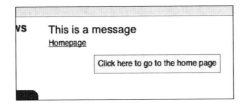

Always load MooTools first

The trick to using jQuery and MooTools together in Joomla! is to make sure that MooTools loads before jQuery does. In the useJqueryAndMooTools() function, if you move the call to JHTML::_('behavior.tooltip'); any time after the call to addScript() that loads in jQuery, an error will occur. Instead, MooTools must load first and define $. Then jQuery.noConflict(); can be called to return $ back to its original assignment.

This is easily managed when you know and can control every instance where MooTools is used. However, if you are building a self-contained extension for others to use, it is quite possible that they are using other extensions that load MooTools. For instance, if someone has a module for a photo gallery that uses MooTools, the MooTools framework will be added to the <head> section of the HTML document after your component with jQuery loads. This will cause a JavaScript error.

The safest way of avoiding this situation is to force the MooTools library to load in your extension before you load jQuery. To do this, simply add JHTML::_ ('behavior.mootools'); in your extension before adding the jQuery framework to <head>. The call to JHTML::_('behavior.mootools'); detects whether MooTools has been loaded yet, and loads it now if it has not.

A downside to this workaround is that the MooTools framework will be included even if it is never used. This will slow down the load time of your site slightly and use resources in the JavaScript environment. If you are building an extension that will not be distributed or reused, you can hard-code the references to jQuery in your template after <jdoc:include type="head" />. In this scenario, jQuery will be loaded on every page and will eventually be used where you determine. If MooTools is loaded by another extension, it will happen before jQuery is initialized.

Summary

Joomla! is ready for your modern JavaScript needs. By using the MooTools JavaScript framework, you can find elements and assign event handlers to them. You can also use pre-built functions within Joomla! to generate the JavaScript necessary for many typical effects. Regardless of the number of effects used, Joomla! will make sure that the MooTools framework is only loaded once, as long as you use the JHTML member functions. You can also use jQuery with MooTools in Joomla!, provided that you take precautions to make sure that the frameworks do not conflict.

Behind the Scenes: Plug-ins

9

So far, our restaurant reviews have been relatively easy to navigate to, and the site is also user-friendly. However, our restaurant critics want us to make things simpler for them. We may periodically want to create feature articles for collections, such as *Late Night Dining Highlights* or *An All Asian Appetite*. We want to make it easier for the critics to link to the reviews within these articles, and we also want to make the reviews searchable, along with the articles.

These new features can be handled through plug-ins. Joomla! provides plug-ins as a way of running pieces of code when certain events occur. Among other tasks, plug-ins can be used to start HTML editors, perform searches, format content, and log users into multiple systems at once. Plug-ins are able to interact with components and modules without modifying their source code. The plug-ins we will write will take us through the following topics:

- Database queries
- A simple link plug-in
- What events can be registered
- An information box plug-in
- Searching reviews

Database queries

Before writing our code, there are some queries that need to be run in order to register the plug-ins in the database. We will be creating three plug-ins—two of them will format content and one will interact with Joomla!'s core search component. The queries will add records pointing to the folders where each plug-in can be found, along with their names.

In your SQL console, enter these three queries:

```
INSERT INTO jos_plugins (name, element, folder, published) VALUES
('Content - Reviews', 'reviews', 'content', 1);
INSERT INTO jos_plugins (name, element, folder, published) VALUES
('Content - Review Information', 'reviewinfo', 'content', 0);
INSERT INTO jos_plugins (name, element, folder, published) VALUES
('Search - Reviews', 'reviews', 'search', 1);
```

If you're using phpMyAdmin, pull up a screen to enter rows into the `jos_plugins` table, and enter the information shown in the following screenshot, in order to register the **Content – Reviews** plug-in in the database:

Field	Type	Function	Null	Value
id	int(11)			
name	varchar(100)			Content – Reviews
element	varchar(100)			reviews
folder	varchar(100)			content
access	tinyint(3) unsigned			0
ordering	int(11)			0
published	tinyint(3)			1
iscore	tinyint(3)			0
client_id	tinyint(3)			0
checked_out	int(11) unsigned			0
checked_out_time	datetime			0000–00–00 00:00:00
params	text			

Using phpMyAdmin, pull up a screen to enter rows into the `jos_plugins` table, and enter the information shown in the following screenshot, in order to register the **Content – Review Information** plug-in in the database:

Field	Type	Function	Null	Value
id	int(11)			
name	varchar(100)			Content – Review Information
element	varchar(100)			reviewinfo
folder	varchar(100)			content
access	tinyint(3) unsigned			0
ordering	int(11)			0
published	tinyint(3)			0
iscore	tinyint(3)			0
client_id	tinyint(3)			0
checked_out	int(11) unsigned			0
checked_out_time	datetime			0000–00–00 00:00:00
params	text			

Using phpMyAdmin, pull up a screen to enter rows into the `jos_plugins` table, and enter the information as in the following screenshot, in order to register the **Search – Reviews** plug-in in the database:

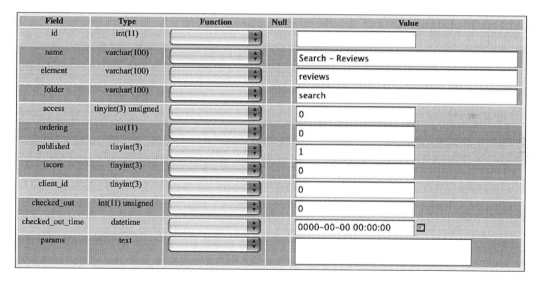

Field	Type	Function	Null	Value
id	int(11)			
name	varchar(100)			Search – Reviews
element	varchar(100)			reviews
folder	varchar(100)			search
access	tinyint(3) unsigned			0
ordering	int(11)			0
published	tinyint(3)			1
iscore	tinyint(3)			0
client_id	tinyint(3)			0
checked_out	int(11) unsigned			0
checked_out_time	datetime			0000–00–00 00:00:00
params	text			

A simple link plug-in

One of our critics suggested that we should code something that would allow them to link to a review by simply typing in the restaurant's name. For instance, when writing an article about lunch spots, the critic doesn't want to hunt down a link to the *Crosstown Deli* review. Instead, by just typing *Crosstown Deli*, he wants it to turn into a link when the article is published. We could modify the code in `com_content` to do this, but the other critics don't know if they want to commit to this system yet. Also, if `com_content` is ever patched with updates from the Joomla! core team, we'll have to modify the code again. Instead, we will create a plug-in to search the output for review titles and automatically turn them into links. To do this, create a file named `reviews.php` in the `/plugins/content` folder in your Joomla! installation, and add the following code to this new file:

```php
<?php
defined( '_JEXEC' ) or die( 'Restricted access' );
$mainframe->registerEvent( 'onPrepareContent', 'pluginReviews' );
```

We use the `registerEvent()` function of the `$mainframe` object to assign `pluginReviews()` to the `onPrepareContent` event. When Joomla! loads a content item from the database, it will trigger all of the functions assigned to the `onPrepareContent` event, including the `pluginReviews()` function. When the function is executed, the row for the current article will be passed in by reference, along with the article parameters. From there, we can add logic to modify any of the article data, and then return `true` when we are finished. Add the code below, for the new function `pluginReviews()`, to the `reviews.php` file:

```php
function pluginReviews( &$row, &$params )
{
    $reviews = contentReviews_getlist();
    $pattern = array();
    $replace = array();
    foreach($reviews as $review)
    {
      $pattern[] = '/' . preg_quote($review) . '/';
      $replace[] = contentReviews_makeLink($review, $reviews);
    }
    $row->text = preg_replace($pattern, $replace, $row->text);
    return true;
}
```

The primary purpose of `pluginReviews()` is to find the names of restaurants in the current article and replace them with links. Two other functions we will add momentarily are used to get a list of restaurants and format the links. We use `contentReviews_getlist()` to get an array of restaurant names keyed by review id. Next, we build two arrays—one with patterns to search for and another with replacement strings. In the `$pattern` array, we're using `preg_quote()` on all of the restaurant names, to escape any characters that would normally be a part of a regular expression. For `$replace`, we call `contentReviews_makeLink()` and pass in the review name as well as the array of names. This will allow `contentReviews_makeLink()` to extract the id and format the link. Once our patterns and replacements are set, we use `preg_replace()` to substitute the links. We set `$row->text` to the result of `preg_replace()` because the object is passed by reference. Although the code for `contentReviews_makeLink()` is brief, putting it in a separate function helps to organize the logic. Add the code below to the `reviews.php` file, to define this function:

```
function contentReviews_makeLink ($title, &$reviews)
{
    $id = array_search($title, $reviews);
    $link = JRoute::_('index.php?option=
     com_restaurants&view=single&id=' . $id );
    $link = '<a href="' . $link . '">' . $title . '</a>';
    return $link;
}
```

Given the review title and an array of titles keyed by review id, `contentReviews_makeLink()` uses PHP's `array_search()` function to get the id that goes with the title. The variable `$link` is then set with a relative URL to the article passed through `JRoute::_()`. The `$link` variable is then set again with HTML for an anchor tag, using the article title as the link text. We then return `$link`.

The `contentReview_makeLink()` function is called within a `foreach()` loop in the `pluginReviews()` function. This loop is cycling through an array of review titles returned by `contentReviews_getlist()`, but we have not yet added this function. Do so by adding the following code:

```
function contentReviews_getlist()
{
    $reviews = array();
    $db =& JFactory::getDBO();
    $query = "SELECT id, name FROM #__reviews";
    $db->setQuery($query);
    $rows = $db->loadObjectList('id');
```

```
        foreach($rows as $id => $row)
        {
          $reviews[$id] = $row->name;
        }
        return $reviews;
    }
```

In `contentReviews_getlist()`, we pass the column `id` into `loadObjectList()` so that the results come back automatically keyed; we only need to reference the name from each row. Once the results are loaded from the database, we cycle through them and build the array `$reviews` which contains review titles keyed by `id`. This allows us to use to use `array_search()` on this array when it gets passed into `contentReviews_makeLink()`.

Notice that the main function is in the format of 'plug-in' followed by the name of the file. Similarly, the other two functions begin with the type of plug-in (content), followed by the filename, an underscore, and a name. Although this convention is not required, it will help us to avoid name conflicts with other plug-ins.

After applying the plug-in, our article will change the restaurant names into links like the example in the following screenshot:

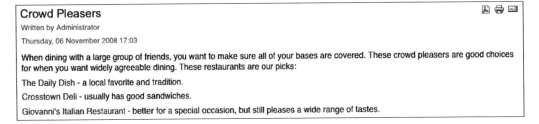

What events can be registered?

In addition to the `onPrepareContent` event we just used, plug-ins in Joomla! can respond to many different kinds of events during a request. Multiple plug-ins can respond to any one event in their group. The ordering of the plug-ins in Joomla!'s back end determines the order in which registered functions are called. For instance, if both plug-in A and plug-in B respond to `onBeforeDisplayContent`, if A's function is registered with `onBeforeDisplayContent` before B's function is, then A will be called first. Here is a listing of when these events occur, grouped by plug-in type:

System

onAfterInitialise – after the framework loads, but before routing and output

onAfterRoute – after routing, but before output

onAfterDispatch – after the Joomla! application is started

onAfterRender – after all output is processed

onGetWebServices – when the XML-RPC function requests a list of valid function calls

onLoginFailure – when a login attempt fails

Search

onSearch – when a search is performed

onSearchAreas – when the search component requests a list of valid search areas

Authentication

onAuthenticate – when a user initially attempts to authenticate, provides a method for authentication

User

onLoginUser – after a user initially authenticates, but before they are fully logged in; all functions must return true to finish authentication

onLogoutUser – when a user attempts to logout; all functions must return true to logout

onBeforeStoreUser – just before a user is stored in the database

onAfterStoreUser – after a user is stored in the database

onBeforeDeleteUser – just before a user is deleted from the system

onAfterDeleteUser – just after a user is deleted from the system

Editor-xtd

onCustomEditorButton – when custom editor buttons are loaded; this allows the addition of buttons

Editor

onInit – when the editor is initialized

onDisplay – when the editor is ready to be displayed

onGetContent – when the contents of the editor are requested

onSetContent – when the contents of the editor are populated

onSave – when the contents of the editor are saved

onGetInsertMethod – just before the editor is output

Content

onPrepareContent – before any output occurs

onAfterDisplayTitle – just after the article title is displayed

onBeforeDisplayContent – just before content is output; this returns the output to be displayed

onAfterDisplayContent – just after content is output; this returns the output to be displayed

An information box plug-in

Another critic was less interested in the links, but was interested in getting a box that would display the "vital details" for the restaurant of her choice. To use this feature, we will instruct the critic to enclose the name of the review in curly braces, preceded by the word reviewinfo and a space. For example, the details for "The Daily Dish" could be added in by entering {reviewinfo The Daily Dish}.

Why curly braces?

Many core plug-ins use curly braces as a way of creating "plug-in tags" in content items, so that they aren't confused with HTML or XML. Frequently, you will see them used alone (as in {runmyplugin}), with parameters (as we're doing with the reviews), or enclosing text ({plugin} like this {/plugin}). PHP's Perl-style regular expression functions are very useful for detecting these patterns. More information about these functions can be found on the PHP website: http://www. php.net/manual/en/ref.pcre.php.

Before we write the code for this, go to the administrator backend, unpublish our first plug-in, and then publish the new one. Go to **Extensions | Plugin Manager**, page through the results, unpublish **Content – Reviews**, and publish **Content – Review Information**.

Then, create the file `reviewinfo.php` in the `/plugins/content` folder, and add this code:

```php
<?php
defined( '_JEXEC' ) or die( 'Restricted access' );
$mainframe->registerEvent( 'onPrepareContent', 'pluginReviewInfo' );
```

As we did for the first plug-in, we register the function `pluginReviewInfo()` to trigger on the `onPrepareContent` event.

```php
function pluginReviewInfo ( &$row, &$params )
{
    preg_match_all('/\{reviewinfo (.*)\}/U', $row->text, $matches);
    foreach( $matches[1] as $name )
    {
        $review = contentReviewInfo_getReviewByName($name);
        $html = contentReviewInfo_createHTML($review);
        $row->text = str_replace("{reviewinfo $name}", $html,
         $row->text);
    }
    return true;
}
```

The triggering event automatically passes the row of content and article parameters into `pluginReviewInfo()`. We use PHP's `preg_match_all()` to get all of the `{reviewinfo ...}` tags in the article, collecting them in `$matches`. The array in `$matches[1]` contains all of the names that were captured between the space after `reviewinfo` and the end of the tag. We cycle through this array and pass the names into `contentReviewInfo_getReviewByName()` to get the information for each review. Next, we get an HTML-formatted snippet of information in `$html` by passing the `$review` object into `contentReviewInfo_createHTML()`. Finally, we use PHP's `str_replace()` to replace all occurrences of the `reviewinfo` tag for that review with the HTML snippet.

```php
function contentReviewInfo_getReviewByName ($name)
{
    $db =& JFactory::getDBO();
    $name = $db->getEscaped($name);
    $query = "SELECT * FROM #__reviews WHERE name = '$name'";
    $db->setQuery($query);
    $review = $db->loadObject();
    return $review;
}
```

Without a review id, we use `contentReviewInfo_getReviewByName()` to fetch the information for the review, given only the name. First, we get a reference to the current database object. Next, we take the `$name` variable, pass it into the function, and run it through the `getEscaped()` member function of the database object so that reviews with apostrophes do not cause the query to fail. We run the query, and use the member function `loadObject()` to load only the first row into the results. We've warned our critic that this may not work as expected if two people write separate reviews for the same restaurant, but she's guaranteed us that the other critics are too narcissistic to write about a place that someone else has already reviewed.

```
function contentReviewInfo_createHTML (&$review)
{
    $html = '<table class="moduletable">';
    $html .= '<tr><th colspan="2">Info</th></tr>';
    $html .= '<tr><td>Address:</td><td>' .
            $review->address . '</td></tr>';
    $html .= '<tr><td>Price Range:</td><td>$' .
            $review->avg_dinner_price . '</td></tr>';
    $html .= '<tr><td>Reservations:</td><td>' .
            $review->reservations . '</td></tr>';
    if ( $review->smoking == 0 )
    {
        $smoking = 'No';
    }
    else
    {
        $smoking = 'Yes';
    }
    $html .= '<tr><td>Smoking:</td><td>' .
            $smoking . '</td></tr>';
    $html .= '</table>';
    return $html;
}
```

Finally, our `contentReviewInfo_createHTML()` function takes a review object row as a parameter and formats it into an HTML table. This HTML table is given the `moduletable` class, which is standard in Joomla! templates. The `address`, `price range`, and `reservations` policy are all included in the HTML as-is. The `smoking` column is tested, with `$smoking` set to `Yes` or `No` depending on the column value. We then use `$smoking` to finish the last row in the table.

Before applying this plug-in, our critic's article would probably look something like the following screenshot:

Dinner on the Cheap

Written by Administrator

Wednesday, 06 August 2008 01:23

Some days, you're not in the mood to cook, but you don't want to spend a lot of money on food. Try these picks for your next meal:

The Daily Dish

Everyone eats there. Not only will you get an inexpensive, filling dinner, but you'll also probably run into one of your friends as well {reviewinfo The Daily Dish}

Crosstown Deli

The sandwiches here are worth trying if you're in the area and need something quick. {reviewinfo Crosstown Deli}

Nana's Bakery

If you still have money in your wallet and room in your stomach after dinner, head on down here for the best dessert in town. {reviewinfo Nana's Bakery}

After publishing the plug-in, the article will transform into something like the following:

Dinner on the Cheap

Written by Administrator

Wednesday, 06 August 2008 01:23

Some days, you're not in the mood to cook, but you don't want to spend a lot of money on food. Try these picks for your next meal:

The Daily Dish

Everyone eats there. Not only will you get an inexpensive, filling dinner, but you'll also probably run into one of your friends as well

Info

Address:	180 Main Street
Price Range:	$10
Reservations:	Accepted
Smoking:	No

Crosstown Deli

The sandwiches here are worth trying if you're in the area and need something quick.

Info

Address:	1923 Crosstown Boulevard
Price Range:	$6
Reservations:	None Taken
Smoking:	No

Nana's Bakery

If you still have money in your wallet and room in your stomach after dinner, head on down here for the best dessert in town.

Info

Address:	48 Huckleberry Lane
Price Range:	$5
Reservations:	None Taken
Smoking:	No

Searching the reviews

Some of our visitors have complained that they cannot find restaurant reviews through the search form. We can fix this by writing a search plug-in to scan the reviews along with the results for content. Create a file name/`plugins/search/reviews.php`, and add the following code to it:

```php
<?php
defined( '_JEXEC' ) or die( 'Restricted access' );

jimport( 'joomla.plugin.plugin' );

class plgSearchReviews extends JPlugin
{
```

In contrast to our content plug-in, for the search plug-in we are extending the JPlugin class instead of calling the registerEvent() member function of the mainframe object. This is a newer method of constructing plug-ins, that is becoming the preferred method.

To start using this style, jimport('joomla.plugin.plugin') is called to load the plug-in code into memory. After this, a class is defined that extends JPlugin. The name format for this class starts with plg, continues with a capitalized form of the plug-in group name (in this case Search), and ends with the name of the plug-in itself (Reviews). Inside of plgSearchReviews, each of the member functions will be named after the event that it responds to. This eliminates the need to create both a set of functions and a set of registered events.

For the search plug-in, we're responding to two events — onSearch and onSearchAreas. The onSearch event is triggered when the search component looks for results for a given phrase. Triggers to the onSearchAreas event are made when the search form is being built, so that a visitor can have a choice over which records are returned.

```php
function onSearchAreas($value='')
    {
        static $areas = array('reviews' => 'Restaurant Reviews');
        return $areas;
    }
```

The `onSearchAreas()` function is used to return an array of valid search areas. Although it is possible to have more than one search area (say, the review text and the review notes), we are going to keep it simple for visitors and just search reviews as a whole. By default, the search component will return results from all published search plug-ins. When the visitor selects one or more search areas, they are limiting their search to only look for records from those areas.

```
function onSearch($text, $phrase = '', $ordering = '', $areas = null)
    {
```

When a search takes place, `onSearch()` is called with up to four parameters. The search keywords are passed into `$text`. We can impose special conditions by using `$phrase`, which can be set to `any` (any of these words), `all` (all of these words), or `exact` (exactly this phrase). Record sorting is determined by `$ordering`, which can be set to `newest`, `oldest`, `popular`, `alpha`, or `category`. Finally, `$areas` is an array of the search areas currently selected by the visitor.

```
    if (!$text)
{
    return array();
}

    if (is_array( $areas ))
    {
        if (!array_intersect( $areas,
         array_keys( $this->onSearchAreas() ) ))
        {
            return array();
        }
    }
```

There are a couple of situations where we may want to quit processing at this instant. First, if there are no search keywords in `$text`, we know there won't be any results, so we return an empty array. Next, we test to see if `$areas` is set as an array. If so, we match this array against the valid search areas for our plug-in. If none of the items in `$areas` are intended for our plug-in, we return an empty array. When `$areas` is set to `null`, all search areas are assumed to be selected.

```
$db =& JFactory::getDBO();

    if ($phrase == 'exact')
    {
        $where = "(LOWER(name) LIKE '%$text%') OR (LOWER(quicktake)
         LIKE '%$text%')" ." OR (LOWER(review) LIKE '%$text%') OR
```

```
            (LOWER(notes) LIKE '%$text%')";
}
else
{
    $words = explode( ' ', $text );
    $wheres = array();
    foreach ($words as $word)
    {
        $wheres[] = "(LOWER(name) LIKE '%$word%')
         OR (LOWER(quicktake) LIKE '%$word%')" . " OR
         (LOWER(review) LIKE '%$word%') OR (LOWER(notes)
         LIKE '%$word%')";
    }
    if($phrase == 'all')
    {
        $separator = "AND";
    }
    else
    {
        $separator = "OR";
    }
    $where = '(' . implode( ") $separator (" , $wheres ) . ')';
}
$where .= ' AND published = 1';
```

After getting the current database object instance from `JFactory::getDBO()`, we build the WHERE clause for a query that will be used for searching the reviews. We test the variable `$phrase` to determine how the visitor wants to have the search terms treated. If they were intending an exact phrase, we simply match the search term as a whole against the `name`, `quicktake`, `review`, and `notes` fields in `jos_reviews`. For 'all' and 'any' searches, we separate out each word in the search term and build an array of WHERE statements, which are joined according to the type of search. Finally, we add a check to make sure we only include published reviews.

```
switch ($ordering)
{
    case 'oldest':
        $order = 'review_date ASC';
        break;
    case 'alpha':
        $order = 'title ASC';
        break;
    case 'newest':
    default:
        $order = 'review_date DESC';
        break;
}
```

After dealing with the search terms, we need to order the reviews properly. Of the five possible orders, only three really make sense for our plug-in—oldest, newest, and alphabetical. Our default is to sort by the review date, reverse-chronologically.

Now that we know the order, we can build our query. Some of the data we want will be in database columns, while we will need to backfill the rest of it. The search component expects the following fields for each row of the result set—title, text, created, section, href, and browsernav.

The first three of these match up to the columns in the jos_reviews table. The **title** field is used for the name of the link that appears in the result; we will use the value of **name** here. The value of **text** is shown as a short excerpt; our **quicktake** field will do nicely. Finally, the **created** field determines the creation date of the record, for sorting; we will use **review_date** for this.

The remaining three columns will need to be constructed. The **section** column is used as a way of differentiating the results of this plug-in apart from the results from other search plug-ins. Because all of our results will be pointing to "Restaurant Reviews", we will hard-code the string "Restaurant Reviews" to be the value of **section** for every row. Also, each result needs a link, which the search component looks for in **href**. MySQL's CONCAT() function will be used to generate these links based on the record's **id**. Finally, the search component will check the value of **browsernav** to determine whether to generate links that open in a new window (**1**) or plain links that stay in the same window (**2**). Because we want plain links for our plug-in, the value for **browsernav** will be set to **2** for every row.

Finish the plug-in with the following code:

```
$query = "SELECT name AS title, quicktake AS text,
 review_date AS created, " .
"\n 'Restaurant Reviews' AS section,"
"\n CONCAT('index.php?option=com_restaurants&view=single&id=',
 id) AS href," .
"\n '2' AS browsernav" .
"\n FROM #__reviews" .
"\n WHERE $where" .
"\n ORDER BY $order";
$db->setQuery( $query );
$rows = $db->loadObjectList();
return $rows;
}
```

Once the query is set, we load the result as an array of objects into $rows, and we return $rows so that they can be included alongside other search results. Now we are ready to test the plug-in.

If you haven't already published a search module for visitors, create one in the administrator backend by going to **Extensions | Module Manager**, then click **New** and choose **Search**. Add a title and then click **Save**. This will provide you with a form for entering searches.

Before the addition of this plug-in, a search on **dish** might have returned a result set similar to the following one:

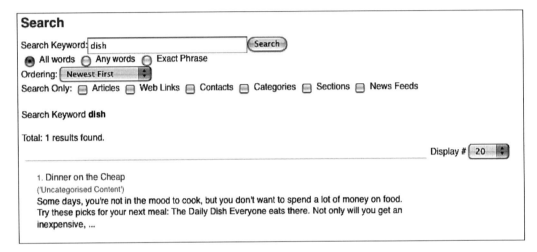

After adding the plug-in, **The Daily Dish** should also appear in the results:

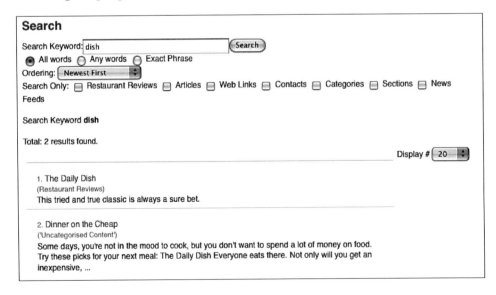

Limiting the search to only reviews should return just **The Daily Dish**:

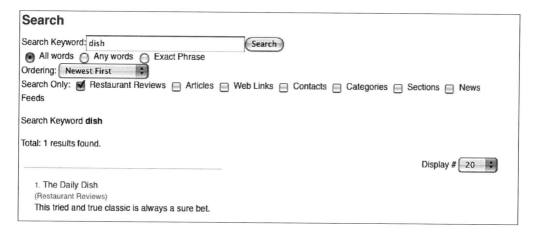

Summary

With our plug-ins in place, the critics are now able to link to the original reviews without even copying the reviews' URLs. We've also given them the option of showing a detail box that matches whichever template we choose. Finally, reviews can now be found in search results along with our articles. Visitors can limit the keyword search to just the reviews if they wish; for example if they remember the word 'croutons' being in a certain review, they will have no problems finding that review.

10
Configuration Settings

Our reviewers are satisfied with all of the features we've provided, but there are some concerns. They would like to have specific control over certain functions. Fortunately, we don't have to add any mundane record management to do this; instead we can concentrate on the logic. Our extensions will need a little rewriting, but nothing too drastic.

- Adding parameters to extensions
- Parameters for modules
- Parameters for plug-ins
- Parameters for components

Adding parameters to extensions

Throughout this book, we've run queries to register extensions in Joomla!. Within the tables where we inserted this data, there is a column named `params`. This column allows us to store configuration parameter values in the database. However, the column itself does not enforce any kind of format for the parameter values. To do this, we will enter the parameter values as a part of an XML document for configuration. This file will sit alongside our other extension files and contain a list of all of the possible settings.

Parameters for modules

The module we wrote for "Restaurant Reviews" already has logic for different display types and different data retrieval scenarios. Defining parameters for the module will make it easy for the administrators to pick and choose their desired setup. To define the parameters, we will need to create a file named `mod_reviews.xml`.

In addition to specifying the parameters to offer to the administrator, this XML file will also identify the copyright and license information for the modules. This is also referred to as the module's "manifest". To create the manifest, go to /modules/ mod_reviews folder, create a file named mod_reviews.xml and enter the following code into this new file:

```xml
<?xml version="1.0" encoding="utf-8"?>
<install type="module" version="1.5">
  <name>Restaurant Reviews</name>
  <author>Sumptuous Software</author>
  <creationDate>January 2008</creationDate>
  <copyright>(C) 2008</copyright>
  <license>MIT</license>
  <authorEmail>support@packtpub.com</authorEmail>
  <authorUrl>www.packtpub.com</authorUrl>
  <version>1.0</version>
  <description>A module for promoting restaurant reviews.
    </description>
  <params>
    <param name="random" type="radio" default="0" label="Randomize"
      description="Show random reviews">
      <option value="0">No</option>
      <option value="1">Yes</option>
    </param>
    <param name="@spacer" type="spacer" default="" label=
      "" description="" />
    <param name="items" type="text" default="1" label="Display #"
      description="Number of reviews to display" />
    <param name="style" type="list" default="default" label=
      "Display style" description="The style to use for displaying
      the reviews.">
      <option value="default">Flat</option>
      <option value="bulleted">Bulleted</option>
    </param>
  </params>
</install>
```

The XML document begins with a standard XML definition, and wraps all of the remaining elements in `<install>` tag. This first element defines that the extension we're describing is a module and that it is intended for Joomla!. Within `<install>`, we have several elements that are intended for identification — name, author, creation date, copyright, license, author email, author URL, version, and description. Except for description, all of these elements will appear in the backend, in the modules section of **Extension Manager**.

After the identification elements, we then add the `<params>` element, which encases several `<param>` elements. For our module we would like to provide options for controlling the display of random restaurants, the number of reviews displayed at a time, and whether the review display is flat-listed or bulleted.

The XML document not only allows us to enforce the data rules for these options, but also allows us to define how they would be used as backend controls. The control for randomizing the reviews makes sense as a yes/no decision, so a radio button is appropriate. We give these parameters the name `random` (to match our earlier code), the type `radio`, the default `0` (for no), the label `Randomize`, and the description `Show random reviews`. Within this parameter element, we define two `<option>` elements, one with `0` as the value and `No` as the text and another with `1` and `Yes` as the value and text respectively, similar to the way in which HTML select options are coded.

Because the other two options have less to do with data retrieval and more with display, we will set these options off with a spacer. The spacer will not have a description, label, or default value, but will be of type `spacer` and will be named `@spacer`.

For the number of items to be displayed, we want the administrator to simply enter in a number. We use a parameter of type `text` and set the default value to `1`. For the choice of style, there should only be a choice of the ones available. We use the `list` type of parameter, and will define the `flat` and `bulleted` options similar to the way we did for the radio button.

What parameters are available for use?

Modules, plug-ins, and components all allow you to define configuration parameters through XML files. Many common parameter types are predefined and can be used in any extension. Every parameter you define must have five basic attributes. First, you must give the parameter a name so that you can reference it later in your code. Next, you need a default value to be displayed and used if no value is chosen. To identify the parameter, you need to give it both a visible label and a description that appears when the mouse cursor hovers over it. Finally, you must specify the type of the parameter. A categorized list of the available parameter types is given below:

- Content
  - `section` - All published sections, in a list
  - `category` - All published categories, in a list
- Text Input
  - `text` - A standard text input
  - `textarea` - A plain text area field

- ◦ `password` - A standard text input where the characters are masked as they are entered
- ◦ `editors` - Provides the administrator's currently chosen WYSIWYG editor for input

- Selections
  - ◦ `menu` - All published menus, in a list
  - ◦ `menuitem` - All published menu items, in a list
  - ◦ `filelist` - A list of files to choose from, given a base folder path
  - ◦ `folderlist` - A list of folders to choose from, given a base folder path
  - ◦ `imagelist` - A list of images to choose from, given a base folder path
  - ◦ `list` - A list of items to choose from (hardcoded into parameter definition)
  - ◦ `radio` - A list of radio selection items to choose from (hardcoded into the parameter definition)
  - ◦ `sql` - Creates a dropdown list out of a provided SQL query

- Predefined
  - ◦ `helpsites` - A list of websites to choose from powering help file translations
  - ◦ `languages` - A list of installed languages to choose from
  - ◦ `spacer` - Creates a visual separation between parameters; no input value is required
  - ◦ `timezones` - A list of all world time zones

- Other
  - ◦ `hidden` - Creates a hidden form element with the value and name provided

After saving the XML document, go to the backend and navigate to **Extensions | Module Manager**. From here, choose **Restaurant Reviews** from the list, and the parameters area on the right should look similar to the following:

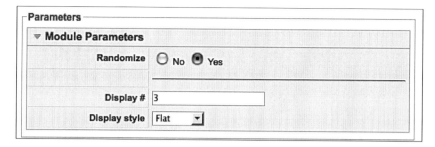

You should be able to set these parameters, save the module, then reopen it, and see the changes. The **Randomize** and **Display #** parameters are already implemented in the helper class we wrote in Chapter 6; the effects of changing them can be seen immediately in the frontend right away:

Restaurant Reviews

Giovanni's Italian Restaurant

Giovanni has renovated this warehouse into a gorgeous restaurant, suitable for formal dining and special occasions.

Nana's Bakery

Pies, cookies, and sweet breads are the main attraction here.

However, changes to the **Display style** parameter are not visible in the frontend. The value of this parameter must be extracted in /modules/mod_reviews/mod_reviews. php. Open this file and change this highlighted line, where $layout is set:

```
$list = modReviewsHelper::getReviews($params);

$layout = $params->get('style', 'default');
$path = JModuleHelper::getLayoutPath('mod_reviews', $layout);
```

For modules, $params is automatically available in global scope. This object has the member function get(), which returns the parameter value given the name (and optionally, a default value). Instead of hard-coding the value for $layout as before, it is now dynamically determined by the value of style set by the administrator in the backend.

After saving the file, go back to the module configuration panel for **Restaurant Reviews** in the backend, set **Display #** to a value of **2**, **Display style** to **Bulleted**, **Randomize** to **No**, and then save the module. In the frontend, the module should now appear similar to the following image:

Restaurant Reviews

- Giovanni's Italian
  Restaurant
- Nana's Bakery

Parameters for plug-ins

For our content review links plug-in, we would like to give the administrators some control over formatting the link. They should be able to add text to the link to show that it goes to a review, or change the anchor tag to have more attributes. The process for adding parameters to our plug-in is similar to what we do for modules. Open the `/plugins/content/reviews.xml` file and add this code:

```
<?xml version="1.0" encoding="utf-8"?>
<install version="1.5" type="plugin" group="content">
  <name>Content - Restaurant Review Links</name>
  <author>Sumptuous Software</author>
  <creationDate>August 2008</creationDate>
  <copyright>(C) 2008</copyright>
  <license>MIT</license>
  <authorEmail>support@packtpub.com</authorEmail>
  <authorUrl>www.packtpub.com</authorUrl>
  <version>1.0</version>
  <description>Searches for titles of restaurants in articles and
    turns them into review links.</description>
  <params>
    <param name="linkcode" type="textarea" default="" rows=
      "5" cols="40" label="Custom Link Code" description=
      "By using {link} and {title}, you can generate custom HTML
      output that includes the URL and review title respectively." />
  </params>
</install>
```

Because our administrators will be adding a bit of code, it will be helpful to have more room than a typical text input provides. To handle this, we create the `linkcode` parameter as type `textarea`. Go to the backend and navigate to **Extensions | Plugin Manager**, and then select **Content – Reviews** from the list. There should be a box labeled **Custom Link Code**, where you can enter the code for the links. Our reviewers have decided that they want to reinforce the fact that the reviews are merely their opinions of the restaurants. They want the text "**(our take)**" to follow the title of each review. Because they're prone to change their minds, the parameter we're defining will give them a way of changing the output without actually getting into the code. We will define the tags {link} and {title} as the relative URL and review title respectively. These tags will be dynamically replaced with the appropriate values when the content is displayed. In the **Custom Link Code** box, enter `<a href="{link}">{title} (our take)</a>`. It should look like the following figure:

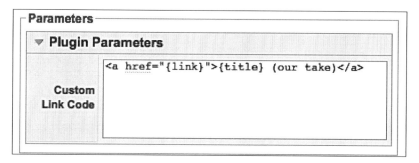

Save the plug-in. Before our formatting can take effect, we need to change the plug-in code to read the parameters and change the link accordingly. Open the `/plugins/content/reviews.php` file, and make the following highlighted changes and additions:

```
function pluginReviews( &$row, &$params )
{
    $plugin =& JPluginHelper::getPlugin('content', 'reviews');
    $pluginParams = new JParameter( $plugin->params );
    $linkcode = $pluginParams->get('linkcode', '');
    $reviews = contentReviews_getlist();
    $pattern = array();
    $replace = array();
    foreach($reviews as $review)
    {
        $pattern[] = '/' . preg_quote($review) . '/';
```

```
        $replace[] = contentReviews_makeLink($review, $reviews,
        $linkcode);
    }
    $row->text = preg_replace($pattern, $replace, $row->text);
    return true;
}

    function contentReviews_makeLink ($title, &$reviews, $linkcode)
    {
    $id = array_search($title, $reviews);
    $link = JRoute::_('index.php?option=com_restaurants&view=
      single&id=' . $id );
    if($linkcode == '')
    {
        $linkcode = '<a href="' . $link . '">' . $title . '</a>';
    }
    else
    {
      $linkcode = str_replace('{link}', $link, $linkcode);
      $linkcode = str_replace('{title}', $title, $linkcode);
    }
    return $linkcode;
    }
```

In `pluginReviews()`, we start by using the `getPlugin()` member function of `JPluginHelper` to get our plug-in object, passing in the plug-in folder `content`, and name `reviews` respectively. The `params` member variable is passed into a constructor for `JParameter`, to get the parameters back as an object. The only parameter we are interested in is `linkcode`, so we extract it and pass it into `contentReviews_makeLink()`. If there is no value for `linkcode`, we return the link as usual. Otherwise, we look for our {`link`} and {`title`} tags and replace them with the appropriate elements.

After saving the plug-in code, make sure that the **Content – Reviews** plug-in is published and that the **Content – Review Information** is unpublished. When you go to an article in the frontend containing the names of the restaurants, links to the reviews should look similar to these:

Learning Joomla! Extension Development

Crowd Pleasers

Written by Administrator

Tuesday, 05 August 2008 01:05

When dining with a large group of friends, you wan to make sure all of your bases are covered. These crowd pleasers are good choices for when you want widely agreeable dining. These restaurants are our picks:

The Daily Dish (our take) - a local favorite and tradition.

Crosstown Deli (our take) - usually has good sandwiches.

Giovanni's Italian Restaurant (our take) - better for a special occasion, but still pleases a wide range of tastes.

Last Updated (Wednesday, 06 August 2008 01:04)

Adding configuration for the Review Information plug-in is similar. This time, we have four possible pieces of data that are displayed with every information box. This might be too much, so we will allow the administrator to turn certain fields off. Open the /plugins/content/reviewinfo.xml file, and add the following code:

```xml
<?xml version="1.0" encoding="utf-8"?>
<install version="1.5" type="plugin" group="content">
  <name>Content - Review Information</name>
  <author>Sumptuous Software</author>
  <creationDate>August 2008</creationDate>
  <copyright>(C) 2008</copyright>
  <license>MIT</license>
  <authorEmail>support@packtpub.com</authorEmail>
  <authorUrl>www.packtpub.com</authorUrl>
  <version>1.0</version>
  <description>Turns {reviewinfo Name of your restaurant}
    into a table with the review's essential
    details.</description>
  <params>
    <param name="address" type="radio" default="1" label=
      "Display Address?" description="Toggles the display of the
      address in summaries.">
      <option value="1">Yes</option>
      <option value="0">No</option>
    </param>
    <param name="price_range" type="radio" default="1"
      label="Display Price Range?" description="Toggles
      the display of the price range in summaries.">
      <option value="1">Yes</option>
      <option value="0">No</option>
    </param>
    <param name="reservations" type="radio" default="1"
      label="Display Reservations?" description="Toggles
      the display of reservation policy in summaries.">
      <option value="1">Yes</option>
      <option value="0">No</option>
    </param>
    <param name="smoking" type="radio" default="1"
      label="Display Smoking?" description="Toggles
      the display of smoking policy in summaries.">
      <option value="1">Yes</option>
      <option value="0">No</option>
    </param>
  </params>
</install>
```

The `<params>` section of this XML file defines four radio buttons, all set to `Yes` by default. These will be used to turn the display of the `address`, `price range`, `reservations`, and `smoking` values in the review summary on and off. After saving the file, open the plug-in by navigating to **Extensions | Plugin Manager**, then select **Content – Review Information**. After selecting **No** for **Display Address**, the parameters box should look similar to the following:

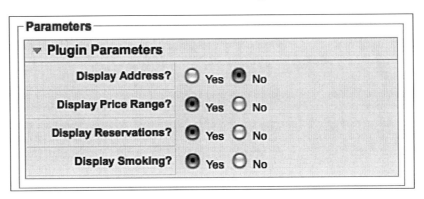

As we did for the link plug-in, we will pull in the parameters once and then pass them into another function. Make the following edits and additions to the `/plugins/content/reviewinfo.php` file:

```
function pluginReviewInfo ( &$row, &$params )
{
    $plugin =& JPluginHelper::getPlugin('content', 'reviewinfo');
    $pluginParams = new JParameter( $plugin->params );
    preg_match_all('/\{reviewinfo (.*)\}/U', $row->text, $matches);
    foreach( $matches[1] as $name )
    {
        $review = contentReviewInfo_getReviewByName($name);
        $html = contentReviewInfo_createHTML($review, $pluginParams);
        $row->text = str_replace("{reviewinfo $name}", $html,
            $row->text);
    }
    return true;
}
function contentReviewInfo_createHTML (&$review, &$pluginParams)
{
    $html = '<table class="moduletable">';
    $html .= '<tr><th colspan="2">Info</th></tr>';
    if($pluginParams->get('address', 1))
```

```
{
    $html .= '<tr><td>Address:</td>
        <td>' . $review->address . '</td></tr>';
}
if($pluginParams->get('price_range', 1))
{
    $html .= '<tr><td>Price Range:</td>
        <td>$' . $review->avg_dinner_price . '</td></tr>';
}
if($pluginParams->get('reservations', 1))
{
    $html .= '<tr><td>Reservations:</td>
        <td>' . $review->reservations . '</td></tr>';
}

if ($pluginParams->get('smoking', 1))
{
    if ( $review->smoking == 0 )
    {
        $smoking = 'No';
    }
    else
    {
        $smoking = 'Yes';
    }

    $html .= '<tr><td>Smoking:</td>
        <td>' . $smoking . '</td></tr>';
}
$html .= '</table>';
return $html;
}
```

What about the $params passed into pluginReviewInfo()?

In the function definition of pluginReviewInfo(), a variable named $params is passed in. These are not the plug-in's parameters; they are the parameters for the content item. Likewise, the $row object is the row in the database in #__content matching the current content item.

After getting the parameters for the plug-in in `pluginReviewInfo()`, we pass them into `contentReviewInfo_createHTML()`, where we test each field for the corresponding configuration value. If all of the fields are set to `Yes`, the information box in the content should appear as shown in the following image:

The Daily Dish

Everyone eats there. Not only will you get an inexpensive, filling dinner, but you'll also probably run into one of your friends as well

Info

Address: 180 Main Street

Price Range: $10

Reservations: Accepted

Smoking: No

When we turn off `Addresses`, it should appear as shown in the following image:

The Daily Dish

Everyone eats there. Not only will you get an inexpensive, filling dinner, but you'll also probably run into one of your friends as well

Info

Price Range: $10

Reservations: Accepted

Smoking: No

Finally, we have the search plug-in. Open the `/plugins/search/reviews.xml` file and add the following XML to it:

```xml
<?xml version="1.0" encoding="utf-8"?>
<install version="1.5" type="plugin" group="search">
  <name>Search - Restaurant Reviews</name>
  <author>Sumptuous Software</author>
  <creationDate>August 2008</creationDate>
  <copyright>(C) 2008</copyright>
  <license>MIT</license>
  <authorEmail>support@packtpub.com</authorEmail>
  <authorUrl>www.packtpub.com</authorUrl>
  <version>1.0</version>
  <description>Allows Searching of Restaurant Reviews</description>
  <params>
    <param name="search_limit" type="text" size="5" default="50"
      label="Search Limit" description="Number of Search items
      to return"/>
  </params>
</install>
```

By default, we set the number of items to return in the search results to 50 (probably more than the number of total items per screen in the search results). With this configuration parameter, we can limit the number of reviews returned all the way down to 1.

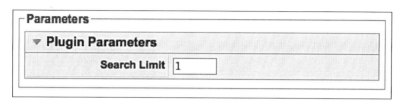

To make our configuration work, open the /plugins/search/reviews.php file, and make the following highlighted adjustments:

```
$query = "SELECT name AS title, quicktake AS text, review_date AS created, " .
"\n 'Restaurant Reviews' AS section," .
"\n CONCAT('index.php?option=com_restaurants&view=single&id=', id) AS href," .
"\n '2' AS browsernav" .
"\n FROM #__reviews" .
"\n WHERE $where" .
"\n ORDER BY $order";
$plugin =& JPluginHelper::getPlugin('search', 'reviews');
$pluginParams = new JParameter( $plugin->params );
$limit = $pluginParams->get( 'search_limit', 50 );
$db->setQuery( $query, 0, $limit );
$rows = $db->loadObjectList();
return $rows;
```

As with the other plug-ins, we first get the parameters for the search reviews and then use `JParameter` to create an object out of them. For the call to `setQuery()`, we're passing in two additional values that will automatically build our limit clause—0 to start with the first row, and `$limit` to go to our configured limit. Before adding our limit of only one restaurant review per search, a search for **restaurant** may have resulted in the following screen:

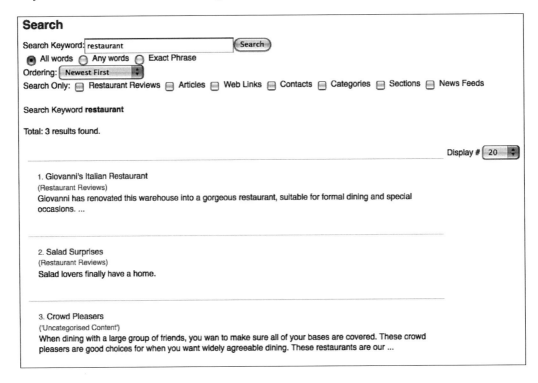

After adding a limit (in this example, of 2), the results would look more like the following:

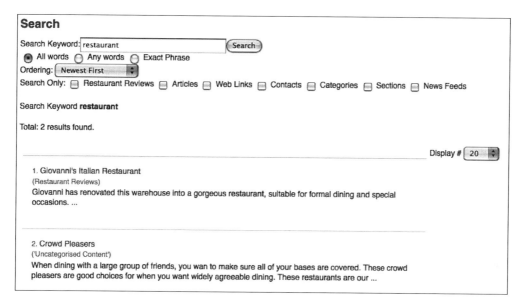

In the two results, the number of content items returned is unchanged; only the number of reviews has changed.

Why did Salad Surprises appear in the first set of results?

You may have noticed that although **Salad Surprises** was returned in the first set of results, the term **restaurants** was not displayed for it on screen. This term matched the full review and not the **quicktake** field that is displayed. This is an issue you will need to consider when testing plug-ins that search multiple fields.

Parameters for components

Implementing parameters for plug-ins and modules is straightforward—you add an XML file with the same name as the PHP file, then modify the code to extract the parameter values, and act accordingly. Components are slightly more complex. Although parameters can be implemented for the component as a whole, individual views can have them as well.

Adding parameters to the list view

Our current `list` view simply outputs a bulleted list of links to published reviews. With only a handful of reviews published, the frontend display looks bare. To fill it in, we can add the text from the **quicktake** field to show a brief description of each linked restaurant. When the reviews become more numerous, the site administrator can turn the quicktakes off to save space.

Instead of adding XML to a manifest file for the component, we will add one for the `default` layout in the `list` view. To do this, go to the `/components/com_restaurants/views/list/tmpl` folder and create a file named `default.xml`, and then load it with the following code:

```xml
<?xml version="1.0" encoding="utf8"?>
<metadata>
    <layout title="All Reviews Layout">
        <message>
        <![CDATA[Shows all reviews.]]>
        </message>
    </layout>
    <state>
        <name>All Reviews</name>
        <description>Shows all published restaurant
         reviews</description>
        <params>
            <param name="display_quicktakes" type="radio" default=
            "0" label="Display Quicktakes?" description="When set to
             'yes', the quicktake field is displayed beneath each
             review.">
                <option value="1">Yes</option>
                <option value="0">No</option>
            </param>
        </params>
    </state>
</metadata>
```

The XML configuration file for a view is much shorter than the one used for an entire extension. First, we enclose all of our data within a `<metadata>` tag. Next, we have a `<layout>` tag with a title parameter, which is set to the name we want to use when referring to this view on the screen where you select a menu link type. The `<message>` tag is placed within this tag and contains the description of the view seen when you hover the mouse over this link.

The contents of the `<state>` tag determine what is displayed and offered on-screen when this view is selected. The `<name>` and `<description>` appear in the top-left portion of the screen. Just like plug-ins and modules, the `<params>` tag determines the parameters displayed for this view.

Go to the backend and select **Menus | Main Menu**, and then click **New**. After selecting **Restaurant Reviews** as the menu type, you should be presented with a screen like the following:

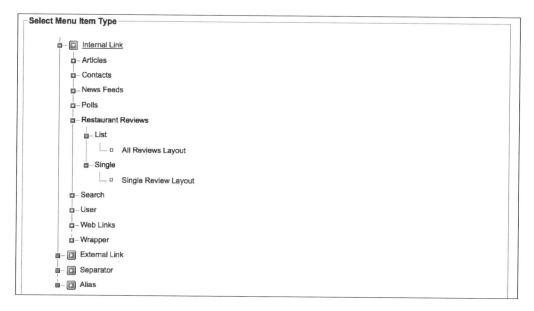

Clicking on **All Reviews Layout** under **List** will give you a configuration screen that includes the menu item parameters box, as seen in the following figure:

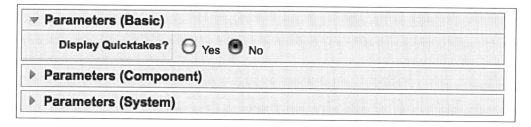

Set **Display Quicktakes?** to **Yes**, enter **Reviews With Quicktakes** as the link title, and then click **Save**. If you follow this link now, the display will be no different from the previously-entered link. We need to make modifications to the view so that the parameter value is tested, to control the output. Go to the `/components/com_restaurants/views/list/view.html.php` file, and make the highlighted changes to the `display()` function:

```
function display($tpl = null)
{
 global $mainframe;

    $rows =& $this->get('data');

    $params =& $mainframe->getParams();
    $quicktake = $params->get('display_quicktakes', 0);

    $this->assignRef('rows', $rows);
    $this->assign('display_quicktakes', $quicktake);

    parent::display($tpl);
}
```

This code first pulls in the `$mainframe` object from global scope. The `getParams()` member function returns an object containing all of the parameters that we need for the request; these are stored in `$params`. Because we are interested in the **display_quicktakes** parameter, we use the `get()` member function to retrieve the value and then store it in `$quicktake`. Finally, we assign this value to the view as `display_quicktakes`.

Some adjustments need to be made to the output as well. Open the file `views/list/tmpl/default.php`, and make the highlighted changes:

```
foreach ($this->rows as $row)
{
    $link = JRoute::_('index.php?option=com_restaurants&id=
    ' . $row->id . '&view=single');
    echo '<li><a href="' . $link . '">' . $row->name . '</a>';

    if ($this->display_quicktakes) {
      echo '<p>' . $row->quicktake . '</p>';
    }

    echo '</li>';
}
```

If the `display_quicktakes` view variable is non-zero, we output the **quicktake** for the review inside paragraph tags within the list item. Save all of the files, and then load the **Reviews With Quicktakes** link in the frontend. Your screen should now look similar to this one:

Restaurants we have reviewed

- Giovanni's Italian Restaurant
  Giovanni has renovated this warehouse into a gorgeous restaurant, suitable for formal dining and special occasions.
- Nana's Bakery
  Pies, cookies, and sweet breads are the main attraction here.
- Crosstown Deli
  Inexpensive sandwiches that are good if you're in the neighborhood.
- The Daily Dish
  This tried and true classic is always a sure bet.
- Salad Surprises
  Salad lovers finally have a home.

Adding parameters to the single view

When you add a link to a menu in the backend, you currently have the option to link to the `single` view, just as you can to the `list` view. At the moment, if you link to the `single` view, you will get a 404 error. This is because the view is looking for an ID in the request to use to load a review and is not finding one.

To fix this, we will add a parameter to the view that will allow the administrator to select a review from a list. Create a file in the `/components/com_restaurants /views/single/tmpl/`folder named `default.xml`, and fill it with the following markup:

```xml
<?xml version="1.0" encoding="utf8"?>
<metadata>
    <layout title="Single Review Layout">
        <message>
        <![CDATA[Shows one review.]]>
        </message>
    </layout>
    <state>
        <name>Single Review</name>
        <description>Shows a single published review</description>
        <url addpath=
          "/administrator/components/com_restaurants/elements">
            <param name="id" type="review" default="" label=
            "Select Review" description="The review to link to" />
        </url>
    </state>
</metadata>
```

This XML file contains most of the elements found in the XML written for the list view. However, instead of a `<params>` element, we have a `<url>` element pointing to `/administrator/components/com_restaurants/elements`. Within this element, we have a single `<param>` defining a parameter named **id** of type `review`. The `<url>` element tells Joomla! that we want to use the enclosed parameters as request variables. The `addpath` attribute of `<url>` loads a specific location at which to find the HTML code to use for generating these parameters. Because Joomla! does not have a built-in parameter type for restaurant reviews, this element will allow us to place code to use in a specified folder instead.

You might notice that we do not yet have a folder of `/administrator/components/ com_restaurants/elements`. Create this folder, then create a file named `review. php` (which matches the type attribute of `<param>`) within this folder, and enter the following code into this new file:

```php
<?php
defined('_JEXEC') or die( 'Restricted access' );

class JElementReview extends JElement
{
    function fetchElement($name, $value, &$node, $control_name)
    {
        $db =& JFactory::getDBO();

        $query = 'SELECT id, name'
            .' FROM #__reviews'
            .' WHERE published = 1'
            .' ORDER BY name';

        $db->setQuery($query);
        $options = $db->loadObjectList();

        return JHTML::_('select.genericlist', $options,
         $control_name. '[' . $name . ']', 'class="inputbox"', 'id',
         'name', $value, $control_name . $name );
    }
}
```

After checking to make sure that the file is being called from within Joomla!, `JElementReview` is declared as an extension of `JElement`. The function `fetchElement()` is automatically called by the Joomla! framework when the element is ready to be rendered. The name of the parameter, the currently selected parameter value, the XML used to define the parameter, and the name used for the current parameter section are all passed in to `fetchElement()`.

Inside of the function, all of the published reviews are selected from the database and loaded into `$options`. Only `id` and `name` are selected from the table, as we need a key and a label for each element in our list. A call to `JHTML::_()` is then used to generate a `<select>` element based on the values from the database, the name of the input, and the currently-selected value.

Save all of the files, and then go to **Menus | Main Menu** in the backend, click **New**, then **Restaurant Reviews**, and finally click on **Single Review Layout**. Your parameters section on the right should now look like this:

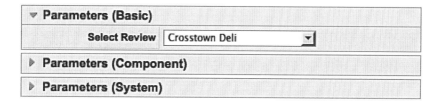

Select one of the restaurants from the list, then give the link a `title` and click **Save**. Clicking the link in the frontend should take you to the specific review you selected:

Adding component global parameters

Some of our restaurant critics are not enthusiastic about the comments feature and would like to be able to turn them off entirely. This can be done through the use of a global component parameter. To add this parameter, create a file named `config.xml` in the `/administrator/components/com_restaurants` folder and add the following code to the new file:

```
<?xml version="1.0" encoding="utf-8"?>
<config>
    <params>
```

```
        <param name="display_comments" type="radio" default=
        "1" label="Enable Comments?" description="When set to 'yes',
         a comment form is displayed beneath each review along with
         existing comments.">
            <option value="1">Yes</option>
            <option value="0">No</option>
        </param>
    </params>
</config>
```

The parameters are enclosed within a <config> element. We only have one <param> defined for display_comments, which has **Yes** and **No** as options (with **Yes** as the default). The parameters for the views were accessible when we created links to them, but where can the parameters for the component be found? Joomla! has a toolbar button that can be added to handle this. Because our restaurant reviewers will frequently be using the **Restaurant Reviews** list screen, we can put the toolbar button there. Edit the /administrator/components/com_restaurants/views/all/tmpl/default.php file, and add the highlighted call to JToolBarHelper::preferences():

```
JToolBarHelper::unpublishList();
JToolBarHelper::preferences('com_restaurants');
JToolBarHelper::editList();
```

Passing com_restaurants into preferences() ensures that the parameters for the "Restaurant Reviews" component are loaded. Save all of the files, then go to **Components | Restaurant Reviews** in the backend. The toolbar should now look like this:

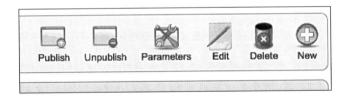

When you click on the **Parameters** button, the parameters should appear in a modal window like the one below:

Set **Enable Comments** to **No** and then click **Save**. There are a couple of adjustments that need to be made to the single view in the frontend to make this setting work. Make the highlighted changes to the `display()` function in the `/components/ com_restaurants/views/single/view.html.php`:

```php
global $mainframe;
$params =& $mainframe->getParams();

$id = (int) JRequest::getVar('id', 0);

$review =& JTable::getInstance('review', 'Table');
$review->load($id);

if ($review->published == 0)
{
    JError::raiseError(404, 'The review you requested is
    not available.' );
}

if ($review->smoking == 1)
{
    $smoking = 'Yes';
}
else
{
    $smoking = 'No';
}

$date = JHTML::Date($review->review_date);
$backlink = JRoute::_('index.php?option=com_restaurants');

$user =& JFactory::getUser();
$comments =& $this->get('Comments');
```

```
$this->assign('display_comments', $params->get('display_comments',
    '1'));
$this->assignRef('review', $review);
$this->assignRef('smoking', $smoking);
```

As we did for the `list` view earlier, the `$mainframe` object is pulled from global scope and the current parameter object is extracted. We then assign the value returned by the `get()` member function when we retrieve the `display_comments` parameter. All we need to do now is to test this value in the layout and act accordingly. Add the highlighted `if()` statement to the `/components/com_restaurants/views/single/tmpl/default.php` file:

```php
<a href="<?php echo htmlspecialchars($this->backlink);
    ?>">&lt; return to the reviews</a>
<?php
if ($this->display_comments)
{
    echo $this->loadTemplate('comments');
    echo $this->loadTemplate('comment_form');
}
```

Load any of the reviews in the frontend and the comments section should now be entirely gone:

The Daily Dish
Sunday, 29 June 2008

This tried and true classic is always a sure bet.

Address: 180 Main Street

Cuisine: Homestyle

Average dinner price: $10

Credit cards: Visa, MasterCard, Discover

Reservations: Accepted

Smoking: No

Chicken fried steak, meatloaf, potatoes, string beans and hot turkey sandwiches are all favorites from this venerable institution the locals swear by. Apple, pumpkin, and pecan pies round out the dessert selection. Dinner there won't break the bank, either.

Notes: Get there early on Friday nights, it's impossible to get a table after 7PM.

< return to the reviews

Summary

Through XML configuration files, we are able to add several options without creating separate tables to hold the values. Parameters can be added to modules, plug-ins, and components with minimally-invasive code. Because modules and plug-ins do not allow for custom backend interfaces written in PHP, parameters provide an essential alternative for administrative control.

Components benefit from both view and global parameters. View parameters make it possible to offer different layouts with specific options. Global parameters are easily added to the component backend; they allow administrators to set options that apply to the component regardless of the view displayed.

The parameters for modules, plug-ins, and components match the style used throughout the Joomla! backend. It is a good idea to use them whenever feasible; they will be familiar to Joomla! site administrators who are comfortable with other extensions.

11
Email, Languages, and JFile

Our reviewers are finally happy with the direction of the website, but there are a few features that they would like to have us add. One of them came up with the idea of allowing visitors to send reviews to their friends through email. Another is interested in adding audio reviews in addition to text.

We are also beginning to look into ways of expanding the market for the software. Internationalizing the component now will make it easy to translate the user interface later.

- Sending emails
- Managing languages
- Creating translations
- Handling file uploads

Sending emails

Joomla!'s core content management has a built-in feature where visitors are able to send articles to their friends through email. A similar feature can be added to the "Restaurant Reviews" component. The component can be modified to display a link to a form where the email address of a friend can be entered along with a short message.

We will create a new view to handle this form. Go to the /components/com_ restaurants/views folder and create a new folder named email. In this folder, create a file called view.html.php, and load it with the following code:

```php
<?php
defined( '_JEXEC' ) or die( 'Restricted access' );

jimport( 'joomla.application.component.view');
```

```
JTable::addIncludePath(JPATH_COMPONENT_ADMINISTRATOR . DS . 'tables');

class RestaurantsViewEmail extends JView
{
    function display($tpl = null)
    {
        $id = JRequest::getInt('id', 0);

        $review =& JTable::getInstance('review', 'Table');
        $review->load($id);

        $this->assignRef('review', $review);

        parent::display($tpl);
    }
}
```

This code first checks to make sure that the file is not being called directly, loads in the framework code for views, and adds /administrator/components/ com_restaurants/tables to the include path list of JTable. After declaring RestaurantsViewEmail as an extension of JView, the display() function pulls in the restaurant review ID from the request. The getInstance() member function of JTable is used to get a reference to a table object for reviews. The review matching the ID is then loaded and assigned to the template using the assignRef() member function. Finally, JView's original display() member function is called.

Although the code in view.html.php now loads the review that our visitors are trying to email, the form still needs to be added. Create a folder named tmpl in the existing /components/com_restaurants/views/email folder, and add create a new file default.php inside with the following code:

```
<?php defined( '_JEXEC' ) or die( 'Restricted access' ); ?>
<form action="index.php" method="post">

    <div class="contentheading">Email review</div>
    <p> </p>
    <p>Fill this form to send this review of <em>
    <?php echo htmlspecialchars($this->review->name) ?>
    </em> to someone you know who will find it useful:</p>

    <div>
        <strong>Your name:</strong>
    </div>
    <p>
        <input type="text" name="sender_name" value="" />
    </p>
```

```
<div>
    <strong>Your email address:</strong>
</div>
<p>
    <input type="text" name="sender_email" value="" />
</p>

<div><strong>Recipient's email address:</strong></div>
<p>
    <input type="text" name="recipient" value="" />
</p>

<div><strong>Message:</strong></div>
<p>
    <textarea name="message" rows="4" cols="40"></textarea>
</p>

<p>
<input type="submit" value="Send Review" class="button" />
</p>

<?php echo JHTML::_( 'form.token' ); ?>
<input type="hidden" name="id" value=
"<?php  echo $this->review->id; ?>" />
<input type="hidden" name="task" value="sendemail" />
<input type="hidden" name="option" value=
"<?php echo $option; ?>" />
</form>
```

Before any output occurs, the code checks to make sure that the request is coming from within Joomla! and is not being called directly. The file then outputs a brief message identifying the review by name, so that the visitors are sure of what they are sending. The form then continues with fields for the visitor's name and email address, the email address of their friend, and an optional message.

Just after the submit button, there is a series of hidden fields. First, JHTML::_('form. token') is called to generate a token for the request. This is the same style of token as is used in the backend to thwart CSRF attacks, only here it is used to cut down on abuse. Next, the ID of the review being emailed is placed into the form. The task variable is set to sendemail, which is a function that we will add to the controller in a moment. Finally, option is set, so that Joomla! loads the com_restaurants component.

Linking the form

If you now load `index.php?option=com_restaurants&view=email` in your browser, you will see this screen:

```
┌─────────────────────────────────────────────────────────┐
│ Email review                                            │
│                                                         │
│ Fill this form to send this review of to someone you know who will find it useful: │
│ Your name:                                              │
│ ┌──────────────────────┐                               │
│ │                      │                               │
│ └──────────────────────┘                               │
│ Your email address:                                     │
│ ┌──────────────────────┐                               │
│ │                      │                               │
│ └──────────────────────┘                               │
│ Recipient's email address:                              │
│ ┌──────────────────────┐                               │
│ │                      │                               │
│ └──────────────────────┘                               │
│ Message (optional):                                     │
│ ┌──────────────────────────────────────────┐           │
│ │                                          │           │
│ └──────────────────────────────────────────┘           │
│ ( Send Review )                                         │
└─────────────────────────────────────────────────────────┘
```

The message at the top of the screen is incomplete as we simply loaded the view without a review id. Although we could add `id` as a parameter onto the end of the URL, our visitors will not be doing this. They will need a link to follow from the review itself. To add this link, we need to make some small adjustments to the `single` view. This view first needs to generate URLs to the `email` view with the ID already included. Do this by making the following highlighted adjustment to the `display()` function in `/components/com_restaurants/views/single/view.html.php`:

```php
$date = JHTML::Date($review->review_date);

$backlink = JRoute::_('index.php?option=com_restaurants');
$emaillink = JRoute::_('index.php?option=com_restaurants&view=email&id=' . $id);

$user =& JFactory::getUser();
$comments =& $this->get('Comments');

$this->assign('display_comments', $params->get('display_comments',
    '1'));
$this->assignRef('review', $review);
$this->assignRef('smoking', $smoking);
$this->assignRef('date', $date);
$this->assignRef('backlink', $backlink);
```

```
$this->assignRef('emaillink', $emaillink);
$this->assignRef('name', $user->name);
$this->assignRef('comments', $comments);

parent::display($tpl);
```

With a URL to the email view now being generated, we now need to display it. Open `/components/com_restaurants/views/single/tmpl/default.php` and add the following highlighted code:

```
<p><?php echo htmlspecialchars($this->review->review); ?></p>
<p><em>Notes:</em> <?php echo htmlspecialchars($this->review->notes);
    ?></p>
<p><a href="<?php echo htmlspecialchars($this->emaillink);
    ?>">Email this to a friend</a></p>
<a href="<?php echo htmlspecialchars($this->backlink);
    ?>">&lt; return to the reviews</a>
```

After saving the files, navigate to one of the restaurant reviews in the frontend. Your screen should now have an **Email this to a friend** link, like the following screenshot:

The Daily Dish
Sunday, 29 June 2008

This tried and true classic is always a sure bet.

Address: 180 Main Street

Cuisine: Homestyle

Average dinner price: $10

Credit cards: Visa, MasterCard, Discover

Reservations: Accepted

Smoking: No

Chicken fried steak, meatloaf, potatoes, string beans and hot turkey sandwiches are all favorites from this venerable institution the locals swear by. Apple, pumpkin, and pecan pies round out the dessert selection. Dinner there won't break the bank, either.

Notes: Get there early on Friday nights, it's impossible to get a table after 7PM.

Email this to a friend

< return to the reviews

When you click on the **Email this to a friend** link, you will get a screen that looks like the following:

```
Email review

Fill this form to send this review of The Daily Dish to someone you know who will find it useful:
Your name:
[                    ]

Your email address:
[                    ]

Recipient's email address:
[                    ]

Message (optional):
[                              ]

( Send Review )
```

Sending email

With the form and the navigation in place, we can now focus on creating the function that creates the email and sends it to the correct place. Throughout the creation of this component, we have used member functions of JRequest to filter our input. We will do the same here, but go one step further by verifying that the email addresses entered are valid.

This extra step is necessary as malicious users can otherwise add invalid newline characters to your email fields, taking control of the message sending process. Once a remote user has control, the message can be sent anywhere with any text. This is known as an "Email Header Injection attack". If you fail to protect your website against this type of attack, your component could be hijacked and used to send thousands of spam messages without your knowledge.

With this caution in mind, we will write the sendemail() function to process the form and send the review. Open /components/com_restaurants/restaurants. php and add this function to the controller class:

```
function sendemail()
{
    JRequest::checkToken() or jexit( 'Invalid Token' );

    JTable::addIncludePath(JPATH_COMPONENT_ADMINISTRATOR . DS .
      'tables');

    $sender_email = JRequest::getString('sender_email', '');
    $recipient = JRequest::getString('recipient', '');
```

```
$sender_name = JRequest::getString('sender_name', '');
$message = JRequest::getString('message', '');
$id = JRequest::getInt('id', 0);

jimport( 'joomla.mail.helper' );

if (!JMailHelper::isEmailAddress($sender_email) ||
 !JMailHelper::isEmailAddress($recipient))
{
    JError::raiseError(500, 'One of the emails you entered is
      invalid. Please try again.');
}

$review =& JTable::getInstance('review', 'Table');
$review->load($id);

$link = JURI::base() . 'index.php?option=com_restaurants&view=
 single&id=' . $id;

$subject = $sender_name . ' wants you to know
 about ' . $review->name;

$body = "Here's a review of {$review->name}:\n\n";
$body .= "{$review->review}\n\n";

if ($message != '')
{
    $body .= $sender_name . " also added this message:\n";
    $body .= '"' . $message . '"' . "\n\n";
}

$body .= "For all of the details, follow this link: {$link}";

$sender_name = JMailHelper::cleanAddress($sender_name);
$subject = JMailHelper::cleanSubject($subject);
$body = JMailHelper::cleanBody($body);
if (JUtility::sendMail($sender_email, $sender_name, $recipient,
 $subject, $body) !== true)
{
    JError::raiseNotice( 500, 'Email failed.' );
}

JRequest::setVar('view', 'email');
JRequest::setVar('layout', 'success');

$this->display();
}
```

Before even checking the variables, the `checkToken()` member function of `JRequest` is called to make sure that the user actually loaded the form. Although this will not prevent spammers from abusing your component, it will slow them down; they will need to load your form and extract the token for each message.

Next, the path /administrator/components/com_restaurants/tables is added to the list of paths JTable will use to find table classes. This is necessary because we will be loading the review in a moment, in order to extract the summary and title.

The email address of the sender, the address of the recipient, the name of the sender, any added message, and the review's ID are all extracted from the HTTP request. With the exception of the id field, all fields are filtered as strings. The id field is more stringently filtered to ensure that the value is also an integer.

Joomla! has a library for handling email data, which we pull in by calling jimport('joomla.mail.helper');. This is used immediately to ensure that the entered email addresses are in a valid format. Both the sender's address and the recipient's address are tested. If either one is in an invalid format or contain newlines, the raiseError() member function of JError is used to stop the script and display a message.

The function continues by generating some review-specific data. The review is loaded from the database, and then a link back to the review is built using the review's ID. A subject line is built with the sender's name and the name of the restaurant. The body of the email starts with the name of the review, followed by the review itself. If the visitor added a personal message then this is added, along with their name. The link to the full review is added at the end.

With all of the content generated, there is one step left before sending the message. The formats of the email addresses have already been validated, but the sender's name, subject, and body all contain user-supplied data. These must be filtered before they are sent off. The cleanAddress(), cleanSubject(), and cleanBody() member functions of JMailHelper strip out any attempts at email header injections.

Finally, the sendMail() member function of JUtility is called to send the email with the sender's address, sender's name, recipient's email address, subject line, and body as the respective parameters. If this function fails for any reason, the raiseError() member function of JError is called and processing stops.

Adding a success message

When you perform an action that sends an email, most web applications will display an "email success" screen letting you know that the message went through. Our component will be no different. At the end of the sendemail() function, we set the view request variable to email, set the layout request variable to success, and then call the display() member function that defaults to JView::display().

Why aren't we calling $this->setRedirect()?

Typically, `$this->setRedirect()` would be called to tell the controller to redirect the user to a specific page. This time, we have chosen to instead set the request variables and call the `display()` function directly. This prevents Joomla! from sending a redirect HTTP header to the browser, which ultimately saves another trip to the server. Because we want to display a message instead of going back to the review straight away, this makes sense. It may also be useful in cases where you have a client-side application that would otherwise be confused by a redirect.

Instead of creating an entirely separate view to handle the success screen, we have opted instead to set the `layout` request variable and point back to the `email` view. This helps us to cut down on the number of views required, and allows us to reuse some of the view code. To add the markup for the success screen, we need to create a new file called `success.php` to the `tmpl` folder of the `email` view. Enter the code below in `success.php`:

```php
<?php defined( '_JEXEC' ) or die( 'Restricted access' ); ?>
<div class="componentheading">Success!</div>
<p>The review for <?php echo htmlspecialchars($this->review->name)
    ?> has been successfully emailed.</p>
<p><a href="<?php echo htmlspecialchars($this->reviewlink) ?>">Return
    to the review for <?php echo
    htmlspecialchars($this->review->name) ?>.</a></p>
```

After checking to make sure that the request to `success.php` is coming from within Joomla!, a confirmation message, including the name, of the review is displayed. A link back to the review is also output. However, the URL for this link has not yet been generated. To do this, go to `/components/com_restaurants/views/email/view.html.php` and add the highlighted code to the `display()` function:

```php
$review->load($id);

$reviewlink = JRoute::_('index.php?option=com_restaurants&view=
    single&id=' . $id);

$this->assignRef('review', $review);
$this->assign('reviewlink', $reviewlink);

parent::display($tpl);
```

Save all of your code, then load one of the reviews and click on the **Email this to a friend** link. Fill the form and click the **Send Review** button. If the email goes through correctly, you should see a screen like the following:

Success!

The review for The Daily Dish has been successfully emailed.

Return to the review for The Daily Dish.

If you sent the review to yourself, the email should look similar to the following:

```
Here's a review of The Daily Dish:


Chicken fried steak, meatloaf, potatoes, string beans and hot turkey
sandwiches are all favorites from this venerable institution the locals
swear by. Apple, pumpkin, and pecan pies round out the dessert selection.
Dinner there won't break the bank, either.


Ralph Elderman also added this message:

"You should really try this place sometime. I take the family there
every week!"


For all of the details, follow this link: http://localhost/index.
php?option=com_restaurants&view=single&id=2
```

Managing languages

Joomla! 1.5 has a centralized approach to internationalization. The default language for the project is English; other languages are distributed separately as extensions. Although these extensions do not translate user-entered content, they do provide phrases for the core Joomla! extensions in other languages. Both the frontend and the backend of Joomla!'s user interface are internationalized; language packs for each are distributed separately.

The following examples assume that the French language packs are installed. If you do not already have them installed, they can be downloaded from Joomlacode at `http://joomlacode.org/gf/project/french/frs`. Be sure to download both the frontend and backend language packs. To install them, go to **Extensions | Install/ Uninstall** in the backend, then use the **Upload Package File** section to install both packages.

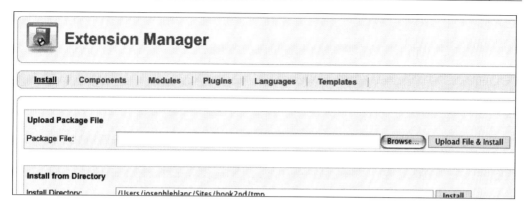

Once both language packs are installed, individual users can choose French, or French can be set as the default for the entire site. To set French as the default language for the frontend, go to **Extensions | Language Manager**, select the radio button next to **French**, then click the **Default** button at the top of the screen. Click on the **Administrator** link (next to **Site**) and repeat the process to make French the default language for the backend.

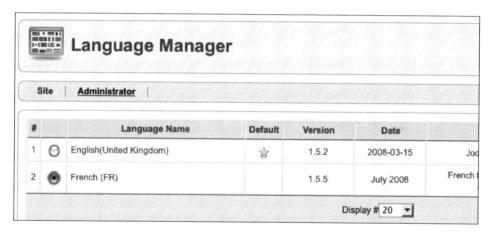

You should now notice that the backend interface is now in French. Go to **Composants | Restaurant Reviews** to see how our reviews component looks compared to the rest of the interface. The portions we wrote will still be in English, with the exception of the toolbar. Because we used standard Joomla! toolbar buttons here, these will be automatically translated, with no further effort required on our part.

Creating translations

When you installed the French language packs, you may have wondered exactly what happened. Joomla! language packs have one file for each core extension. There are two folders named `language` where these files are placed—one at Joomla!'s root and one inside the `administrator` folder. The `language` folders contain one folder for each language pack installed.

These folders are named for the language's ISO language code. For instance, the British English pack is in `en-GB` and French French is in `fr-FR`. The language files for the individual extensions are located within these folders. There is one additional file in each language folder that defines phrases that are not exclusively used by any single extension.

To begin translating the interface for the "Restaurant Reviews" component into French, open the file `/administrator/components/com_restaurants/views/all/tmpl/default.php`. Make the following highlighted change to the header row of the second table:

```
<tr>
  <th width="20">
    <input type="checkbox" name="toggle" value=
      "" onclick="checkAll(<?php echo count( $this->rows ); ?>);" />
  </th>
  <th class="title"><?php echo JText::_('Name') ?></th>
  <th width="15%">Address</th>
  <th width="10%">Reservations</th>
  <th width="10%">Cuisine</th>
  <th width="10%">Credit Cards</th>
  <th width="5%" nowrap="nowrap">Published</th>
</tr>
```

The `_()` function of `JText` is used throughout Joomla! for translating strings in the user interface. If Joomla! cannot find a translation for the string you pass in, it simply outputs the base string. For now, we have passed `Name` into `_()`, but we have not created a translation for it in the French language file yet. Save the file and refresh the main screen of **Restaurant Reviews**. The header row of the table should look like this:

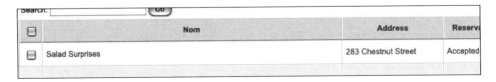

You may be wondering how **Name** has suddenly become **Nom**. Even though we did not create a translation for `Name`, Joomla! found one in the file `/administrator/language/fr-FR/fr-FR.ini`. This file is always loaded for translations regardless of which extensions are in use.

Now pass the rest of the table headers through `JText::_()`. The code changes to do this are highlighted below:

```
<tr>
  <th width="20">
    <input type="checkbox" name="toggle"
        value="" onclick="checkAll(<?php echo  count( $this->rows );
        ?>);" />
  </th>
  <th class="title"><?php echo JText::_('Name') ?></th>
  <th width="15%"><?php echo JText::_('Address') ?></th>
  <th width="10%"><?php echo JText::_('Reservations') ?></th>
  <th width="10%"><?php echo JText::_('Cuisine') ?></th>
  <th width="10%"><?php echo JText::_('Credit Cards') ?></th>
  <th width="5%" nowrap="nowrap"><?php echo JText::_('Published') ?></th>
</tr>
```

After saving the file and refreshing the page, the remainder of the headers should look like this:

	Address	Reservations	Cuisine	Credit Cards	Publié

Notice that **Published** is now translated as **Publié**, but the four remaining headers are still in English. We need to define translations for these strings in a file specific to the **Restaurant Reviews** component. Create a file named `/administrator/languages/fr-FR/fr-FR.com_restaurants.ini` and add the following text:

```
ADDRESS=Adresse
RESERVATIONS=Réservations
CUISINE=Cuisine
CREDIT CARDS=Cartes de credit
```

Notice that although the strings passed into `JText::_()` are mixed case, the definitions in `fr-FR.com_restaurants.ini` are uppercase. If you attempt to use a mixed case string for your definitions, `JText` will not read them during translation. Punctuation marks in the definitions are acceptable.

Save your language file, and then reload the screen. You should now see all of the table headers translated:

When we originally created the toolbar for this component, the title of the screen was passed through `JText::_()`. This string can now be translated with the following highlighted addition to `fr-FR.com_restaurants.ini`:

```
ADDRESS=Adresse
RESERVATIONS=Réservations
CUISINE=Cuisine
CREDIT CARDS=Cartes de crédit
RESTAURANT REVIEWS=Revues des restaurants
```

After saving the file, refresh the page. The title at the top of the screen should now appear as translated:

Adding comments to language files

If you want to add a comment in your language file, simply add a # at the beginning of the line you wish to comment. This is particularly helpful when you have a component with several views. Simply add a comment before adding a set of definitions for a specific view , to identify the view to which the definitions belong.

Debugging languages

One thing you may notice in our translations is that 'cuisine' is a French word spelled the same way in English. Although this cuts down on the amount of work for the translators, it can be rather confusing if you are trying to determine what is being passed through `JText::_()`. Even more importantly, how can you tell when a language definition is missing from your language file?

Joomla!'s Debug Language feature solves this. Each string that goes through `JText::_()` is wrapped in either bullets or question marks. Bullets represent a translated string and question marks represent missing language definitions.

To turn Debug Language on, go to **Site | Global Configuration (Configuration globale)**, then click on the **System (Système)** link beneath the tile. On the right, there will be a box labeled **Debug Settings (Paramètres de débogage)**, with **Debug Language (Débogage de la langue)** as an option. Set this option to **Yes (Oui)**, then click **Save**. Finally, go back to the Restaurant Reviews component. You should now see bullets surrounding much of the text in the user interface:

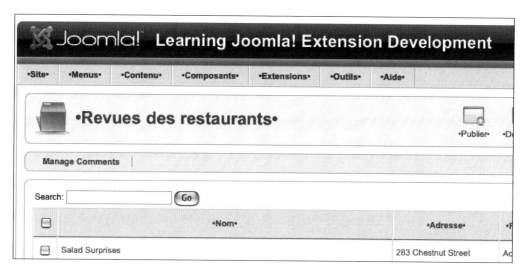

To see what the output looks like when a language definition is missing, temporarily remove the line ADDRESS=Adresse from the /administrator/languages/fr-FR/ fr-FR.com_restaurants.ini file. After saving the file, reload the component. The Address column should now look like this:

The debug language feature will work regardless of which language you have loaded as your default. This makes it possible for you to debug each language individually. When beginning to internationalize your component, leave **Debug Language** on and start with your preferred language. This will help you to build a complete set of language definitions that you can send to a translator.

Translating the frontend

The frontend uses a set of language packs that is separate from the backend. However, the translation process is the same—pass the string to be translated through `JText::_()` and add a definition to the language file. Language debugging also works in the frontend.

To translate the header **Restaurants we have reviewed** in the `list` view, open `/components/com_restaurants/views/list/tmpl/default.php` and make the change highlighted below:

```
<?php defined( '_JEXEC' ) or die( 'Restricted access' ); ?>
<div class="componentheading"><?php echo JText::_('Restaurants we
    have reviewed') ?></div>
<ul>
```

If you now follow a link to the Restaurant Reviews component in the frontend (or go to `index.php?option=com_restaurants&view=list`) and have Language Debugging turned on, your screen should look now similar to the following:

??Restaurants we have reviewed??

- Giovanni's Italian Restaurant
- Nana's Bakery
- Crosstown Deli
- The Daily Dish
- Salad Surprises

To translate the header and get rid of the question marks, create the file `/languages/fr-FR/fr-FR.com_restaurants.ini`, and add the following definition to it:

`RESTAURANTS WE HAVE REVIEWED=Restaurants que nous avons passés en revue`

After saving the file, reload the frontend. Your screen should now have the updated header, wrapped in bullets:

·Restaurants que nous avons passés en revue·

- Giovanni's Italian Restaurant
- Nana's Bakery
- Crosstown Deli
- The Daily Dish
- Salad Surprises

Once the interface has been translated to your satisfaction, turn off **Debug Language** and set the default language to your preferred one.

Handling file uploads

Although most needs for data storage can be handled through the database, sometimes you will want to allow users to upload files to the server. Joomla! provides a library that makes it easy to safely handle file uploads.

For the Restaurant Reviews component, we want to make it possible for the critics to upload MP3 files to go with the reviews. To handle this, we need to adjust the form on which reviews are entered so that it accepts files. Also, the `save()` function in our controller for the backend needs to be adjusted to look for the file and copy it to the correct place.

First, open the file `/administrator/components/com_restaurants/views/single/tmpl/default.php` and make the following highlighted adjustments:

```
<form action="index.php" method="post" name="adminForm" id="adminForm"
enctype="multipart/form-data">
  <fieldset class="adminform">
    <legend>Details</legend>
    <table class="admintable">
    <tr>
      <td width="100" align="right" class="key">
        Name:
      </td>
      <td>
        <input class="text_area" type="text" name="name" id="name"
        size="50" maxlength="250" value="<?php echo
        $this->row->name;?>" />
      </td>
    </tr>

......

    <tr>
      <td width="100" align="right" class="key">
        Published:
      </td>
      <td>
        <?php echo $this->published; ?>
      </td>
    </tr>
    <tr>
      <td width="100" align="right" class="key">
        Audio File:
      </td>
      <td>
```

```
    <input type="file" name="audiofile" value="" />
  </td>
 </tr>
 </table>
</fieldset>
```

Before we can accept files, we need to set the form so that it will accept more than just text strings. Setting `enctype` to `multipart/form-data` in the `<form>` tag allows us to send both text strings and entire files from our inputs. Once this is in place, any `<input>` elements of type `file` will function as intended. The added code created another row in the table with a file input through which MP3s can be uploaded.

Load the Restaurant Reviews component in the backend and click on **New**. There should now be an input field, at the bottom of the page, for uploading files:

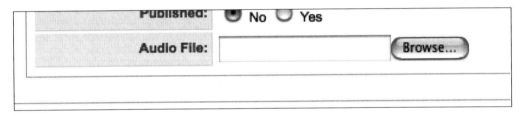

If you tried to upload an MP3 file now, it would not be saved as we have not yet modified the `save()` function in our controller to handle the file as well. To do this, open the file `/administrator/components/com_restaurants/controllers/reviews.php` and add the highlighted code:

```
if(!$row->review_date)
{
    $row->review_date = date( 'Y-m-d H:i:s' );
}

if(!$row->store())
{
    JError::raiseError(500, $row->getError() );
}

$file = JRequest::getVar( 'audiofile', '', 'files', 'array' );

if(isset($file['name']) && $file['name'] != '')
{
    jimport('joomla.filesystem.file');

    $ext = JFile::getExt($file['name']);
```

```
$filename = JPATH_SITE . DS . 'components' . DS . $option . DS .
  'audio' . DS . $row->id . '.' . $ext;

if (!JFile::upload($file['tmp_name'], $filename))
{
    $this->setRedirect("index.php?option=$option", "Upload
      failed, check to make sure that /components/$option/audio
      exists and is writable.");
    return;
}

}

if ($this->getTask() == 'apply')
{
    $this->setRedirect('index.php?option=' . $option .
      '&task=edit&cid[]=' . $row->id, 'Changes Applied');
}
else
{
    $this->setRedirect('index.php?option=' . $option,
      'Review Saved');
}
```

First, the file information is extracted from the HTTP request using JRequest::
getVar(). The first parameter is the name of the file that was entered, while the
second is a default. The third tells getVar() to extract audiofile from PHP's
$_FILES superglobal. The fourth parameter ensures that the file information is in
an array.

Before attempting to process the file, we make sure that the name element of the $file
array exists and is not empty. If so, the code continues by loading in the file system
library that provides the file handling functions through the JFile class. The extension
of the uploaded file is extracted using the getExt() member function of JFile and
stored in $ext.

Next, the complete path and name of the final destination for the file is constructed.
The constant JPATH_SITE points to the base of the Joomla! installation, and DS is set
to the operating system's appropriate directory separator. The rest of the constructed
path points to /components/com_restaurants/audio. After the path is complete,
the current record's id is used from $row->id, followed by a period and ending with
the file extension. This will ensure that only one file is uploaded for the restaurant
review and that it does not clash with the name for any other review.

Finally, the file is copied into the correct place using `JFile::upload()`. The first parameter is the location of the temporary file; temporary files are created by PHP automatically on file upload. The location is found in the `tmp_name` element of the `$file` array. The second parameter is the full path and filename where the file is to be copied.

Why is the function named JFile::upload()?

It may seem a little odd that we are using a function named `upload()` instead of `copy()`. This is because Joomla! uses a built-in FTP layer to handle file management. This FTP layer exists to get around a common issue where shared hosts assign the 'nobody' or 'apache' username to all PHP processes. If this username does not have privileges to write files to the destination directories, the copy will fail. Joomla! solves this problem by opening an FTP connection to the local server and uploading the file during the PHP process. You do not need to have an FTP client installed on your computer because it all happens on the server. The FTP layer is optional; if it is turned off, Joomla! will fall back on using standard PHP file management functions.

If the upload fails, the `setRedirect()` member function of the controller is called to take the user back to the Restaurant Reviews management screen and display a message. To halt further execution of the `save()` function, `return` is called straight away.

With this code in place, files can be successfully uploaded to the server. You may have noticed that the `audio` folder under `/components/com_restaurants` is referenced but we never explicitly created it. When a path that does not exist is passed into `JFile::upload()`, Joomla! attempts to create the folders necessary to complete it. If you have problems uploading files to the server, create the `audio` folder yourself, and try again. Also, make sure that your file is not too large. PHP file and POST size limits that are frequently set as low as two megabytes. These can be adjusted in your `php.ini` file.

Although you may now have some files uploaded to the server in the `audio` folder, there is currently no way for visitors to download them. To fix this, we need to make slight adjustments to the `single` view in the frontend. First, a link to the file must be generated when one is available. Open `/components/com_restaurants/ views/single/view.html.php` and make the highlighted adjustments to the `display()` function:

```
$user =& JFactory::getUser();

$comments =& $this->get('Comments');

jimport('joomla.filesystem.file');
```

```
$download = '';

if (JFile::exists(JPATH_COMPONENT . DS . 'audio' . DS . $id .
    '.mp3'))
{
    $download = JURI::base() . 'components/com_restaurants/audio/'
    . $id . '.mp3';
}

$this->assign('display_comments', $params->get('display_comments',
    '1'));
$this->assignRef('review', $review);
$this->assignRef('smoking', $smoking);
$this->assignRef('date', $date);
$this->assignRef('backlink', $backlink);
$this->assignRef('emaillink', $emaillink);
$this->assignRef('name', $user->name);
$this->assignRef('comments', $comments);
$this->assign('download', $download);

parent::display($tpl);
```

This code first imports the `JFile` libraries using `jimport('joomla.filesystem.file')`. Then, `$download` is set to a null string as a fallback value. Next, the function `JFile::exists()` is called to test whether a file for this specific review exists. The filename is assembled using the path to the component frontend (stored in `JPATH_COMPONENT`), along with the current review's id and the extension `.mp3`. If the file does exist, `$download` is set to the URL from where the file can be downloaded, using `JURI::base()` to get the Joomla! root URL. The `$download` variable is then assigned to the view.

Although this generates the link, it must still be output. Open `/components/com_restaurants/views/single/tmpl/default.php` and add this highlighted code:

```
<p><?php echo htmlspecialchars($this->review->review); ?></p>
<p><em>Notes:</em> <?php echo htmlspecialchars($this->review->notes);
    ?></p>
<?php if ($this->download != ''): ?>
    <p><a href="<?php echo htmlspecialchars($this->download)
    ?>">Listen to the review</a></p>
<?php endif ?>
<p><a href="<?php echo htmlspecialchars($this->emaillink); ?>">Email
    this to a friend</a></p>
<a href="<?php echo htmlspecialchars($this->backlink); ?>">&lt;
    return to the reviews</a>
```

This code checks to make sure that the `download` variable is not set to a null string. If this is the case, it continues by outputting an anchor tag. The URL is passed through PHP's `htmlspecialchars()` function to escape common HTML entities.

Once all of the adjustments have been made, save all of the files. Then go to the frontend and load one of the Restaurant Reviews for which you also uploaded an MP3 file. You should now see a link beneath the review where the file can be downloaded:

> the locals swear by. Apple, pumpkin, and pecan pies round out the desser
>
> *Notes:* Get there early on Friday nights, it's impossible to get a table after
>
> Listen to the review
>
> Email this to a friend

Using the original filename

In this upload file example, the MP3 files were simply renamed to reflect the ID of the associated database record. In many cases, you will actually want to use the original name of the file when it is written to the server. The user's browser will send the local filename in the HTTP request for you.

However, as with all incoming data, you cannot trust that the given filename is valid. If you were to trust this data, a malicious hacker could forge the name as something like `../../../configuration.php` or any other path on your server. If you accept this name as the filename and the file permissions on `configuration.php` are not secure, a hacker can overwrite it with anything they like and take over the site.

To avoid such a scenario, clean the incoming filename using `JFile::makeSafe()`. When you pass in the filename from the HTTP request as the parameter, this function will return it, after stripping out all of the slashes and invalid characters. To implement this in our example of the audio file, `$filename` would need to be set with this line of code:

```
$filename = JPATH_SITE . DS . 'components' . DS . $option . DS
            . 'audio' . DS . JFile::makeSafe($file['name']);
```

A major drawback of this method is that you have to decide how to manage filename conflicts. For example, if someone uploads the file `interview.mp3` for one review and then someone else also uploads `interview.mp3` for a different review, the second one will overwrite the first. One way around this would be to create a separate folder for each review, numbering them according to the ID of the review. When doing this, you will still need to scan the record's folder each time someone loads the review to determine whether or not a given audio file is available for download.

Summary

Our reviewers are pleased to see the email feature in place. Visitors are sending reviews to their friends, and traffic to the site is up. In addition, email address validation is deterring abuse of the feature.

Also, the structure is now in place for reviewers to add brief audio reviews. Because we use the `JFile` class, we can rest assured that the audio files will make it on to the server and be named according to our conventions.

Finally, we have started work on internationalizing the component. Although this does not translate the restaurant reviews themselves, it does help us to make the user interface friendlier to people for whom English is not their primary language. Defining the symbols now gives us a head start. When we are ready to launch the component into new markets, we only need to find someone who can translate the labels.

12
Packing Everything Together

Our restaurant reviewers are now quite satisfied with the development of the site—satisfied enough to recommend it to their colleagues in other cities. Our email accounts are now flooded with requests to produce similar sites. Instead of producing each individual website, we will package the module, component, and plug-ins so that they can be distributed to other webmasters. Our packaging process will cover the following tasks:

- Listing all of the files
- Packaging the module
- Packaging the plug-ins
- Packaging the component
- Including SQL queries
- Creating backend menu options
- Providing extra installation scripts
- Distribution

Listing all of the files

To create the installation packages for our elements, we will start with the XML manifest files we previously created to hold the configuration parameters. All of the three extension types require you to list files and folders in the package. The installer will not copy over any files or folders in the package that are not listed in the manifest.

Packaging the module

For our module, take the existing `mod_reviews.xml` file and add the following highlighted code:

```xml
<?xml version="1.0" encoding="utf-8"?>
<install type="module" version="1.5">
  <name>Restaurant Reviews</name>
  <author>Sumptuous Software</author>
  <creationDate>August 2008</creationDate>
  <copyright>(C) 2008</copyright>
  <license>MIT</license>
  <authorEmail>support@packtpub.com</authorEmail>
  <authorUrl>www.packtpub.com</authorUrl>
  <version>1.0</version>
  <description>A module for promoting restaurant
    reviews.</description>
  <files>
    <filename module="mod_reviews">mod_reviews.php</filename>
    <filename>helper.php</filename>
    <filename>mod_reviews.xml</filename>
    <folder>tmpl</folder>
  </files>
  <params>
    <param name="random" type="radio" default="0" label="Randomize"
      description="Show random reviews">
      <option value="0">No</option>
      <option value="1">Yes</option>
    </param>
    <param name="@spacer" type="spacer" default="" label=
      "" description="" />
    <param name="items" type="text" default="1" label="Display #"
      description="Number of reviews to display" />
    <param name="style" type="list" default="default" label="Display
      style" description="The style to use for displaying
      the reviews.">
      <option value="default">Flat</option>
      <option value="bulleted">Bulleted</option>
      <option value="detail">Detail</option>
    </param>
  </params>
</install>
```

Each file is listed in a `<filename>` element, and all of these elements are enclosed in a `<files>` element. The `tmpl` folder is also listed, but enclosed within `<folder>` tags instead; this copies the folder and all of the contained files. For `mod_reviews.php`, we give the `<filename>` element a parameter of `module`, which is set to `mod_reviews`. This creates the directory `mod_reviews` in the `modules` directory and also registers our module in the database. By doing this, we automate the steps while writing the first module.

Packaging the plug-ins

The adjustments to the XML files for the plug-ins are very similar. Open the `/plugins/content/reviews.xml` file and make the following highlighted changes:

```
<?xml version="1.0" encoding="utf-8"?>
<install version="1.5" type="plugin" group="content">
  <name>Content - Restaurant Review Links</name>
  <author>Sumptuous Software</author>
  <creationDate>August 2008</creationDate>
  <copyright>(C) 2008</copyright>
  <license>MIT</license>
  <authorEmail>support@packtpub.com</authorEmail>
  <authorUrl>www.packtpub.com</authorUrl>
  <version>1.0</version>
  <description>Searches for titles of restaurants in articles and
    turns them into review links.</description>
  <files>
    <filename plugin="reviews">reviews.php</filename>
  </files>
  <params>
    <param name="linkcode" type="textarea" default="" rows="5"
    cols="40" label="Custom Link Code" description="By using {link}
    and {title}, you can generate custom HTML output that includes
    the URL and review title respectively." />
  </params>
</install>
```

On the opening `<install>` tag, we add the `group` parameter and set it to `content`. This ensures that the plug-in is added to the correct directory. For the single file of code, we have the parameter `plugin` set to the plug-in name, which is used along with the group in the database to identify it.

The process is identical for the `reviewinfo` plug-in:

```xml
<?xml version="1.0" encoding="utf-8"?>
<install version="1.5" type="plugin" group="content">
    <name>Content - Review Information</name>
    <author>Sumptuous Software</author>
    <creationDate>August 2008</creationDate>
    <copyright>(C) 2008</copyright>
    <license>MIT</license>
    <authorEmail>support@packtpub.com</authorEmail>
    <authorUrl>www.packtpub.com</authorUrl>
    <version>1.0</version>
    <description>Turns {reviewinfo Name of your restaurant} into a
     table with the review's essential details.</description>
    <files>
        <filename plugin="reviewinfo">reviewinfo.php</filename>
    </files>
    <params>
        <param name="address" type="radio" default="1" label="Display
         Address?" description="Toggles the display of the address in
         summaries.">
            <option value="1">Yes</option>
            <option value="0">No</option>
        </param>
        <param name="price_range" type="radio" default="1"
         label="Display Price Range?" description="Toggles the
         display of the price range in summaries.">
            <option value="1">Yes</option>
            <option value="0">No</option>
        </param>
        <param name="reservations" type="radio" default="1"
         label="Display Reservations?" description="Toggles the
         display of reservation policy in summaries.">
            <option value="1">Yes</option>
            <option value="0">No</option>
        </param>
        <param name="smoking" type="radio" default="1" label="Display
         Smoking?" description="Toggles the display of smoking policy
         in summaries.">
            <option value="1">Yes</option>
            <option value="0">No</option>
        </param>
    </params>
</install>
```

The changes to the XML file for the `search` plug-in are similar to the first two, except that here you set the `group` parameter in the `<install>` tag to `search`. Notice that we are using the same name for a plug-in in the `search` group as in the `content` group. This is possible because of the manner in which XML is written.

```xml
<?xml version="1.0" encoding="utf-8"?>
<install version="1.5" type="plugin" group="search">
  <name>Search - Restaurant Reviews</name>
  <author>Sumptuous Software</author>
  <creationDate>August 2008</creationDate>
  <copyright>(C) 2008</copyright>
  <license>MIT</license>
  <authorEmail>support@packtpub.com</authorEmail>
  <authorUrl>www.packtpub.com</authorUrl>
  <files>
    <filename plugin="reviews">reviews.php</filename>
  </files>
  <version>1.0</version>
  <description>Allows Searching of Restaurant Reviews</description>
  <params>
    <param name="search_limit" type="text" size="5" default="50"
label="Search Limit" description="Number of Search items to return"/>
  </params>
</install>
```

Packaging the component

Although preparing modules and plug-ins mainly involves listing the files, components need some extra attention. Components are typically used to manage records in the database, so queries to add the accompanying tables are necessary. We will require links to the component backend. Finally, we may wish to run some additional set-up code to be run just after the installation has completed, or a clean-up script to be run when the component is removed. For the moment, create a folder outside of your Joomla! root called `component` and create file named `restaurants.xml`, and load it with the following code:

```xml
<?xml version="1.0" encoding="utf-8"?>
<install type="component" version="1.5.0">
  <name>Restaurants</name>
  <author>Sumptuous Software</author>
  <creationDate>August 2008</creationDate>
  <copyright>(C) 2008</copyright>
  <authorEmail>support@packtpub.com</authorEmail>
  <authorUrl>www.packtpub.com</authorUrl>
  <version>1.5.0</version>
```

```
<license>MIT</license>
<description>A component for writing and managing
  restaurant reviews.</description>
<installfile>install.restaurants.php</installfile>
<uninstallfile>uninstall.restaurants.php</uninstallfile>
<install>
  <sql>
    <file driver="mysql" charset="utf8">install.mysql.sql</file>
  </sql>
</install>
<uninstall>
  <sql>
    <file driver="mysql" charset="utf8">uninstall.mysql.sql</file>
  </sql>
</uninstall>
<files folder="site">
  <filename>restaurants.php</filename>
  <filename>router.php</filename>
  <folder>models</folder>
  <folder>views</folder>
</files>
<administration>
  <menu>Restaurant Reviews</menu>
  <submenu>
    <menu link="option=com_restaurants">Manage Reviews</menu>
    <menu view="comments">Manage Comments</menu>
  </submenu>
  <files folder="admin">
    <filename>config.xml</filename>
    <folder>elements</folder>
    <folder>controllers</folder>
    <filename>install.mysql.sql</filename>
    <filename>uninstall.mysql.sql</filename>
    <folder>models</folder>
    <filename>restaurants.php</filename>
    <filename>install.restaurants.php</filename>
    <filename>uninstall.restaurants.php</filename>
    <folder>tables</folder>
    <folder>views</folder>
  </files>
</administration>
</install>
```

What has changed from Joomla! 1.0?

For the most part, XML component installation files for Joomla! 1.5 are similar to the ones used in 1.0. For the installation and uninstallation queries, the SQL has now been migrated to external files, with the flexibility to include different SQL files for different database types. Also, the backend code is now sorted into a separate folder that you can specify in the folder parameter of the `<files>` tag in the `<administration>` section. This helps to avoid filename conflicts. Finally, you can now use the `<folder>` tag instead of `<filename>` to copy an entire folder at once. This saves you the effort of listing each individual file.

As with modules and plug-ins, we list all of the files related to the extension. However, with components, we have backend files as well as the frontend files. The backend files are placed within the `<administration>` tag in a `<files>` tag where the `folder` attribute is set to `admin`. The files for the frontend of the site are also listed inside of a `<files>` tag, but this one has an attribute of `site`. The files enclosed within the `<installfile>` and `<uninstallfile>` tags are used to identify the custom installation and uninstallation files that we will create in a moment.

Below the tags for the custom installation and uninstallation files are the `<install>` and `<uninstall>` tags. Within these tags are `<sql>` and `<file>` tags. These are used to add SQL queries to the installation and uninstallation processes. Because Joomla! supports different database types, you can include a different file for each type (we will only create one for MySQL). Note that both the `install.mysql.sql` and `uninstall.mysql.sql` files are listed within the `<install>` and `<uninstall>` tags, as well as in the `<files>` tag within the `<administration>` tag. If these files are not listed in the `<administration>` section, they will not be copied on installation and the queries will consequently not be run. This is also the case with `install.restaurants.php` and `uninstall.restaurants.php`, which are only found in the `<installfile>` and `<uninstallfile>` tags.

Including SQL queries

To add the tables that we need for managing the reviews, some SQL queries should be run. To do this, we will add the queries to some files that will be run when the component is installed and uninstalled. Create a new file named `install.mysql.sql` in the `/administrator/components/com_restaurants` folder, and enter the following queries into this file:

```
CREATE TABLE IF NOT EXISTS `#__reviews` (
    `id` int(11) NOT NULL auto_increment,
    `name` varchar(255) NOT NULL,
    `address` varchar(255) NOT NULL,
```

```
  `reservations` varchar(31) NOT NULL,
  `quicktake` text NOT NULL,
  `review` text NOT NULL,
  `notes` text NOT NULL,
  `smoking` tinyint(1) NOT NULL default 0,
  `credit_cards` varchar(255) NOT NULL,
  `cuisine` varchar(31) NOT NULL,
  `avg_dinner_price` tinyint(3) NOT NULL default 0,
  `review_date` datetime NOT NULL,
  `published` tinyint(1) NOT NULL default 0,
  PRIMARY KEY  ('id')
);

CREATE TABLE IF NOT EXISTS `#__reviews_comments` (
  `id` int(11) NOT NULL auto_increment,
  `review_id` int(11) NOT NULL,
  `user_id` int(11) NOT NULL,
  `full_name` varchar(50) NOT NULL,
  `comment_date` datetime NOT NULL,
  `comment_text` text NOT NULL,
  PRIMARY KEY  ('id')
);
```

There are two differences between these queries and the originals encountered earlier. First, we've added the additional qualifier IF NOT EXISTS. If a person has problems uninstalling the component or already has these tables (perhaps from a backup), this qualifier will prevent an error from occurring. Also, in the above queries, we're using the #__ table prefix notation, which will be replaced with the table prefix on the host Joomla! system.

In addition to the installation SQL, we want to provide an uninstallation SQL script that will remove the tables so that no trace of the component is left. Create the file uninstall.mysql.sql in /administrator/components/com_restaurants folder, and add the following to the new file:

```
DROP TABLE #__reviews;
DROP TABLE #__reviews_comments;
```

The code in both of these files will be used when our component is installed or uninstalled, as we've defined them within the <install> and <uninstall> tags we added to the XML file.

Creating backend menu items

Within the `<administration>` tags in the XML file, we define the items found under the **Components** menu item in the backend. If we were only managing one type of record, the following piece of XML would be sufficient for linking to the backend:

```
<menu>Restaurant Reviews</menu>
```

However, our component manages both reviews and comments. To handle this, we want the `Restaurant Reviews` item to expand into two submenu items. In the following XML, we enclose the menu items in a `<submenu>` tag. The first item uses `link` to define a hard link to `index.php?option=com_restaurants`, and the second uses `view` to form a link to `index.php?option=com_restaurants&view=comments`.

```
<submenu>
   <menu link="option=com_restaurants">Manage Reviews</menu>
   <menu view="comments">Manage Comments</menu>
</submenu>
```

Extra installation scripts

When installing a component, Joomla! displays a standard success message along with the description found in the XML file. A generic uninstallation message is also generated upon removal. We can override both of these with custom code. Create a new file named `install.restaurants.php` in the `/administrator/components/com_restaurants` folder, and enter the following code into this new file:

```php
<?php
defined( '_JEXEC' ) or die( 'Restricted access' );
function com_install()
{
  ?>
  <div class="header">Congratulations, Restaurant Reviews is
          ready to roll!</div>
  <p>
    Congratulations on not only purchasing, but also installing,
    Restaurant Reviews! Undoubtedly, you are about to
    embark on many joyous hours of authoring and
    organizing all of the hot spots for your city.
    To get started, navigate to Components, Restaurant
    Reviews, Manage Reviews and click the "New" button
    at the right-hand corner of the screen. Also, be
    sure to install the accompanying plugins and module
    to promote your reviews throughout the website!
  </p>

  <?php
}
```

For uninstallation, create a new file named `uninstall.restaurants.php` in the `/administrator/components/com_restaurants` folder, and load it with the following code:

```php
<?php
defined( '_JEXEC' ) or die( 'Restricted access' );
function com_uninstall()
{
  ?>
  <div class="header">The reviews are now removed from your
    system.</div>
  <p>
    We're sorry to see you go! To completely remove the software
    from your system, be sure to also uninstall the plugins and
    module.
  </p>
<?php
}
```

These scripts are referenced by the XML in the following two lines that we added below the `<description>` tag, earlier:

```
<installfile>install.restaurants.php</installfile>
<uninstallfile>uninstall.restaurants.php</uninstallfile>
```

Joomla! will load the `install.restaurants.php` file on installation, and `uninstall.restaurants.php` on removal, but will also call the functions `com_install()` and `com_uninstall()` respectively. You can use these functions to do more than simply display messages. The `com_install()` function is called just after the installation process is complete, so it can be used to guide users through first-time configuration. Likewise, the `com_uninstall()` function is called just before the component is removed; any output generated will be buffered and displayed after the component is removed. If `com_install()` or `com_uninstall()` returns false, the process is rolled back. This can be used to prevent components from being installed when the target system does not meet the minimum requirements. It can also be used to prevent the removal of a component that is pointed to by published menu items.

Distribution

We now have all of the files that we need to package our extensions. For the module, put all of the files and folders /modules/mod_reviews into a .zip archive. For the plug-ins, create three separate .zip archives—one for the review information, another for the review links, and a third one for the review searches. Each of these archives should contain the .php and .xml files for the corresponding plug-in.

The component needs a little extra attention. Because both the frontend and backend code are contained within folders named com_restaurants, we need to create separate folders for them within the archive. Because the file listing has the administrative files designated as being in the admin folder and the frontend files in site, these are the ones we will create. Copy the files and folders from /components/com_restaurants into your separate component folder, under site. The contents of the /administrator/components/com_restaurants folder should be copied into the admin folder. The structure of your component archive should look like the following:

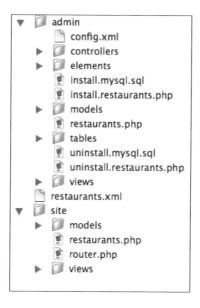

Once your component folder is prepared, compress it the way you did for the module and plug-ins.

After creating the five archives, all of the code created in this book will be ready for installation on any Joomla! system. Set up a clean installation of Joomla! (separate from the one you used to develop the component) and install the component by going to **Extensions | Install/Uninstall** and using use the **Upload Package File** form to upload the .zip archive containing the reviews component. If everything works correctly, you should see the following screen:

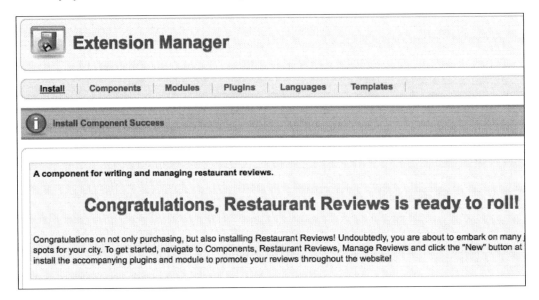

Summary

We now have several .zip files ready to go, containing everything necessary to set the Restaurant Reviews system up on another website. We've spared our end users from confusing queries—they simply upload the files through the **Extension Manager** and start writing reviews! This is made possible through the XML configuration file, which defines the scripts to run, queries to add, and files to copy during installation.

Index

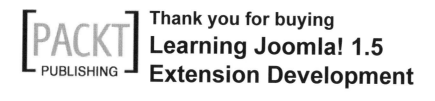

Thank you for buying
Learning Joomla! 1.5
Extension Development

Packt Open Source Project Royalties

When we sell a book written on an Open Source project, we pay a royalty directly to that project. Therefore by purchasing Learning Joomla! 1.5 Extension Development, Packt will have given some of the money received to the Joomla project.

In the long term, we see ourselves and you—customers and readers of our books—as part of the Open Source ecosystem, providing sustainable revenue for the projects we publish on. Our aim at Packt is to establish publishing royalties as an essential part of the service and support a business model that sustains Open Source.

If you're working with an Open Source project that you would like us to publish on, and subsequently pay royalties to, please get in touch with us.

Writing for Packt

We welcome all inquiries from people who are interested in authoring. Book proposals should be sent to author@packtpub.com. If your book idea is still at an early stage and you would like to discuss it first before writing a formal book proposal, contact us; one of our commissioning editors will get in touch with you.

We're not just looking for published authors; if you have strong technical skills but no writing experience, our experienced editors can help you develop a writing career, or simply get some additional reward for your expertise.

About Packt Publishing

Packt, pronounced 'packed', published its first book "Mastering phpMyAdmin for Effective MySQL Management" in April 2004 and subsequently continued to specialize in publishing highly focused books on specific technologies and solutions.

Our books and publications share the experiences of your fellow IT professionals in adapting and customizing today's systems, applications, and frameworks. Our solution-based books give you the knowledge and power to customize the software and technologies you're using to get the job done. Packt books are more specific and less general than the IT books you have seen in the past. Our unique business model allows us to bring you more focused information, giving you more of what you need to know, and less of what you don't.

Packt is a modern, yet unique publishing company, which focuses on producing quality, cutting-edge books for communities of developers, administrators, and newbies alike. For more information, please visit our website: www.PacktPub.com.

Building Websites with Joomla 1.5

ISBN: 978-1-847195-30-2   Paperback: 363 pages

This best selling book has now been updated for the latest Joomla 1.5 release

1. Learn Joomla! 1.5 features

2. Install and customize Joomla! 1.5

3. Configure Joomla! administration

4. Create your own Joomla! templates

Mastering Joomla! 1.5 Extension and Framework Development

ISBN: 978-1-847192-82-0   Paperback: 380 pages

The Professional Guide to Programming Joomla!

1. In-depth guide to programming Joomla!

2. Design and build secure and robust components, modules and plugins

3. Includes a comprehensive reference to the major areas of the Joomla! framework

Please check **www.PacktPub.com** for information on our titles

Joomla! Template Design

ISBN: 978-1-847191-44-1 Paperback: 250 pages

A complete guide for web designers to all aspects of designing unique website templates for the free Joomla! 1.0.8 PHP Content Management System

1. Create Joomla! Templates for your sites
2. Debug, validate, and package your templates
3. Tips for tweaking existing templates

Joomla! Web Security

ISBN: 978-1-847194-88-6 Paperback: 248 pages

Secure your Joomla! website from common security threats with this easy-to-use guide

1. Learn how to secure your Joomla! websites
2. Real-world tools to protect against hacks on your site
3. Implement disaster recovery features

Please check **www.PacktPub.com** for information on our titles